Exam Ref SC-200
Microsoft Security
Operations Analyst

Yuri Diogenes
Jake Mowrer
Sarah Young

Exam Ref SC-200 Microsoft Security Operations Analyst

Published with the authorization of Microsoft Corporation by:
Pearson Education, Inc.

ISBN-13: 978-0-13-756835-2
ISBN-10: 0-13-756835-5

Library of Congress Control Number: On file

1 2021

TRADEMARKS

WARNING AND DISCLAIMER

SPECIAL SALES

For information about buying this title in bulk quantities, or for special sales opportunities (which may include electronic versions; custom cover designs; and content particular to your business, training goals, marketing focus, or branding interests), please contact our corporate sales department at corpsales@pearsoned.com or (800) 382-3419.

For government sales inquiries, please contact governmentsales@pearsoned.com.

For questions about sales outside the U.S., please contact intlcs@pearson.com.

CREDITS

EDITOR-IN-CHIEF
Brett Bartow

EXECUTIVE EDITOR
Loretta Yates

DEVELOPMENT EDITOR
Rick Kughen

SPONSORING EDITOR
Charvi Arora

MANAGING EDITOR
Sandra Schroeder

PROJECT EDITOR
Dan Foster

COPY EDITOR
Rick Kughen

INDEXER
Valerie Haynes Perry

PROOFREADER
Scout Festa

TECHNICAL EDITOR
Nicholas DiCola

EDITORIAL ASSISTANT
Cindy Teeters

COVER DESIGNER
Twist Creative, Seattle

COMPOSITOR
Danielle Foster

Contents at a glance

Contents

Chapter 2   Mitigate threats using Azure Defender   121

Acknowledgments

The authors would like to thank Loretta Yates and the entire Microsoft Press/Pearson team for their support in this project, and Nicholas DiCola for reviewing the book.

Yuri would also like to thank: My wife and daughters for their endless support; my great God for giving me strength and guiding my path on each step of the way; and my great friends and co-authors Sarah Young and Jake Mowrer for this amazing partnership. My manager Rebecca, for always encouraging me to achieve more and stretch myself to the next level. Thanks for the support from our learning team, especially Brandon Neeb, for their contribution to this project. Last but not least, thanks to my parents for working hard to give me an education, which is the foundation I use every day to keep moving forward in my career.

Sarah would like to thank Grayson, who has sat providing (mostly) silent writing support every day; Erica for being the greatest friend and security inspiration; and both Yuri and Jake for being the best co-authors anyone could ever ask for. My many Microsoft colleagues who have championed and supported me to get me to the role I am in today. There are many, but in particular, my manager Kara and mentors Pen, Colleen, Shelly, Gary, Hany, Ping, Mark, Harry, and Hana-San. My most special thanks are saved for my parents and grandparents, who gave so much for my education, taught me the value of hard work and integrity, and continue to support me in every way possible.

Jake thanks his wife, Jennifer, and four sons, Ryker, Mikey, Dylan, and Zach, for their love and encouragement. To Yuri Diogenes: Without his leadership and drive, this book would not have been possible. A big thank you to the leadership and my colleagues in the Microsoft Defender Customer Acceleration Team, whose knowledge and mentorship shaped the content in this book. To Moti, Raviv, and all friends and colleagues in the Israel Research and Development Center, Redmond, and India Development Center at Microsoft for constantly innovating to protect customers. A very special thank you to my parents, who taught me that hard work, positive attitude, dedication, and kindness would lead to success.

About the authors

Yuri Diogenes, MsC is a Master of science in cybersecurity intelligence and forensics investigation (UTICA College), and a Principal Program Manager in the Microsoft CxE ASC Team, where he primarily helps customers onboard and deploy Azure Security Center and Azure Defender as part of their security operations/incident response. Yuri has been working for Microsoft since 2006 in different positions. He spent five years as senior support escalation engineer on the CSS Forefront Edge Team, and from 2011 to 2017, he worked on the content development team, where he also helped create the Azure Security Center content experience since its GA launch in 2016. Yuri has published a total of 26 books, mostly covering information security and Microsoft technologies. Yuri also holds an MBA and many IT/Security industry certifications, such as CISSP, E|CND, E|CEH, E|CSA, E|CHFI, CompTIA Security+, CySA+, Cloud Essentials Certified, Mobility+, Network+, CASP, CyberSec First Responder, MCSE, and MCTS. You can follow Yuri on Twitter at @yuridiogenes.

Sarah Young is a senior program manager in the Azure Sentinel CxE team, where she works with Microsoft customers to remove technical blockers for deployment. Having worked with Azure Sentinel since it was announced at RSA 2019, Sarah has extensive knowledge of the platform and has helped it develop and grow. Sarah is an experienced public speaker and has presented on a range of IT security and technology topics at industry events, both nationally and internationally. She holds numerous industry qualifications, including CISSP, CCSP, CISM, and Azure Solutions Architect. In 2019, Sarah won the Security Champion award at the Australian Women in Security Awards. She is an active supporter of both local and international security and cloud-native communities. You can follow Sarah on Twitter at @_sarahyo.

Jake Mowrer is a Principal Program Manager in the Microsoft 365 Defender Customer Acceleration Team and a 25-year IT veteran. He helps some of the world's largest companies deploy Microsoft Defender for Endpoint and assists security operations teams with integrating Microsoft 365 Defender into their existing processes. Jake's deep knowledge in Microsoft Defender for Endpoint originated in 2016 when he was trained by Microsoft's development team in Herzliya, Israel, and he has since delivered technical sessions for private and public entities, as well as at technical conferences around the world. In 2020, Jake founded IronSpire Internet Security, a company focused on protecting homes and small businesses from cyber threats. You can follow Jake on Twitter at @JakeMowrerMSFT and @IronspireS.

Introduction

The SC-200 exam deals with technologies that are relevant for Microsoft Security Operations Analysts who collaborate with organizational stakeholders to secure information technology systems for the organizations. This exam cover topics that will help to reduce organizational risk by rapidly remediating active attacks in the environment, advising on improvements to threat protection practices, and referring violations of organizational policies to appropriate stakeholders. The exam also covers topics such as investigation and response for threats using Microsoft Azure Sentinel, Azure Defender, Microsoft 365 Defender, and third-party security products.

This book covers every major topic area found on the exam, but it does not cover every exam question. Only the Microsoft exam team has access to the exam questions, and Microsoft regularly adds new questions to the exam, making it impossible to cover specific questions. You should consider this book a supplement to your relevant real-world experience and other study materials. If you encounter a topic in this book that you do not feel completely comfortable with, use the "Need more review?" links you'll find in the text to find more information and take the time to research and study the topic. Great information is available on *docs.microsoft.com*, at MS Learn, and in blogs and forums.

Organization of this book

This book is organized by the "Skills measured" list published for the exam. The "Skills measured" list is available for each exam on the Microsoft Learning website: *http://aka.ms/examlist*. Each chapter in this book corresponds to a major topic area in the list, and the technical tasks in each topic area determine that chapter's organization. If an exam covers six major topic areas, for example, the book will contain six chapters.

Preparing for the exam

Microsoft certification exams are a great way to build your résumé and let the world know about your level of expertise. Certification exams validate your on-the-job experience and product knowledge. Although there is no substitute for on-the-job experience, preparation through study and hands-on practice can help you prepare for the exam. This book is not designed to teach you new skills.

We recommend that you augment your exam preparation plan by using a combination of available study materials and courses. For example, you might use the Exam Ref and another study guide for your "at home" preparation and take a Microsoft Official Curriculum course for the classroom experience. Choose the combination that you think works best for you. Learn more about available classroom training and find free online courses and live events at *http://microsoft.com/learn*. Microsoft Official Practice Tests are available for many exams at *http://aka.ms/practicetests*.

Note that this Exam Ref is based on publicly available information about the exam and the authors' experience. To safeguard the integrity of the exam, authors do not have access to the live exam.

Microsoft certification

Microsoft certifications distinguish you by proving your command of a broad set of skills and experience with current Microsoft products and technologies. The exams and corresponding certifications are developed to validate your mastery of critical competencies as you design and develop, or implement and support, solutions with Microsoft products and technologies both on-premises and in the cloud. Certification brings a variety of benefits to the individual and to employers and organizations.

> **MORE INFO   ALL MICROSOFT CERTIFICATIONS**
>
> For information about Microsoft certifications, including a full list of available certifications, go to *http://www.microsoft.com/learn*.

Check back often to see what is new!

Errata, updates & book support

We've made every effort to ensure the accuracy of this book and its companion content. You can access updates to this book—in the form of a list of submitted errata and their related corrections—at:

MicrosoftPressStore.com/ExamRefSC200/errata

If you discover an error that is not already listed, please submit it to us at the same page.

For additional book support and information, please visit *MicrosoftPressStore.com/Support*.

Please note that product support for Microsoft software and hardware is not offered through the previous addresses. For help with Microsoft software or hardware, go to *http://support.microsoft.com.*

Stay in touch

Let's keep the conversation going! We're on Twitter: http://twitter.com/MicrosoftPress.

CHAPTER 1

Mitigate threats using Microsoft 365 Defender

In recent years, the proliferation of endpoint protection, detection, and response tech-nologies enabled security operations teams to gain better visibility into attacks that target endpoints. This is one reason that *dwell time*—the measurement of time between the start of an incident and when a security operations team detects the intrusion—has decreased from a 78-day median in 2019 to 56 days in 2020 (Source: FireEye 2020 M-Trends). Unfortunately, this trend also encouraged malicious actors to increase their use of other attack vectors, such as email, cloud applications, and identities. These additional attack vectors pressure security teams to cover more ground in these additional domains, making it increasingly difficult for incident responders to effectively protect, detect, and respond to these threats.

Microsoft 365 Defender helps security operations teams respond to threats across these domains by providing the following features:

- Consolidated incident model
- Consolidated portal
- Automated self-healing
- Cross-product hunting

Skills covered in this chapter:

- Detect, investigate, respond, and remediate threats to the productivity environment using Microsoft Defender for Office 365
- Detect, investigate, respond, and remediate endpoint threats by using Microsoft Defender for Endpoint
- Detect, investigate, respond, and remediate identity threats
- Manage cross-domain investigations in Microsoft 365 Defender Security portal

Skill 1-1: Detect, investigate, respond, and remediate threats to the productivity environment using Microsoft Defender for Office 365

Attackers use email and Microsoft Office documents to gain initial entry into targeted systems. Microsoft Defender for Office 365 can identify, alert, block, and remediate these attacks. If an attacker is successful gaining a foothold in the targeted system, sensitive data could be at risk to theft. Configuring data loss prevention policies, sensitivity labels, and insider risk policies can protect this data, and alert security and compliance teams of the attempted exfiltration.

Examine a malicious spear phishing email

One popular attack vector is credential harvesting via spear phishing coupled with a forged login page. MITRE ATT&CK defines spear phishing as "an attempt to trick targets into divulging information, frequently credentials, or other actionable information." The spear phishing email in Figure 1-1 appears to be from Bob Smith, the Contoso Corporation CEO. The email was sent to Paul DePaul, CFO of Contoso Corporation, and asks him to click a link and use his email account to log in.

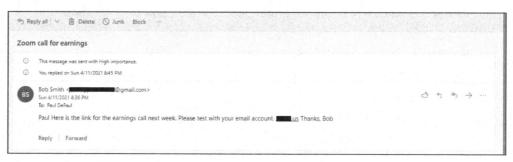

FIGURE 1-1 Spear phishing email

There are two suspicious properties in this email:

- The email is marked as having been sent with **High Importance**. This is a method to encourage the user to read and respond to the email right away. Creating a sense of urgency is commonly seen in social engineering–based attacks.

- The **sender** name is spoofed. The email appears to be from Contoso CEO Bob Smith, though the sender address ends in gmail.com.

When the user clicks the link in the email, they are presented with the web page shown in Figure 1-2.

This website is intended to look real enough so the user will type in their Office 365 username and password. Once the user types in their credentials and clicks **Sign In**, the credentials are sent to the attacker so they can log in to Office 365 as that user.

FIGURE 1-2 Credential harvesting website

To protect users from links in spear phishing emails, you need a technology that will scan links in emails when the email is delivered and when a user clicks the link. This ensures the links are safe to click, which takes the decision out of the user's hands. Safe Links is a feature in Defender for Office 365 that provides the best protection against these types of spear phishing attacks with malicious links.

The Safe Links feature in Microsoft Defender for Office 365 protects user email in two ways:

- Links that are sent in email are scanned before they are delivered to the user's mailbox.

- Links are scanned again when a user clicks the link. Scanning the link upon click is critical because a common attack technique to evade email protection is to activate the malicious content on the hosting site *after* the email passes through a company's email security layer.

These protections can be configured for emails sent to the company from outside email systems (inter-organization) as well as emails sent within the company (intra-organization).

Configuring a Safe Links policy

To configure a Safe Links policy, you must be a member of the **Organization Management** or the **Security Administrator** role groups configured in the **Permissions & Roles** section of the **Microsoft 365 Security Portal** (*https://security.microsoft.com*). For read-only access to Safe Link policies, you must be a member of either the **Global Reader** or **Security Reader** role groups. Note these are role groups in Office 365 and are separate from Azure Active Directory roles. However, the **Global Admin** and **Security Administrator** roles in Azure Active

Directory are members of the **Organization Management** and **Security Administrator** role groups by default, respectively.

> **MORE INFO** **CUSTOM ROLES IN THE ROLE-BASED ACCESS CONTROL FOR MICROSOFT 365 DEFENDER**
>
> For more information on Office 365 roles, please see the information at *https://docs.microsoft.com/en-us/microsoft-365/security/defender/custom-roles?view=o365-worldwide*.

Use the following steps to configure a Safe Links policy:

1. Log in to *https://security.microsoft.com* with the required permissions.
2. Under **Email & Collaboration**, click **Policies & Rules** > **Threat Policies**.
3. In **Threat Policies**, under **Policies**, click the **Safe Links** icon.
4. Click **Create** to start the **Create A New Safe Links Policy** wizard, as shown in Figure 1-3.

FIGURE 1-3 Name Your Policy

5. Provide a **Name** and **Description** for your Safe Links policy. You can have more than one policy that targets specific users in your organization, so keep this in mind when choosing your naming scheme. Click **Next** to move to the **Settings** page, as shown in Figure 1-4.
6. On the **Settings** page, set the **Select The Action For Unknown Potentially Malicious URLs in Messages** option to **On**. This allows the policy to check for malicious links.
7. Set the **Select The Action For Unknown Or Potentially Malicious URLs Within Microsoft Teams** setting to **On**. This setting will allow Safe Links to protect links shared in Microsoft Teams.

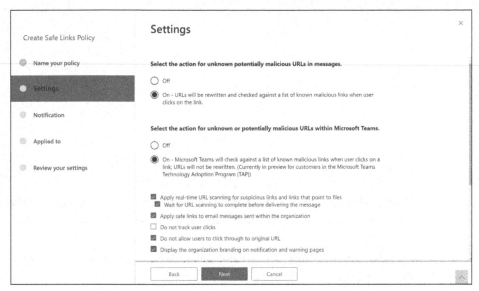

FIGURE 1-4 Create Safe Links Policy wizard's Settings page

8. To allow Safe Links to protect clicks on URLs that point to files, select the **Apply Real-Time URL Scanning For Suspicious Links And Links That Point To Files** option.

9. Waiting for URL scanning to complete before delivering the message will reduce the chances for false negatives because it will allow Safe Links to scan the link completely before delivering the email to the user. False negatives occur when a malicious link is delivered because it was scanned and found not to be malicious (sometimes referred to as a *miss*). We strongly recommend that you enable **Apply Real-Time URL Scanning For Suspicious Links And Links That Point To Files**.

10. Select the **Apply Safe Links To Email Messages Sent Within The Organization** option to prevent malicious links from being sent between mailboxes in the same company. Once they have breached one mailbox, it is common for attackers to start to phish other mailboxes in the same company. Users are very likely to click malicious links in emails, especially when they are sent from a coworker!

11. The **Do Not Track User Clicks** option should be left unchecked to ensure you know what links users are clicking.

12. Select the **Do Not Allow Users To Click Through To Original URL option**, which prevents users from bypassing the Safe Links block page, thereby accepting the risk of visiting a website believed to be malicious. This typically results in undesirable consequences.

13. The **Display The Organization Branding On Notification And Warning Pages** option allows you to customize the block page branding with a company logo. Scrolling down the **Settings** page exposes the **Do Not Rewrite The Following URLs** option shown in Figure 1-5.

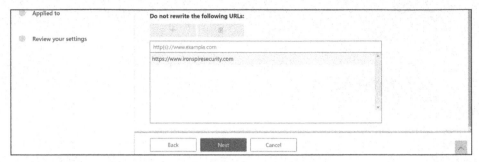

FIGURE 1-5 Do Not Rewrite The Following URLs

The **Do Not Rewrite The Following URLs** option allows you to add URLs that should not be rewritten to interact with Safe Links. Typically, this setting is used to allow access to third-party phishing test sites.

14. Once you have the **Settings** page options set as needed, click **Next** to display the **Notification** page shown in Figure 1-6.

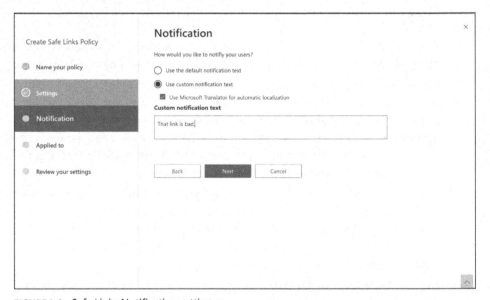

FIGURE 1-6 Safe Links Notification settings

15. On the **Notification** page, there are two options: **Use The Default Notification Text** or **Use Custom Notification Text**. The **Custom Notification Text** box allows you to enter the custom text you want to be displayed to users when they interact with a link that is blocked by Safe Links. Select the **Use Microsoft Translator For Automatic Localization** option to allow your custom notification text to be translated to the user's locale. Click **Next** to advance to the **Applied To** page shown in Figure 1-7.

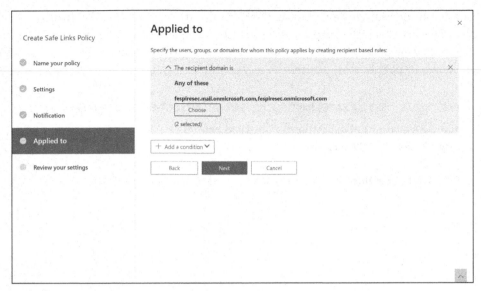

FIGURE 1-7 Safe Links Applied To page

16. On the **Applied To** page, you configure which **groups**, **users,** or **domains** this Safe Links policy will apply to. In this example, the policy will apply to all users who have email addresses with these domains: *fespiresec.mail.onmicrosoft.com* and *fespiresec.onmicrosoft.com*. Combinations of conditions can be used to include specific users and groups of users. Exceptions can be used to exclude specific users, groups, or domains from this Safe Links policy. Click **Next**.

17. The **Review Your Settings** page lists all the configuration settings made so far in the Safe Links configuration wizard. You can edit any of the settings from this screen. When the settings are configured as desired, click **Finish** to create the Safe Links policy.

Multiple Safe Link policies can be created, as shown in Figure 1-8.

FIGURE 1-8 Safe Link policy view

Safe Link policies can be enabled or disabled using the **Status** slider. The **Priority** determines in what order the policies are applied. The policy with Priority 0 is applied first, followed by the policy with Priority 1, and so on. Once a policy's **Applied To** condition is met, no additional policies are processed.

> **MORE INFO**   SET UP SAFE LINKS POLICIES IN MICROSOFT DEFENDER FOR OFFICE 365
>
> You can learn more about setting up Safe Links policies at
> *https://aka.ms/sc200_setupsafelinks*.

Click **Global Settings** to open a side menu, as shown in Figure 1-9.

FIGURE 1-9   Safe Links Global Settings

Under the **Global Settings For Users Included In Active Safe Links Policies** setting, you can configure URLs that will always be blocked in emails and Office 365 Apps. A possible use case for this feature is that if a false negative (miss) occurs, you can add the URL to this list, and it will be blocked, regardless of the verdict from Safe Links.

The **Settings That Apply To Content In Supported Office 365 Apps** options control whether links inside Office 365 Apps are protected by Safe Links. For example, if a PowerPoint presentation contains a slide with a link to a malicious site, these settings will control whether Safe Links will protect the link.

> **MORE INFO   CONFIGURE GLOBAL SETTINGS FOR SAFE LINKS IN MICROSOFT DEFENDER FOR OFFICE 365**
>
> You can learn more about these global settings at *https://aka.ms/sc200_SLglobalsettings*.

Malicious attachments

Attackers sometimes use malicious files attached to emails to gain unauthorized access into a system. This type of attack entry is beneficial because it establishes a foothold for the attacker to carry out additional attacks on other connected systems to the compromised system. Signature-based detections are often not enough to catch these malicious files. Fortunately, the Safe Attachments feature in Defender for Office 365 provides additional protection against this type of attack.

Safe Attachments uses dynamic analysis coupled with Machine Learning to detect threats in files and prevent the files from landing in a user's inbox. Since this is a resource-intensive operation, the Safe Attachments analysis occurs only on files that do not already have an anti-malware signature. Files that do have an anti-malware signature are blocked by Exchange Online Protection before they reach Safe Attachments.

Configuring a Safe Attachments policy

To configure a Safe Attachments policy, you must be a member of the **Organization Management** or the **Security Administrator** role groups configured in the **Permissions & Roles** section of the **Microsoft 365 Security Portal** (*https://security.microsoft.com*).

> **NOTE   ROLE GROUP MEMBERSHIPS**
>
> For read-only access to Safe Attachment policies, you must be a member of either the Global Reader or Security Reader role groups. Note these are role groups in Office 365 and are separate from Azure Active Directory roles.

Use the following steps to configure a Safe Attachment policy:

1. Log in to *https://security.microsoft.com* with the required permissions.
2. Under **Email & Collaboration**, click **Policies & Rules** > **Threat Policies**.
3. In **Threat Policies**, under **Policies**, click the **Safe Attachments** icon.
4. Click **Create** to start the **Create A New Safe Attachments Policy** wizard shown in Figure 1-10.

FIGURE 1-10 Name your Safe Attachments policy

5. On the **Name Your Policy** screen, enter a **Name** for the policy and add a **Description**. You can have more than one policy that targets specific users in your organization, so keep this in mind when choosing your naming scheme. Click **Next** to advance to the **Settings** page shown in Figure 1-11.

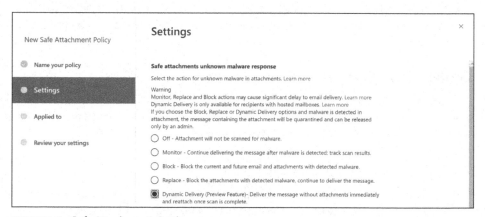

FIGURE 1-11 Safe Attachments Settings page

6. The **Safe Attachments Unknown Malware Response** setting controls how the Safe Attachments feature will interact with an email containing a file attachment.

   ■ **Off—Attachment Will Not Be Scanned For Malware** This setting essentially disables Safe Attachments.

   ■ **Monitor—Continue Delivering The Message After Malware Is Detected; Track Scan Results** This setting is an "audit mode" that allows you to do a what-if analysis of attachments that would be blocked without actually blocking the attachments.

- **Block—Block The Current And Future Email And Attachments With Detected Malware**   This is the most intrusive Safe Attachments mode. If an email contains an attachment that is found to be malicious by Safe Attachments, the email and the attachment will not be delivered to the recipient(s). This is the default and recommended setting.

- **Replace—Block The Attachments With Detected Malware, Continue To Deliver The Message**   In this mode, Safe Attachments will deliver the email, but the attachment will be replaced with a text file indicating the file was infected and was removed.

- **Dynamic Delivery (Preview Feature)—Deliver The Message Without Attachments Immediately And Reattach Once Scan Is Complete**   This setting delivers the email body while the attachment is scanned. A preview of the attachment is provided until the Safe Attachments analysis is complete. If the attachment is found to be malicious, a text file will instead be placed in the message indicating the file was infected and removed.

7. The last few options on the settings page are seen in Figure 1-12.

FIGURE 1-12   Redirect Attachment On Detection

8. If the **Redirect Attachment On Detection** option is selected, the detected malicious files will be sent to a mailbox that you configure, so you can collect these samples for further analysis.

9. Selecting the **Apply The Above Selection If Malware Scanning For Attachment Times Out Or Errors Occur** option ensures that files that time out or error out during scanning are treated the same as what you configured in the policy. Be sure to select the **Redirect Attachment On Detection** if a file is not malicious so that you can recover the file for the user.

10. Once you have the options configured to meet your needs, click **Next** to show the **Applied To** page shown in Figure 1-13.

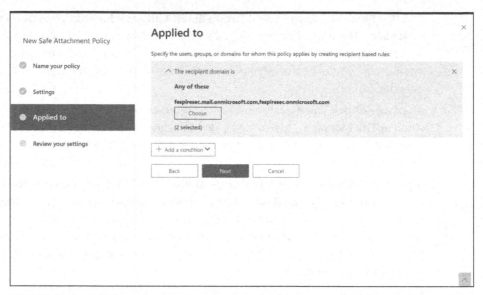

FIGURE 1-13 Applied To page

11. The **Applied To** page is where you configure which **groups**, **users,** or **domains** this Safe Attachments policy will apply to. In this example, the policy will apply to all users with email addresses with the domains *fespiresec.mail.onmicrosoft.com* and *fespiresec. onmicrosoft.com*. Combinations of conditions can be used to include specific users and groups of users. Exceptions can be used to exclude specific users, groups, or domains from this Safe Attachments policy. Click **Next**.

12. The **Review Your Settings** page lists all the configuration settings made so far in the Safe Attachments configuration wizard. You can edit any of the settings from this screen. When the settings are configured as desired, click **Finish** to create the Safe Attachments policy.

Multiple Safe Attachments policies can be created, as shown in Figure 1-14.

FIGURE 1-14 Safe Attachments policy view

Safe Attachments policies can be enabled or disabled using the slider under **Status**. The Priority determines the order in which the policies are applied. The policy with Priority 0 is applied first, followed by the policy with Priority 1, and so on. Once a policy's **Applied To** condition is met, no additional policies are processed.

Clicking **Global Settings** opens a side menu, as shown in Figure 1-15.

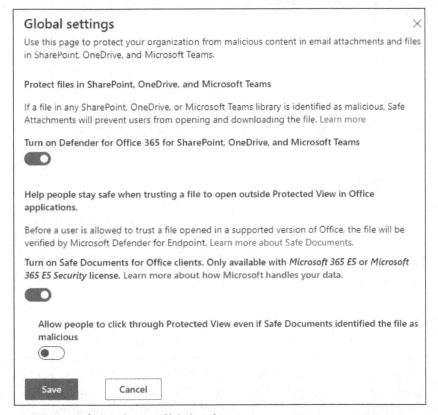

FIGURE 1-15   Safe Attachments Global settings

These Global settings apply to files stored on SharePoint, OneDrive, and Microsoft Teams and prevent users from accessing malicious files in these locations tenant wide. The key difference between these settings and Safe Attachments policies are that these setting focus on *files outside of emails*. Here are the protections you can enable in **Global Settings**:

- **Turn On Defender For Office 365 For Sharepoint, OneDrive, And Microsoft Teams** applies Safe Attachments' malicious file-detection capabilities for files stored in these locations. With this option enabled, if a malicious file is stored in these locations, the user would be unable to open the file. This option should be set to **Enabled**.

- **Turn On Safe Documents For Office Clients** enables the files opened by Office 365 apps to be scanned by Cloud Protection, a component of Microsoft Defender for Endpoint that provides an added layer of protection on top of Safe Attachments protection. This option should be set to **Enabled**.

- **Allow People To Click Through Protected View Even If Safe Documents Identified The File As Malicious** would allow users to override Safe Documents' verdict of a file. We recommend that you do not enable this option.

> **MORE INFO** **TURN ON SAFE ATTACHMENTS FOR SHAREPOINT, ONEDRIVE, AND MICROSOFT TEAMS**
>
> You can learn more about setting up Safe Attachments policies for these products at *https://aka.ms/sc200_safeattach4sps*.

> **MORE INFO** **SAFE DOCUMENTS IN MICROSOFT 365 E5**
>
> You can learn more about setting up Safe Documents at *https://aka.ms/sc200_safedocs*.

Anti-phishing policies

Exchange Online Protection (EOP), which is included with the Office 365 Exchange Online service, provides a moderate amount of protection against phishing. Microsoft Defender for Office 365 takes anti-phishing protection to the next level by adding the following features:

- Impersonation protection
- Configurable advanced phishing thresholds

Impersonation protection

Impersonation protection applies to two types of impersonation: user impersonation and domain impersonation. User impersonation occurs when an attacker sends an email where the user portion of an email address mimics a user who is credible to the recipient. In the previous spear phishing example, the attacker used Bob Smith as the sender's name to mimic the Contoso CEO. The attacker could have further impersonated Bob Smith by creating the email account *bobsmith@fabrikam.com* to increase the chances of the recipient responding to the message.

With domain impersonation, an attacker registers a domain that closely resembles a legitimate domain. For example, instead of *contoso.com*, the attacker could register *consoto.com*, which means at first glance, the recipient would recognize the Contoso name and interact with the message. Combinations of symbols and numbers are also used in this technique, such as *bobsmith@C0NTOSO.com*. (A zero is used instead of the first letter 'O' in CONTOSO.)

Configurable advanced phishing thresholds

Advanced phishing thresholds allow you to define how aggressive the machine learning models should be when determining if an email is a phish. The machine learning models driving the phishing detection in Defender for Office 365 have the ability score on a scale of low, medium, high, or very-high confidence levels. The more aggressive you configure this setting, the higher the chances of false positives. False positives occur when a legitimate email is falsely determined to be a phishing email and is kept out of the recipient's inbox. False negatives can occur if the setting is not aggressive enough, so this setting is a double-edged sword. Each organization is different in terms of how much risk they are willing to accept, which will drive the decision when setting this threshold.

Below are the advanced phishing thresholds available:

- **1—Standard**   The machine learning model will treat phish based on the determined confidence level. This is the default setting.
- **2—Aggressive**   High-confidence phish and above will be treated like very high–confidence phish.
- **3—More aggressive**   Medium-confidence phish and above will be treated like very high–confidence phish.
- **4—Most aggressive**   All emails determined to be any level of phish will be treated like very-high-confidence phish.

> **MORE INFO   RECOMMENDED SETTINGS FOR CONFIGURING EOP AND DEFENDER FOR OFFICE 365**
>
> The Microsoft recommended settings for anti-phishing can be found at *https://aka.ms/sc200_antiphishrecommended*.

Configuring an anti-phishing policy

To configure a Safe Links policy, you must be a member of the **Organization Management** or the **Security Administrator** role groups configured in the **Permissions & Roles** section of the **Microsoft 365 Security Portal** (*https://security.microsoft.com*). For read-only access to Safe Link policies, you must be a member of either the **Global Reader** or **Security Reader** role groups.

Use the following steps to configure an anti-phishing policy:

1. Log in to *https://security.microsoft.com*.
2. Under **Email & Collaboration**, click **Policies & Rules** > **Threat Policies**.
3. In **Threat Policies**, under **Policies**, click the **Anti-Phishing** icon.
4. Click **Create** to start the **Create A New Anti-phishing Policy** wizard and display the **Name Your Policy** screen, as shown in Figure 1-16.

FIGURE 1-16 Name your anti-phishing policy.

5. Type in a **Name** and a **Description** for the policy. You can have more than one policy that targets specific users in your organization, so keep this in mind when choosing your naming scheme. Click **Next** to advance to the **Applied To** page shown in Figure 1-17.

FIGURE 1-17 Applied To page

6. The **Applied To** page is where you configure which **groups**, **users**, or **domains** this anti-phishing policy will apply to. The policy will apply to all users with email addresses with the domains *fespiresec.mail.onmicrosoft.com* and *fespiresec.onmicrosoft.com*. Combinations of conditions can be used to include specific users and groups of users. Exceptions can be used to exclude specific users, groups, or domains from this anti-phishing policy. Click **Next.**

7. The **Review Your Settings** page lists the configurations made so far in the anti-phishing configuration wizard. You can edit any of the settings from this screen. When the settings are configured as desired, click **Create This Policy**, which will create the policy with default settings.

8. On the **Anti-Phishing Policy** screen, click the anti-phishing policy you just created. This will open a fly-out menu where you configure the **Impersonation** settings and **Advanced Settings,** as shown in Figure 1-18.

FIGURE 1-18 Edit page for an anti-phishing policy

9. Click **Edit** next to the **Impersonation** settings to open the **Edit Impersonation Policy** wizard; the wizard starts with the **Editing Add Users To Protect** page shown in Figure 1-19.

FIGURE 1-19 Editing Add users to protect in the anti-phishing impersonation policy

10. Click the toggle button to **On**. This will expose a section where you can add users who you want to protect from user impersonation. You can add up to 60 email accounts to this list. Typically, you want to add users with high public visibility, such as the CEO, as well as external users associated with your company, such as board members. **Bob Smith** was added because he is the Contoso CEO. When finished adding email accounts, click **Add Domains To Protect**, shown in Figure 1-20.

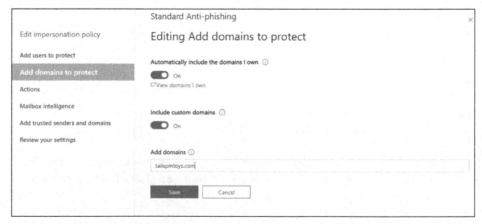

FIGURE 1-20 Editing Add Domains To Protect in the anti-phishing impersonation policy

11. On the **Add Domains To Protect** page of the wizard, enter the domains you want to protect from domain impersonation. You can add up to 50 domains to protect. To add the domains configured in your Office 365 tenant, click the toggle switch under **Automatically Include The Domains I Own** to **On**. To enter email domains that are external to your company that you normally do business with, click the toggle switch under the **Include Custom Domains** to **On**. **Tailspintoys.com** was entered under **Add Domains** because they are a major supplier to Contoso. When you are finished adding domains, click the **Actions** option on the left, as shown in Figure 1-21.

FIGURE 1-21 Editing Actions in the anti-phishing impersonation policy

12. The **Actions** wizard page is where you configure what action you want performed when an email is believed to be impersonating a user or domain. Both cases are set to **Move Message To The Recipients' Junk Email Folders**. You can set the same action on both user and domain impersonation, or you can set a different action for each. The choices for **Actions** include:

- **Redirect Message To Other Email Addresses**
- **Move Message To The Recipients' Junk Email Folders**
- **Quarantine The Message**
- **Deliver The Message And Add Other Addresses To The BCC Line**
- **Delete The Message Before It's Delivered**
- **Don't Apply Any Action**

The **Turn On Impersonation Safety Tips** text is a clickable link that when clicked opens the **Safety Tips** configuration window shown in Figure 1-22.

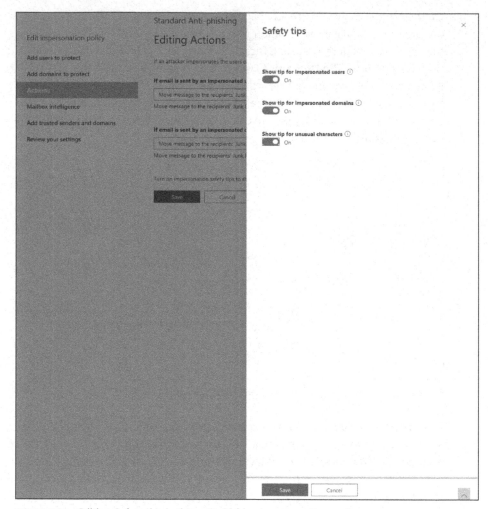

FIGURE 1-22 Editing Safety tips in the anti-phishing impersonation policy

These options allow a banner to be added to emails when a user or domain is impersonated or when unusual characters are present in the sender email address, such as bobsmith@C0NTOSO.com (where a zero is used instead of the first O in CONTOSO). Set the toggle switch to **On** for each of these settings and click **Save** when you are finished. This will return you to the **Actions** wizard page.

When you have the options set on the **Actions** wizard page, click the **Mailbox Intelligence** option on the left, as shown in Figure 1-23.

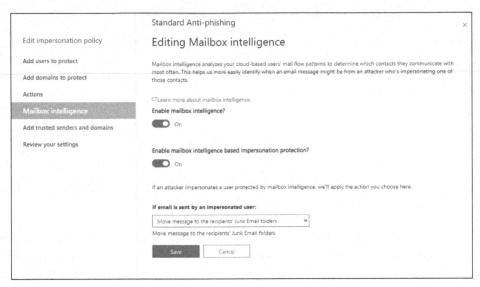

FIGURE 1-23 Editing the Mailbox Intelligence

13. **Mailbox Intelligence** is an additional layer of artificial intelligence–driven protection that learns the sending and receiving patterns of the users configured to be protected by the impersonation policy. This pattern learning improves the efficacy of the impersonation policy and should be turned on. If Mailbox Intelligence is what catches the impersonation, the action configured under **If Email Is Sent By An Impersonated User** is taken. The actions are configurable as follows:

- **Redirect Message To Other Email Addresses**
- **Move Message To The Recipients' Junk Email Folders**
- **Quarantine The Message**
- **Deliver The Message And Add Other Addresses To The Bcc Line**
- **Delete The Message Before It's Delivered**
- **Don't Apply Any Action**

Once you have the action configured, click the **Add Trusted Senders And Domains** option on the left, as shown in Figure 1-24.

14. Adding sender email addresses and domains to exempt them from the impersonation policy should only be used for reoccurring false positives. Exempting too many domains increases your exposure to impersonation. It is best to start out with no exceptions if possible. Click the **Review Your Settings** text on the left.

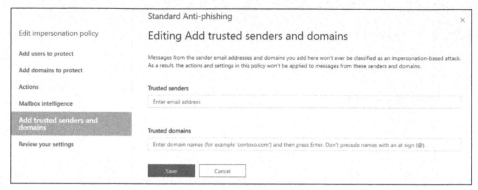

FIGURE 1-24   Add Trusted Senders And Domains

15. The **Review Your Settings** page lists all the configuration settings made so far in the **Edit Impersonation Policy Configuration** wizard. You can edit any of the settings from this screen. When the settings are configured as desired, click **Save** to apply the impersonation settings to the anti-phishing policy and return you to the **Edit Your Policy Standard Anti-Phishing** page shown in Figure 1-25.

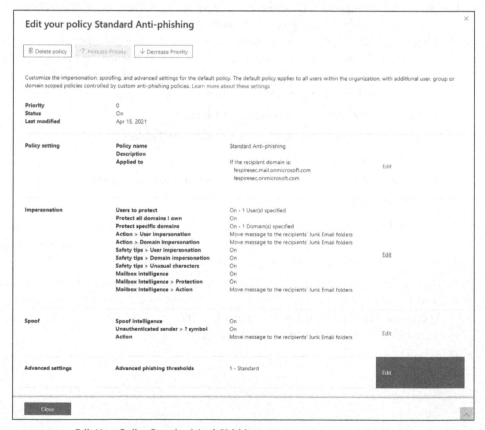

FIGURE 1-25   Edit Your Policy Standard Anti-Phishing page

16. Lastly, you need to configure the **Advanced Settings** of the **Anti-Phishing Policy**. Click **Edit** next to **Advanced Settings** to open the **Editing Advanced Phishing Thresholds** window shown in Figure 1-26.

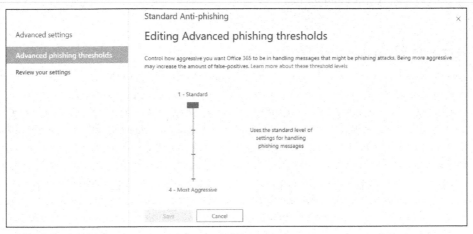

FIGURE 1-26 Editing Advanced Phishing Thresholds

17. Depending on the tolerance for false positives (in other words, emails not reaching the attended recipients), set this policy to the appropriate aggressiveness. One approach is to leave the settings at the default setting—**1-Standard**—and increase aggressiveness if there are false negatives. Repeat this process until the efficacy is acceptable. After setting the aggressiveness, click the **Review Your Settings** option on the left.

18. The **Review Your Settings** page lists all the configuration settings made so far in the **Advanced Settings** wizard. You can edit any of the settings from this screen. When the settings are configured as desired, click **Save** to apply the **Advanced Settings** to the anti-phishing policy.

19. Click **Close** to complete the configuration of the anti-phishing policy.

20. Multiple anti-phishing policies can be created, as shown in Figure 1-27.

FIGURE 1-27 Anti-phishing policies

21. Anti-phishing policies can be enabled or disabled using the slider under **Status**. The Priority determines in what order the policies are applied. The policy with priority 0 is applied first, followed by the policy with priority 1, and so on. Once a policy's **Applied To** condition is met, no additional policies are processed.

Attack Simulation Training

Having a cybersecurity awareness program is an essential part to your overall plan to combat email-based attacks. Earlier in this chapter, we covered ways to prevent malicious emails from reaching users. But a good cybersecurity defensive posture demands that you examine every layer of your defenses and come up with a plan for how you will mitigate a threat that makes it through each layer. This raises the question, "How can I help end users not click everything that is delivered to their Inbox?" While this is a frustrating and constant battle, it is important to keep in mind that users do not have years of cybersecurity knowledge (which tends to result in having lots of skepticism). They need help separating good emails from an email that just does not seem right. This is the reason the Attack Simulation Training feature in Microsoft Defender for Office 365 was created. You can use this tool to send benign emails with suspicious qualities to train your users to look for signs that an email should be reported rather than interacted with (for example, clicking the link, opening the attachment, or gladly typing their corporate credentials into every web-based credential page). The Attack Simulation Training feature is an impressive improvement to the initial Attack Simulator that was released in 2019.

Launching a simulation

To create a new attack training simulation, you must be a member of one of the following roles:

- **Organization Management**
- **Security Administrator**
- **Attack Simulator Administrators**

Follow these steps to create a new simulation:

1. Log in to *https://security.microsoft.com*.
2. Under **Email & Collaboration**, click **Attack Simulation Training**, as shown in Figure 1-28.

FIGURE 1-28 Create an attack simulation.

3. Click **Simulations > Launch A Simulation**, which brings up the **Select Technique** step in the attack simulation creation wizard shown in Figure 1-29.

FIGURE 1-29 Creating an attack simulation

4. Under **Select Technique**, choose the simulation technique you want to run against your users. For this simulation, choose **Credential Harvest** and click **Next** to bring up the **Name Simulation** page shown in Figure 1-30.

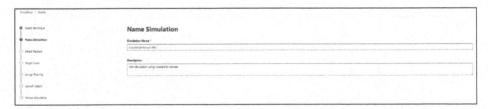

FIGURE 1-30 Add a Simulation Name and Description for the simulation.

5. Enter a name for the simulation under **Simulation Name** and enter a **Description**. Click **Next** to advance to the **Select Payload** page shown in Figure 1-31.

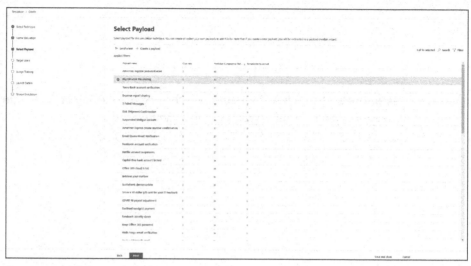

FIGURE 1-31   Select a payload for the simulation.

6. Select a payload for the simulation. This is what will be used to bait the user for the **Credential Harvest** technique. You can sort the payloads by the **Predicted Compromise Rate (%)** column, which is calculated based on the compromised percentage of all Microsoft Defender for Office 365 customers. You can click **Send A Test** to the currently logged-in user to see the payload sample before you commit. Based on the 42 percent predicted compromise rate, select **Payroll Work File Sharing** and then click **Next**.

7. In the **Target Users** page, you can choose to **Include All Users In My Organization** or **Include Only Specific Users And Groups**. In this case, select **Include Only Specific Users And Groups** and click **Add Users** to open the **Add Users** fly-out pane, as shown in Figure 1-32.

FIGURE 1-32 Target users for the simulation.

8. In the **Add Users** fly-out pane, there are some thoughtful suggestions on which users to target. For example, you can target **Users Not Targeted By A Simulation In The Last Three Months** or **Repeat Offenders**, which are users who continue to fall for the simulations. In this case, there is a user group created in Azure Active Directory to run the first simulation on pilot users. Once the desired user group is selected, click **Add User(s)** and then click **Next** to advance to the **Assign Training** page as shown in Figure 1-33.

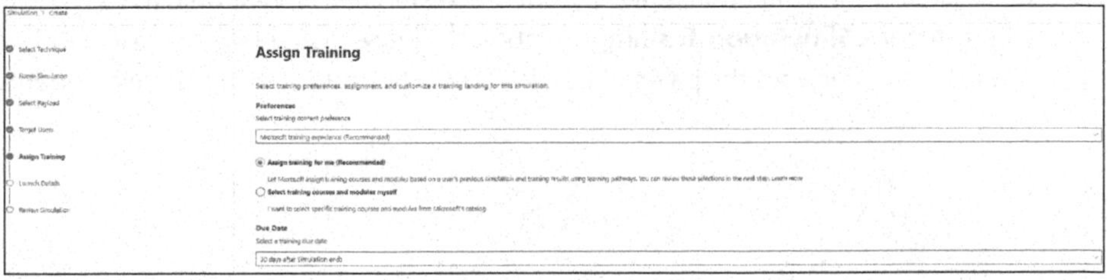

FIGURE 1-33 Assign Training

9. **Assign Training** is a welcome addition to the Attack Simulation Training feature. You can assign training to users who fall for the simulations by interacting with the email and/or payload. You can choose to use the **Microsoft Training Experience**, **Redirect To A Custom URL** (handy if you have a Learning Management System, or LMS), or **No Training**. For the **Microsoft Training Experience** option, you can then choose to allow the system to **Assign Training For Me** based on the technique and payload used or **Select Training Courses And Modules Myself**. A **Due Date** can also be set for when the training must be completed by the user. Click **Next**.

10. On the **Training Landing Page**, you can see the text the user will see if they fall for the simulation. You can customize the **Header** and **Body** of the page and view a preview. Type the text you want the user to see and click **Next**.

11. The last options to configure are the Launch Details for when you want the simulation to launch and when you want it to end. You can also select the option to **Enable Region Aware Timezone Delivery** so the simulation does not deliver to users outside your time zone during off-work hours, which might cause them to miss the email. Click **Next** to advance to the **Review Simulation** page, as seen in Figure 1-34.

FIGURE 1-34 Review Simulation

12. **Review Simulation** allows you to edit the settings you have configured thus far in the simulation. You can also choose **Send A Test** to ensure the simulation operates as you expect before unleashing it on your users. Once you are satisfied with the configuration, click **Submit** to finalize the simulation.

Reviewing the Attack Simulation Training results

You can track how the simulation is playing out by clicking the simulation name on the main page of the **Attack Simulation Training** dashboard. Figure 1-35 shows one user who was tricked into interacting with the payload by clicking the link and supplying their credentials.

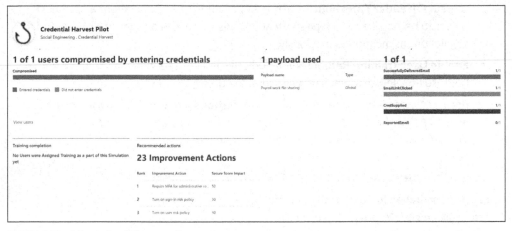

FIGURE 1-35 Attack simulation results

Attack Simulation Training settings

The Attack Simulation Training feature settings are largely configured as part of the simulations, however there are some overall settings that are important to mention.

In the Attack Simulation Training section, clicking **Settings** shows the following options, which are also shown in Figure 1-36.

FIGURE 1-36 Attack Simulation Training settings

- **Repeat Offender Threshold** is the number of consecutive simulations a user must fall for to be classified as a repeat offender. These users can be specifically targeted for simulations as mentioned previously.

- **Enable User Training Reminders** periodically emails users who have training due because they fell for a simulation and interacted with the simulation payload.

- Because you cannot delete simulations, **Simulations Excluded From Reporting** comes in handy if you have a simulation that is tainted for some reason (such as the URL was blocked by proxy) and you do not want this simulation to skew the reporting.

> **MORE INFO**   **GET STARTED USING ATTACK SIMULATION TRAINING**
>
> Full documentation for the Attack Simulation Training feature can be found at *https://aka.ms/sc200_attacksimtraining*.

Data protection, labeling, and insider risk

Data and intellectual property are among the most valuable assets in a company. With data being accessed from virtually anywhere on any device, protecting these assets is key. Microsoft 365 Compliance features allow you to scan for sensitive data types, apply sensitivity labels to the data, and protect the data so that only authorized users have access. These steps help protect honest users from accidentally oversharing data.

Sensitivity labels

Sensitivity labels allow for users to label their data according to company data handling policies. You can also auto label documents with a sensitivity label if they match your defined criteria.

Follow these steps to create a sensitivity label:

1. Log in to *https://compliance.microsoft.com* as a member of the **Global Administrator** role in Azure Active Directory. You can also use an account that is a member of the **Compliance Data Administrator, Compliance Administrator**, or **Security Administrator** role groups. Note these are Office 365 role groups, and they are separate from Azure Active Directory roles.

2. In the menu on the left side of the page, click **Show All**.

3. Under **Solutions**, click **Information Protection**.

4. On the **Labels** page, click **Create A Label**, which opens the **New Sensitivity Label** wizard shown in Figure 1-37.

5. In the **New Sensitivity Label** wizard, provide a **Name, Display Name, Description For Users,** and **Description For Admins**.

6. Select **Files & Emails** and click **Next**.

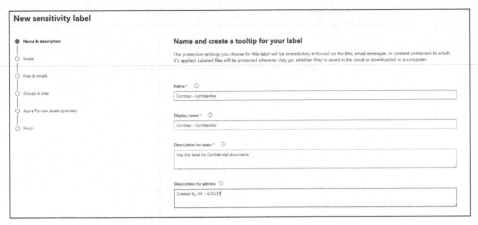

FIGURE 1-37 Name & Description page in the New Sensitivity Label wizard

7. Select **Mark The Content Of Files** and click **Next**.

8. Select the content marking options you want to appear on files and emails classified with this sensitivity label and click **Next**.

9. When auto-labeling files and emails, you want users to be able to choose their labels at first, so leave the auto-labeling option unselected and click **Next**.

10. On the **Define Protection Settings For Groups And Sites** page, click **Next**.

11. On **Review Your Settings And Finish** page, make sure the options are configured to your specifications, and then click **Create Label**.

12. Click **Done** once the label is created.

Before users can use the labels, you need to publish the label using Label policies.

1. Select the label you created and click the **Publish Labels** button shown in Figure 1-38.

FIGURE 1-38 Publish Labels

2. On the **Choose Sensitivity Labels To Publish** page, make sure your label is listed and click **Next**.

3. On the **Publish To Users And Groups** page, leave the default of **All Users And groups**, and click **Next** to open the **Policy Settings** page shown in Figure 1-39.

FIGURE 1-39 Policy Settings

4. On the **Policy Settings** page there are three options:

   ▪ **Users Must Provide A Justification To Remove A Label Or Lower Its Classification** This setting is meant to force the user to type in a justification if they set the classification of the document to a less sensitive label or remove the label entirely.

   ▪ **Require Users To Apply A Label To Their Emails And Documents** Before users can save documents or send emails, this option forces them to set a label.

   ▪ **Provide Users With A Link To A Custom Help Page** This setting allows you to set up a help page for users to explain the various sensitivity labels and how to use them.

5. Once you select the options desired, click **Next**.

6. Under **Apply This Label As The Default Label To Documents And Emails**, choose the label you created. This ensures all emails and documents are labeled.

7. On the **Name Your Policy** page, provide a **Name** and **Description** for the label policy, and then click **Next**.

8. On the **Review And Finish** page, ensure the settings are as you want them and click **Submit** to create the label policy.

9. Once the policy is created, click **Done**.

Users can now use the sensitivity label you created to label their documents and emails.

> **MORE INFO** **LEARN ABOUT SENSITIVITY LABELS**
>
> For additional information about sensitivity labels, see *https://aka.ms/sc200_sensitivelabels*.

Managing data loss prevention alerts

One of the responsibilities of a data loss prevention administrator is to respond to alerts indicating sensitive data, such as customer credit card numbers, were exposed to parties unintentionally.

Follow these steps to review data loss prevention alerts:

1. Log in to *https://compliance.microsoft.com* as a member of the **Global Administrator** role in Azure Active Directory. You can also use an account that is a member of the **Compliance Data Administrator, Compliance Administrator**, or **Security Administrator** role groups. Note these are role groups in Office 365 and are separate from Azure Active Directory roles.

2. In the menu on the far-left side of the page, under **Solutions**, click **Data Loss Prevention**.

3. At the top of the page, click the **Alerts** tab (see Figure 1-40).

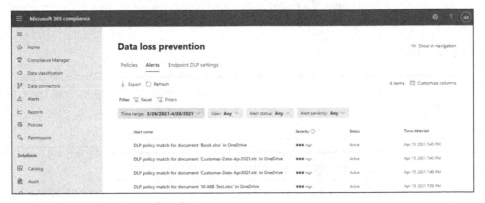

FIGURE 1-40 Data loss prevention alerts

4. In Figure 1-40, high-severity alerts are shown, indicating a DLP policy match. Click the **first alert**, and then click **View Details** to open the alert page shown in Figure 1-41.

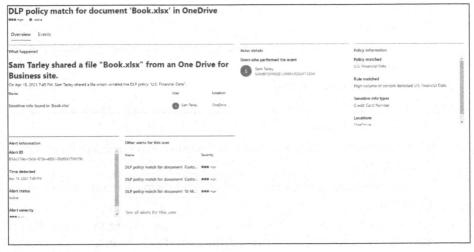

FIGURE 1-41 Data loss prevention alert overview

This alert indicates that **Sam Tarley shared** a file named Book.xlsx **from One Drive for Business**. This file contains **U.S. financial data** in the form of **credit card numbers**. Under **Other Alerts For This User**, it appears that Sam has shared **several other files with sensitive data in them**. Once you have spoken to Sam, you can close this alert out.

5. Under **Manage Alert**, set the **Status** to **Resolved**, **assign** the alert to yourself, and provide **comments** in the **Comments** text box; click **Save**.

> **MORE INFO   CREATE, TEST, AND TUNE A DLP POLICY**
>
> For additional information about DLP policies and alerts, see *https://aka.ms/sc200_dlppol.*

Insider risk

Data leakage can also occur because of an insider threat. Insider threats are when a user with access to company data assets purposefully steals these assets for personal gain. The motivations of these individuals vary. Following are some examples:

- A disgruntled employee looking to embarrass the company publicly
- An employee who feels they are underpaid and who seeks to make money from selling company intellectual property to the highest bidder

You can use insider risk management policies to generate alerts when activity is detected per the policy settings. Follow these steps to create an insider risk policy:

1. Log in to *https://compliance.microsoft.com* as a member of the **Global Administrator** role in Azure Active Directory. You can also use an account that is a member of the **Compliance Data Administrator, Compliance Administrator**, or **Security Administrator** role groups. Note these are role groups in Office 365 and are separate from Azure Active Directory roles.

2. In the menu on the far-left side of the page, under **Solutions**, click **Insider Risk Management.**

3. Click **Policies** > **Create Policy**.

4. Under **Choose A Policy Template**, under **Categories**, select **Data Leaks**. Under **Templates**, select **General Data Leaks** and click **Next**.

5. On the **Name Your Policy page**, provide a **Name** and **Description** for your policy, and then click **Next**.

6. On the **Choose Users And Groups** page, select **Include All Users And Groups** and click **Next**.

7. On the **Specify Content To Prioritize** page, leave the **I Want To Specify Sharepoint Sites, Sensitivity Lables, And/Or Sensitive Info Types As Priority Content** option at its default setting and click **Next**.

8. On the **SharePoint Sites To Prioritize (Optional)** page, click **Next**.

9. On the **Sensitive Info Types To Prioritize (Optional)** page, click **Next**.

10. On the **Sensitivity Labels To Prioritize (Optional)** page, click **Add Or Edit Sensitivity Label**. Select the sensitivity label you created earlier and click **Next**.

11. On the **Indicators And Triggering Event For This Policy** page, under **Choose Triggering Event**, select **User Performs An Exfiltration Activity**. Under **Policy Indicators**, select **all the indicators** in each section and click **Next**.

12. On the **Decide Whether To Use Default Or Custom Indicator Thresholds** page, select **Use Default Thresholds For All Indicators**, click **Next**.

13. On the **Review Settings And Finish** page, ensure the selections made are as you need them and then click **Submit**.

This policy will begin to assess the indicators configured in the policy and raise an alert if a user performs an exfiltration activity, such as downloading files from SharePoint or emailing a significant number of attachments outside the organization.

> **MORE INFO INSIDER RISK MANAGEMENT IN MICROSOFT 365**
>
> For additional information about insider risk management, see *https://aka.ms/sc200_insiderisk*.

Investigate and remediate an alert raised by Microsoft Defender for Office 365

Alerts raised from Microsoft Defender for Office 365 are viewed in the Microsoft 365 Defender Security portal at *https://security.microsoft.com*. They are aggregated into incidents and investigated by the built-in Automated Investigation and Response technology.

Following the steps below, you will triage and resolve an email security incident:

1. Log in to *https://security.microsoft.com* as a member of the **Organization Management** or the **Security Administrator** role groups.

2. In the menu on the far left, expand **Incidents & Alerts** and click **Incidents** to open the incidents page shown in Figure 1-42.

FIGURE 1-42   Incident list view

3. On the **Incidents** page, note one of the detection sources is **Office 365**. Click the incident named **Multi-Stage Incident On One Endpoint Reported By Multiple Sources** to open the incident view, as shown in Figure 1-43.

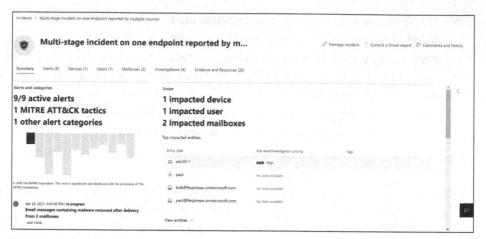

FIGURE 1-43 Incident details page

4. This view tells you there are **nine alerts** in this incident, all falling into the **Initial Access Stage** of the MITRE ATT&CK Framework. Below the framework bar chart is a timeline of the alerts, starting with the alert that occurred first. The **Scope** shows the impacted assets are **one device, one user,** and **two mailboxes**. Click the **Manage Incident** link at the top-right of the page.

5. The **Manage Incident** fly-out window allows you to assign the incident to yourself. This lets other incident responders know you are working on this incident. You can also change the name of the incident. Click the **Assign To Me** slider and click **Save** to assign the incident to yourself.

6. Back on the incident page, click the **Alerts** section near the top of the page to view the alerts in this incident, as shown in Figure 1-44.

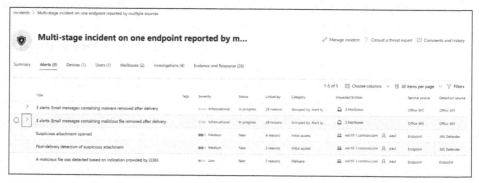

FIGURE 1-44 Incident alerts view

7. Alerts with the same title are grouped. Looking at the alert titles, it appears that an email with a malicious attachment was delivered to user mailboxes, and at least one of the users opened the attachment. Defender for Office 365 learned the attachment was malicious but only after this occurred.

At this point, you would typically begin searching mailboxes for this email and remove the messages. Thankfully, the Automated Investigation and Response feature in Defender for Office 365 has already found the messages and is waiting for your approval to remove them.

8. Click the **Investigations** section to view the investigations for the incident shown in Figure 1-45.

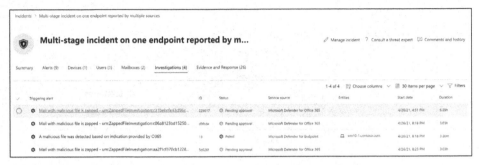

FIGURE 1-45   Incident investigations view

9. There are three investigations with the Microsoft Defender for Office 365 service source, and all are pending approval. Click the **first investigation** in the list to open the **Investigation Summary** shown in Figure 1-46.

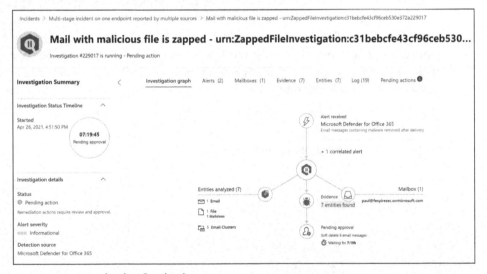

FIGURE 1-46   Investigation Graph tab

10. The investigation graph walks you through the steps taken by Automated Investigation to ensure that all the malicious emails were located and evaluated for malicious content. If malicious emails (including attachments) are found, they are marked **Pending Action**. Pending actions allow you to either approve or reject the recommended action for

each artifact. Click the **Pending Actions** section and then click the first pending action, as shown in Figure 1-47.

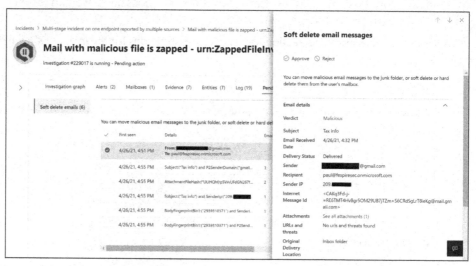

FIGURE 1-47 Pending Actions

11. You can review each action that Automated Investigation wants to take to clean up this incident. In this example, this email was found to be **malicious,** and the pending action is to **soft delete** the email. It was originally delivered to the **inbox**, though the **Zero-Hour Auto Purge (ZAP)** action removed it post-delivery from the user's inbox and placed it in **quarantine**. You can click each of the **Pending Action** items and approve them manually, or you can click the **Select All** check box and approve them all as one object, as shown in Figure 1-48.

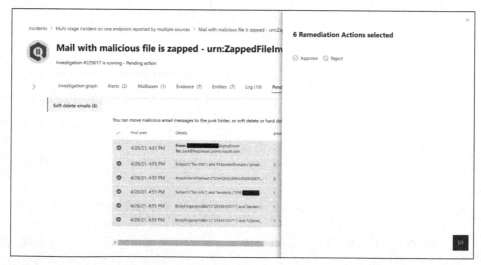

FIGURE 1-48 Approve all actions

12. Choose **Select All** > **Approve**.

13. In the menu on the far left, click **Action Center**.

14. The Action Center allows you to approve all pending actions and view the **history** of actions already approved or rejected, as shown in Figure 1-49.

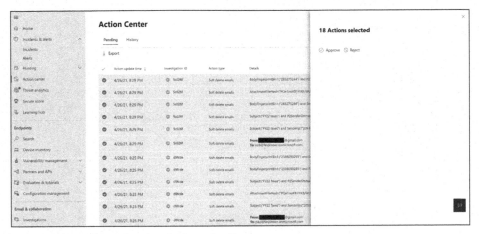

FIGURE 1-49 Approve all actions in the Action Center.

15. Click **Select All**, and then click **Approve**.

16. Now that you have approved all the pending actions for this incident, the incident is ready to be marked as **Resolved**. Click back to the **Incident**.

17. On the incident view, click **Manage Incident** to open the **Manage Incident** fly-out window, as shown in Figure 1-50.

18. Click the **Resolve Incident slider**. Set the **Classification** to **True Alert** and select **Malware** under **Determination**. Provide **Comments** if necessary and click **Save**.

> **MORE INFO REMEDIATION ACTIONS IN MICROSOFT DEFENDER FOR OFFICE 365**
>
> For additional information about remediation actions in Defender for Office 365, see *https://aka.ms/sc200_mdoremediate*.

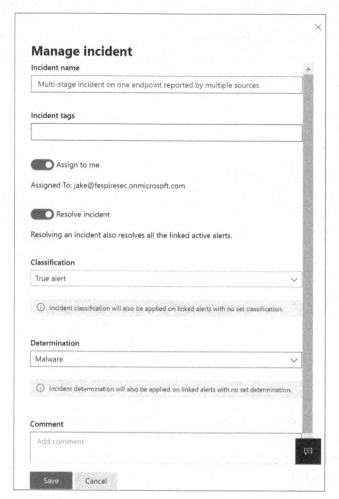

FIGURE 1-50 Manage Incident

Skill 1-2: Detect, investigate, respond, and remediate endpoint threats using Microsoft Defender for Endpoint

Threats to endpoints have continued to become more sophisticated and harder to detect. Techniques like "living off the land," which involves built-in operating system utilities to avoid detection, are increasingly being used. To meet this challenge, security teams invest millions of dollars in endpoint detection capabilities leading to multiple security agents running on endpoints. The increasing number of agents results in the negative effect of poor performance and patching troubles.

Microsoft Defender for Endpoint provides not only next-generation anti-virus (NGAV) and endpoint detection and response (EDR) but also additional capabilities, including:

- 180 days of data retention stored in trusted Azure data centers
- Antimalware coverage far beyond signature detections, powered by cloud protection and attack surface reduction
- Tamper protection and detection
- Manual response and AI-driven self-healing
- Fast querying via advanced hunting
- Threat and vulnerability management
- Rich APIs and a partner ecosystem
- Next-level threat Intelligence via threat analytics
- Multi-platform coverage, including Mac, Linux, iOS, Android, and Windows
- Opt-in targeted attack notifications through Microsoft Threat Experts
- Integration with Intune and conditional access

This list is not exhaustive and continues to grow as Microsoft Defender for Endpoint continues to release features at a blistering pace.

> **MORE INFO** **MICROSOFT DEFENDER FOR ENDPOINT AND OTHER MICROSOFT SOLUTIONS**
>
> For additional information about integration with other Microsoft solutions, see https://aka.ms/sc200_mdeintegrations.

Configuring Microsoft Defender for Endpoint

There are two main areas of Microsoft Defender for Endpoint that require configuration:

- Configuration in the Microsoft 365 Security portal
- Settings on the monitored endpoints

The focus of this chapter will be on configuring Microsoft Defender for Endpoint in the Microsoft 365 Security portal.

Setting up the Microsoft Defender for Endpoint subscription

There are two critical settings to take note of when performing the initial subscription configuration of Microsoft Defender for Endpoint. These settings include:

- Data location
- Data retention period

Data location is selected during the initial subscription configuration and cannot be changed without offboarding all your endpoints and losing all your data. At the time of this writing the regions available are:

- United States
- European Union
- United Kingdom

You should check with your privacy officer to ensure you select the correct region to store your data. This list is for commercial offerings and does not include government offerings.

> **IMPORTANT REGION CANNOT BE CHANGED!**
>
> You cannot change the region your data is stored in once you configure your subscription without offboarding all endpoints and losing all data in the subscription!

> **MORE INFO MICROSOFT DEFENDER FOR ENDPOINT DATA STORAGE AND PRIVACY**
>
> More details on Microsoft Defender for Endpoint data storage and privacy can be found at *https://aka.ms/sc200_mdeprivacy*.

The data retention period is also selected during initial subscription configuration. Unlike the data location, the retention period can be changed at any time, even after completing the subscription configuration wizard. The **default retention period is 180 days (6 months)** and can be changed to 30, 60, 90, 120, or 150 days.

Once the subscription configuration wizard is complete, you can change the data retention period by performing the following steps:

1. Log in to *https://security.microsoft.com* as a member of the **Global Administrator** or **Security Administrator** Azure Active Directory roles.

2. In the menu on the left, click **Settings > Endpoints**.

3. Under **General**, click **Data Retention**, as shown in Figure 1-51.

4. Note that you cannot change the **Data Storage** location as previously mentioned (selections are unavailable). To change the **Data Retention** period, click the **drop-down menu** and select the number of days that is appropriate to your environment.

5. When you are finished, click **Save Preferences**.

> **MORE INFO SET UP MICROSOFT DEFENDER FOR ENDPOINT DEPLOYMENT**
>
> Full details of the Microsoft Defender for Endpoint subscription configuration wizard can be found at *https://aka.ms/sc200_mdeconfigwiz*.

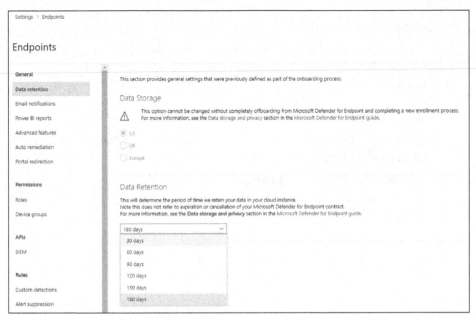

FIGURE 1-51 Data Retention selection for Microsoft Defender for Endpoint

Role-Based Access Control

Like all Microsoft enterprise Software as a Service (SaaS) offerings, Microsoft Defender for Endpoint uses Azure Active Directory for authentication and authorization. Initial configuration provides the following Azure Active Directory built-in roles access to the endpoint-specific data and settings in the Microsoft 365 Security portal:

- **The Global Administrators** and **Security Administrators** roles have **full access.**
- **The Security Reader** role has **read-only access.**

Typically, this model is too rigid for larger companies, especially those with multi-tiered security operations teams. In these companies, each tier has set responsibilities and needs to have the least amount of privilege to carry out those responsibilities. Thankfully, Microsoft Defender for Endpoint's role-based security model was designed for various sizes of security teams.

Roles in Microsoft Defender for Endpoint consist of two major parts:

- **Roles** that provide Azure Active Directory groups with specific rights to Microsoft Defender for Endpoint data and settings.
- **Device Groups** are used to segment enrolled devices so they can have Azure Active Directory groups and their roles assigned to them.

This model allows for least privilege access to only the devices that the security analyst should possess.

> **IMPORTANT** **ACCESS LOSS**
>
> Enabling roles will cause users with the **Security Reader** Azure Active Directory role to lose access to Microsoft Defender for Endpoint data and settings in the Microsoft 365 Security portal.

To enable roles, follow these steps:

1. Log in to *https://security.microsoft.com* as a member of the **Global Administrator** or **Security Administrator** Azure Active Directory roles.

2. In the menu on the left, click **Settings** > **Endpoints**.

3. Under **Permissions**, click **Roles**, as shown in Figure 1-52.

FIGURE 1-52 Enabling roles for Microsoft Defender for Endpoint

4. Note the **Users With Read-Only Permissions Will Lose Access To The Portal Until They Are Assigned One Of The New Roles Through Their Azure AD Groups** warning. These are users who gained access via the Azure Active Directory **Security Readers** role. If you have users in this situation, you should create an Azure Active Directory group for these read-only users *before* you enable roles to get them back to being operational as quickly as possible. When you are ready, click **Turn On Roles**.

Now that roles are enabled, the **Microsoft Defender For Endpoint Administrator (Default)** role is automatically created, which provides full rights to the endpoint data and settings (see Figure 1-53).

This role can be used instead of the built-in Azure Active Directory **Global Administrator** or **Security Administrator** roles, which is ideal because these Azure Active Directory roles provide access beyond endpoint data and should be used sparingly. If a user needs full permissions to manage the endpoint data and related settings, they can be placed in this role.

FIGURE 1-53 Default role for Microsoft Defender for Endpoint

To provide read-only rights to the endpoint data, create a role with read-only access using the following steps:

1. Log in to *https://security.microsoft.com* as a member of the **Global Administrator** or **Security Administrator** Azure Active Directory roles.

2. In the menu on the left, click **Settings** > **Endpoints**.

3. Under **Permissions**, click **Roles**.

4. Click the **Add Item** button and the fly-out menu will appear, as shown in Figure 1-54.

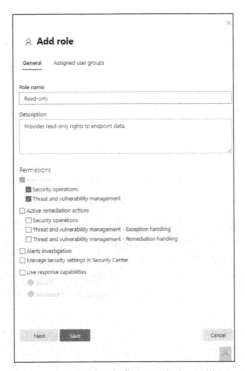

FIGURE 1-54 Add Role fly-out window with permission list

5. Provide a **Role Name** and **Description**.

6. For **Permissions**, notice you can provide the **View Data** permission for either **Security Operations** data, **Threat And Vulnerability Management** data, or both. This is important if your security operations team is separate from your threat and vulnerability management team. In this case, you want to allow both types of data, so leave them both selected.

7. Click **Assigned User Groups**, as shown in Figure 1-55.

FIGURE 1-55 Assigned User Groups tab

8. Because you likely have many security groups, you can type the partial name of the group in the text field, which will filter the list below. **Secops** was entered into this text box to filter the list for all groups containing "Secops" in the group title. Once you find the group or groups you need, select the box next to the Azure Active Directory group you want to assign the role to and then click the **Add Selected Groups** button. When you are finished, click the **Save** button.

Secops-Tier1 user named Ryker now has read-only access to the endpoint data in the Microsoft 365 Security portal. Note in Figure 1-56, Ryker can view data for the computer win10-1 but cannot perform any actions.

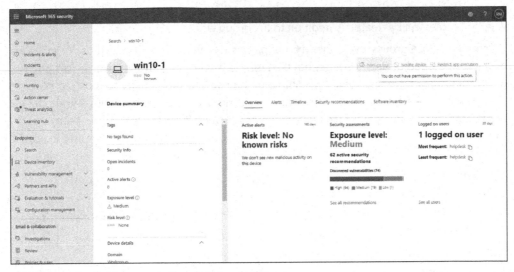

FIGURE 1-56 Read-only access to the win10-1 endpoint

EXAM TIP

Be sure to know what rights to endpoint data and settings each permission provides.

MORE INFO **CREATE AND MANAGE ROLES FOR ROLE-BASED ACCESS CONTROL**

Full details of each permission can be found at *https://aka.ms/sc200_mderbac*.

Under **Device Groups**, notice there are no groups currently, as shown in Figure 1-57.

FIGURE 1-57 Device Groups

This is because no device groups have been created yet. Once we create a device group, a default group will be created in addition to the group we create.

Without device groups, everyone who has permissions via a role will have those permissions over all onboarded devices. This may not be desirable, especially with sensitive devices, such as devices operated by executives of the company. Contoso has an executive support staff consisting of Mikey, Zach, and Dylan. They require access to the executive machines and should be the only ones with access. Because of this, you need to keep Ryker in Tier 1 from having access to these endpoints. You have already created the Executive Support role for the three executive support staff members and added the Azure Active Directory group. Now you need to create a device group for these executive devices.

To create a device group, follow these steps:

1. Log in to *https://security.microsoft.com* as a member of the **Global Administrator** or **Security Administrator** Azure Active Directory roles.

2. In the menu on the left, click **Settings** > **Endpoints**.

3. Under **Permissions**, click **Device Group,** and then click **Add Device Group** to open the fly-out menu shown in Figure 1-58.

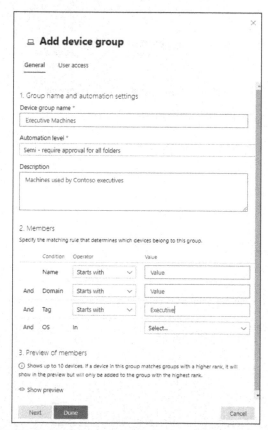

FIGURE 1-58 Add device group fly-out menu

4. In the **Add Device Group** fly-out menu, type a **Device Group Name**, choose an **Automation Level**, and type a **Description**.

5. In the **Members** section, devices can automatically be placed in this device group based on these values:

   - **Name** Name of the device
   - **Domain** Active Directory domain name the device is a member of
   - **Tag** A label that is assigned to the device
   - **OS** Operating system that runs on the device

   The **Name**, **Domain**, and **Tag** values support **Starts With, Ends With, Equals,** and **Contains** operators. Note these conditions are ***Boolean*** AND ***conditions***. For the device to be placed in this Device group, it must meet **all the conditions** you specify in the **Value** text box. You can use the **Executive** value for **Tag**.

6. **Preview Of Members** allows you to see up to 10 devices that will be placed in this device group based on the **Members** logic.

7. Click the **User Access** tab at the top of the **Add Device Group** fly-out menu, as shown in Figure 1-59.

FIGURE 1-59 User Access tab

8. Click the check box next to **Executive Support**, click the **Add Selected Groups** button, and then click **Done**.

9. You should now be on the **Device Groups** page shown in Figure 1-60.

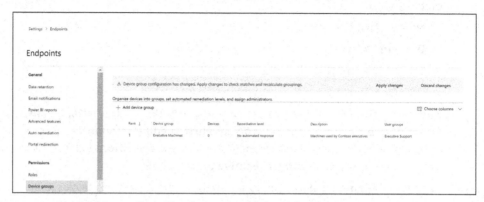

FIGURE 1-60 Applying or discarding changes

10. You will see a warning at the top of the page indicating that you need to **Apply Changes** or **Discard Changes**. Click **Apply Changes**.

Once you click **Apply Changes**, a message with a green background appears where the warning was once located indicating that it will take a bit of time to apply the changes; once the changes are complete, the message disappears. You should now see two device groups—the one you created for **Executive Machines** and one you did not create called **Ungrouped Devices (Default)**. They are ranked **1** and **Last**, respectively, as seen in Figure 1-61.

FIGURE 1-61 Device Groups list

Devices are placed in device groups starting with groups with the lowest **rank** then working their way down. Once the device meets the criteria for a device group per its criteria, the device becomes a member of that group, and processing for that device stops. Therefore, it is important to put the most specific device group (such as those that match tags) at the top and place less-specific device groups (such as those that match domains) toward the bottom. The **Ungrouped Devices (Default)** is the "catch-all" device group that is created by default once you create a device group. This device group contains all devices that do not match a criterion in the device groups you create. You can change the rank of the device groups by selecting the device group you want to change and clicking either the **Promote Rank** or **Demote Rank** buttons shown in Figure 1-62.

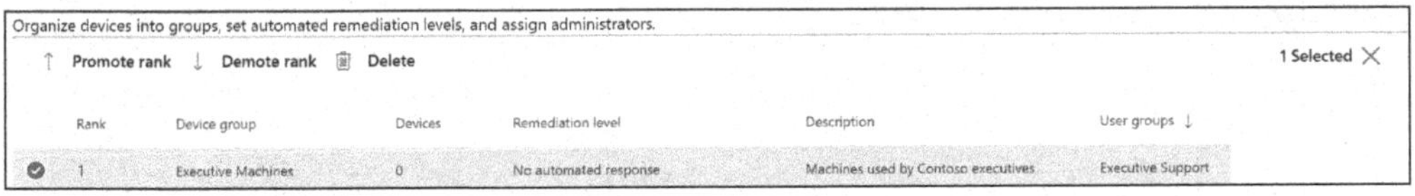

Organize devices into groups, set automated remediation levels, and assign administrators.

↑ Promote rank	↓ Demote rank	🗑 Delete				1 Selected ✕
Rank	Device group	Devices	Remediation level	Description	User groups ↓	
✔ 1	Executive Machines	0	No automated response	Machines used by Contoso executives	Executive Support	

FIGURE 1-62 Promote Rank or Demote Rank buttons

With the changes complete, Mikey, Zach, and Dylan on the executive support staff are the only users with access to the executive devices.

> **MORE INFO   ADVANCED RBAC EXAMPLE**
>
> See the following blog for an advanced RBAC use case: *https://aka.ms/sc200_mderbacadv*.

Alert notifications

It is assumed that the security operations team has better things to do than to stare at a dashboard all day, waiting for something to happen. So how will they know when alerts are triggered in Microsoft Defender for Endpoint that need their attention? The Email notifications feature in Microsoft Defender for Endpoint can send emails based on alerts that are generated. These notifications are created through rules which can be customized to send alerts to different email addresses based on their severity and Device group affected.

To receive Alert notifications, follow these steps:

1. Log in to *https://security.microsoft.com* as a member of the Azure Active Directory **Global Administrator** or **Security Administrator** roles or as a member of an Endpoint role with the **Manage Security Settings** permission.

2. In the menu on the left, click **Settings** > **Endpoints**.

3. Under **General**, click **Email Notifications**.

4. On the **Alerts** page, click **Add Item** to bring up the **New Notification Rule** fly-out menu shown in Figure 1-63.

FIGURE 1-63 New Notification Rule

5. In the **Rule Name field**, type **Tier 1 Alerts**.

6. Options for **Include Organization Name**, **Include Organization-Specific Portal Link**, and **Include Device Information** allow you to choose what items you want to appear in the email body. While you might wonder why you wouldn't include this information by default, you might want to limit this information for privacy reasons given that emails can be forwarded.

7. Under **Devices**, select **Notify For Alerts On All Devices**, though if you plan to notify different email addresses based on different device groups, choose **Notify For Alerts On Selected Device Group** and choose the device group(s) to use for this notification rule. Also, select **Notify For Alerts On All Devices** since this is going to the Tier 1 security operators.

8. **Alert Severity** allows you to choose what severity the alert must be to trigger this rule. Click **Check/Uncheck All** to select all severities and click **Next** to advance to the **Recipients** settings shown in Figure 1-64.

FIGURE 1-64 Recipients tab

9. On the **Recipients** tab, in the **Recipient Email Address** field, type in the **email addresses** that you want to be emailed with this alert notification rule is matched and click **Add**. Also, you can also click **Send Test Email** to preview your settings for the rule.

10. When you are finished, click **Save**. This returns you to the Email Notifications page. Note there is also a Vulnerabilities page where you can add notification rules when new vulnerabilities are found in the endpoint environment.

> *MORE INFO*   **CONFIGURE ALERT NOTIFICATIONS**
>
> See the following article for more information on configuring notifications: *https://aka.ms/sc200_mdenotify.*

Advanced settings

Microsoft Defender for Endpoint's sensor is used for more than just Endpoint Detection and Response (EDR). Features are being added constantly, and they can be enabled or disabled based on your needs. To enable or disable the advanced capabilities, follow these steps:

1. Log in to *https://security.microsoft.com* as a member of the **Global Administrator** or **Security Administrator** Azure Active Directory roles or as a member of a Microsoft Defender for Endpoint role with the **Manage Security Settings** permission.

2. In the menu on the left, click **Settings** > **Endpoints**.

3. Under **General**, click **Advanced Features**.

There are two types of advanced features:

- **Endpoint features**   Enable or disable Microsoft Defender for Endpoint capabilities.
- **Integration features**   Allow for data sharing between other Microsoft products, such as Intune, Microsoft Cloud App Security, and the like.

Following are examples of **Endpoint features**:

- **Automated investigation**   The auto-remediation capability that responds to alerts and attempts to return the endpoint back to a healthy state.
- **Automatically resolve alerts**   If automated investigation can return an endpoint to a healthy state, it will automatically mark the alert as being resolved, so incident responders know it was dealt with.
- **EDR in block mode**   Enables Defender to block attacks even when there is a third-party anti-virus agent installed.
- **Live Response and Live Response for Servers**   Allows for an incident responder to open a limited interactive shell with an endpoint.
- **Allow or block file**   Uses cloud Protection to allow or block files on endpoints.
- **Preview features**   Allows your subscription to receive features before they become generally available.
- **Microsoft threat experts**   Allows Microsoft human hunters pseudonymized access to your endpoint data, so that in the event of a breach, these hunters can send targeted attack notifications (TANs) alerts into your tenant to draw your security operations team's attention to the incident.

Examples of **integration features** include the following:

- **Show user details**   Allows Microsoft Defender for Endpoint to call into Azure Active Directory to fill out user information such as job title, department, name, and so on.
- **Microsoft Cloud App Security**   Network data relating to the cloud application access can be shared with Cloud App Security for discovery. Also, it allows for blocking unsanctioned cloud apps.
- **Microsoft Defender for Identity integration**   Shares Endpoint data with Microsoft Defender for Identity to improve detections, enhance identity pages, and provide additional evidence in incidents.
- **Share Endpoint alerts with Microsoft Compliance Center**   Allows risk officers to view Endpoint alerts in the Microsoft 365 Compliance portal and enhances insider risk insights.
- **Microsoft Intune Connection**   This setting shares the onboarding information with Microsoft Intune to onboard devices into Microsoft Defender for Endpoint, as well as shares the device's risk score. Intune uses this risk score to mark a device as being compliant or not compliant, based on your risk compliance policy settings in Intune.

> **MORE INFO**   **CONFIGURE ADVANCED FEATURES IN DEFENDER FOR ENDPOINT**
>
> See the following article for more information on configuring advanced features: *https://aka.ms/sc200_mdeadvfeatures*.

Respond to incidents and alerts

Now that Microsoft Defender for Endpoint is configured, it is time to look at how to investigate endpoint-related alerts and incidents. There are built-in simulations that you can use to generate benign alerts and incidents; just be sure to run the simulation in a test environment, so you can avoid an unpleasant conversation with your company's security operations team!

You need to train your security operations team on how to triage alerts and incidents using Microsoft Defender for Endpoint. The simulation you can use to practice responding to alerts and incidents can be accessed by following these steps:

1. Log in to *https://security.microsoft.com* as any user who has at least the **View Data** permissions for Endpoint data.

2. Under **Endpoints**, expand **Evaluation & Tutorials** and click **Tutorials & Simulations** to bring up the **Simulations & Tutorials** page shown in Figure 1-65.

FIGURE 1-65 Simulations & Tutorials

3. Click the **Get Simulation File** button under the **Automated Investigation (Backdoor) Simulation** in the **Microsoft section**.

4. Once the file downloads, click the **Learn More** button to open the **guide** for this simulation.

5. Follow the guide for how to run the simulation, it includes the **password** necessary to open the file and instructions for how to **enable the macro** that carries out the benign attack. It will take a few minutes for the alerts to populate and for the automated investigation to complete.

6. To investigate the incident, select **Incidents & Alerts** in the menu on the left, and then click **Incidents**.

7. You will see an incident titled **Multi-Stage Incident Involving Initial Access & Persistence On One Endpoint**, as shown in Figure 1-66.

FIGURE 1-66 Incidents view in Microsoft 365 Security portal

8. Expand the incident by clicking the **icon** next to the **Incident Name**. Note that there are multiple alerts in this incident. While it is possible to manually associate alerts with incidents, in Microsoft 365 Defender, there are machine-learning models and detection logic running against all alerts that are ingested. Alerts that the machine-learning model believes are related will be grouped into a single incident. This is important because it starts to formulate an attack story for the incident responder, instead of relying on the incident responders to draw this correlation for themselves.

9. To view more information on this incident, you can click the bubble to the left of the incident noted by the arrow in Figure 1-67 to open the incident fly-out menu.

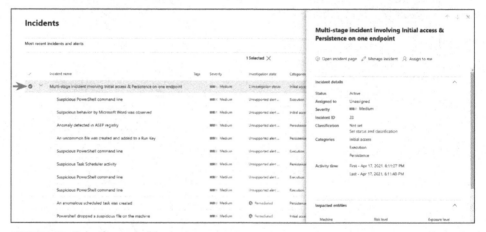

FIGURE 1-67 Selecting an incident

10. Click **Assign To Me**. A pop-up window will appear indicating that the incident and all alerts in the incident will be assigned to you. Click **Assign To Me** in that pop-up. This is a quick way to take ownership of an incident and all linked alerts, which lets your fellow security operators know that you are working this incident.

11. From the fly-out page, click **Open Incident**.

12. You are now viewing the incident with all the associated alerts, starting with the **Summary** view. The goal of this view is to ensure the incident responder has as much information as needed to determine if the incident can be resolved or if it requires more investigation. If it requires more investigation, additional details are all available in this view as shown in Figure 1-68 to assist in formulating the incident response plan.

FIGURE 1-68 Viewing the incident summary

13. First, look at the **Alerts And Categories** section shown in Figure 1-69.

FIGURE 1-69 Alert timeline and MITRE ATT&CK mapping

14. **Alerts And Categories** is a vertical list of alerts in chronological order, with the top alert occurring first in the chain of alerts. Above the vertical list are the alerts mapped to the **MITRE ATT&CK framework** showing what stages of the framework the alerts in this incident apply to. The bars signify **each stage** of the framework; hovering over the bars will show you what stage has alerts and how many alerts are in that stage.

> ***MORE INFO*** **MITRE ATT&CK FRAMEWORK**
>
> More information on the MITRE ATT&CK Framework can be found at *https://attack.mitre.org/.*

---

15. Next on the summary screen you see the **Scope** and **Evidence** that are involved in this incident. Under **Scope**, the individual devices and users can also be seen by clicking the applicable **Devices** and **Users** sections, as indicated by the arrows in Figure 1-70. Under **Evidence**, you can click the **View All Entities** link to see the files, processes, IP addresses, and other evidence related to this incident.

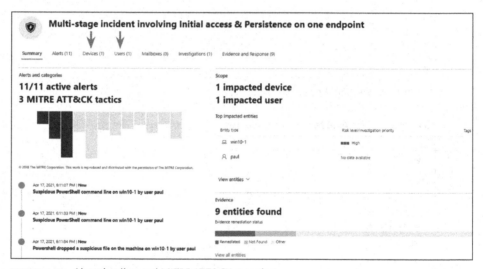

FIGURE 1-70 Alert timeline and MITRE ATT&CK mapping

16. Click the **Alerts** section.
17. In the **Alerts** section, you can see a list of alerts that make up this incident. Note how the first alert—**Suspicious PowerShell Command Line**—has several entries, and they are grouped under a **single entry**. This is so you can manage alerts resulting from the **same detector logic** as a single entity or as separate artifacts.
18. **Select the bubble** next to the first **Suspicious PowerShell Command Line** alert. A flyout page showing additional information about this alert appears, as shown in Figure 1-71.

FIGURE 1-71 Selected alert fly-out page

19. You can classify the alert as a **True Alert** or **False Alert** (or in other words, "true-positive" or "false-positive"), which you can use for reporting. This also feeds back into the detector logic in Microsoft Defender for Endpoint and helps Microsoft determine the **signal-to-noise ratio** of each detector, which is used to measure how effective it is and whether it should be optimized.

Status allows you to set the alert to **In Progress** or **Resolved**, which can also be used for reporting and to let other incident responders know the status of the alert.

> **TIP   SET CLASSIFICATION AND STATUS ON AN INCIDENT**
>
> When possible, set the Classification and Status on an incident versus the individual alerts in the incident. Once an incident is classified and the status is set, all alerts in the incident will adopt those settings. This will minimize the amount of overhead when managing incidents and alerts.

20. On the fly-out page, click **Open Alert Page**.

21. The alert page shows you all the information available for the alert, as shown in Figure 1-72.

FIGURE 1-72 Alert page

22. At the top of the page, there is a **breadcrumb trail** of where you were before you clicked this alert. This is consistent in the Microsoft 365 Security portal to ensure you keep your place in your investigation and can quickly backtrack if necessary. There is also a View Incident Page link that will return you to the incident that alert is part of. In the **Alert Story**, you can see the process tree as well as the alert and which event in the process tree triggered the alert. In this case, the **Suspicious PowerShell Command Line** alert was triggered because of the partially obfuscated command line.

23. Click the **Suspicious PowerShell Command Line** item and notice how the pane on the right changes. As you click each entity, the pane on the right shows additional information about the entity you have selected in the **Alert Story**.

24. With the **Suspicious PowerShell Command Line** item selected, click the **ellipsis (...)** indicated by the arrow in Figure 1-73.

25. Clicking **See In Timeline** allows you to pivot from this alert to the **device timeline** for when this event occurred, triggering the alert. This is helpful when you want to see what events happened around the time the alert occurred. Clicking **Consult A Threat Expert** sends this alert to a Microsoft Threat Expert to ask a question, though it is important to note this is an additional service you must pay for on top of your license cost.

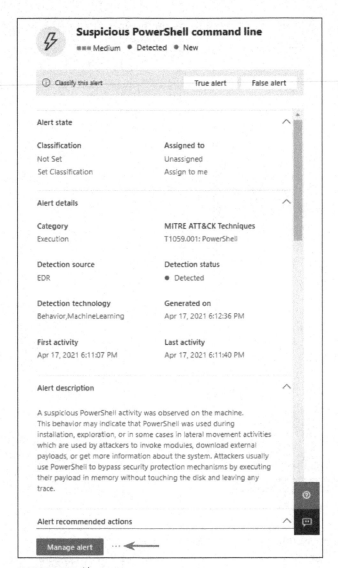

FIGURE 1-73 Alert page

26. **Click Create Suppression Rule** when there is an EDR sourced alert that is a **benign true positive** in your environment. A benign true positive is an alert that is a true alert, though it is a normal operation in your environment and can safely be ignored. A theoretical example of this would be a medical application that uses PowerShell to download its application updates encoded in Base64. More than likely, this will raise an alert, and while this is certainly not the best way to do software updates, it is normal operation for the application, so the resulting alert is a benign true positive.

27. Click **Create Suppression Rule**, which opens the menu shown in Figure 1-74.

FIGURE 1-74 Create Suppression Rule for an alert

28. Great care must be taken when creating suppression rules because they are effectively muting detections in your environment. Like exclusions in an anti-virus program, suppression rules should be created with criteria that is as specific as possible. To illustrate this point, you are creating a suppression rule that involves powershell.exe. It is possible to suppress all alerts related to powershell.exe, though this would be a very bad idea because it would create a major blind spot in your detections!

29. **Suppression conditions** can be used to increase the specificity on the suppression rule. In this case, coupling the command line with the file name and folder path should provide criteria that are specific enough to make this suppression rule as safe as possible. Note that **SHA1** is not selected because the SHA1 of Powershell.exe will change each time it is patched.

30. Under **Action**, you can select either to **Hide Alert** or **Resolve Alert**. If you do not want to see the alert at all, select Hide Alert. If you want to see the alerts but have them set to be resolved automatically, choose **Resolve Alert**.

31. **Scope** is another great way to limit your exposure in a suppression rule. You can configure the suppression rule to only apply when an endpoint in a device group is the machine the alert involves. If there is only one endpoint that should run this type of command, you can scope the suppression rule to the individual endpoint.

32. **Name** and **Comment** help you document the suppression rule. It is a best practice to add as much information in the Comment text box as possible. In this case, because Contoso uses a change management system to track changes performed in their production environment, the change ID that documents this change was added.

33. Do not save this suppression rule; instead, click **Cancel** to return to the alert.

34. Back on the **Alert** page, click the **ellipsis (...)** menu next to the device object near the top of the page, as shown in Figure 1-75.

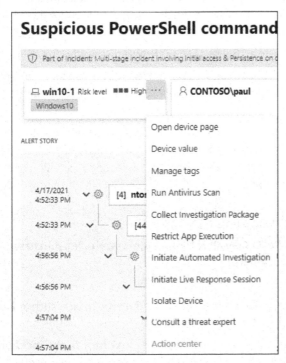

FIGURE 1-75 Device action menu

35. Below are descriptions for each option:

- **Open Device Page**   This will pivot the view from the alert page to the device page.
- **Device Value**   You can set a value on devices as **High**, **Normal**, or **Low** based on the importance of the device. For example, domain controllers could be marked **High** because they should be one of the most protected assets in your network. Executive officer machines are another example on which you would want to set a value. This setting also affects your organization's exposure level score based on the findings on these devices. Exposure scores will be covered in the "Managing risk through security recommendations and vulnerability management" section later in this chapter.
- **Manage Tags**   Allows you to add or remove tags from the device.
- **Run Antivirus Scan**   Runs either a **quick** or **full** scan on the device.
- **Collect Investigation Package**   Various preprogrammed scripts and commands run on the device that collect items like registry keys, scheduled tasks, DNS cache, and the like. This information is zipped and uploaded to the portal for download by an incident responder.
- **Restrict App Execution**   Applies a code integrity policy on the device to only allow Microsoft applications to run, which helps stop malicious binaries from running.
- **Initiate Automated Investigation**   Manually kick off the artificial intelligence–driven Automated Investigation process on the device. Typically, automated investigations are initiated by supported alert types.
- **Initiate Live Response Session**   Starts a live response session with the device.
- **Isolate Device**   Instructs the Windows Firewall to block all inbound and outbound traffic to and from the device except for communications with the Defender for Endpoint cloud service.
- **Consult A Threat Expert**   This option allows you to submit a question about this device to the Microsoft Threat Experts (MTE) service. For example, if you thought this device showed suspicious behavior but were not sure, selecting this option will send a request to an MTE team member.

> *NOTE*   **MICROSOFT THREAT EXPERTS (MTE)**
>
> **The Microsoft Threat Experts (MTE) Consult A Threat Expert service is a purchased service and is not covered on the exam.**

- **Action Center**   Review what actions were performed on the device, such as **Isolate Device**, **Collect Investigation Package**, and so on.

36. Click the **View Incident Page** at the top of the alert page to **return to the incident**. If needed, you can return to the incident by clicking **Incident & Alerts** on the left.

37. Click the **Investigations** section and then click the **bubble** next to **Powershell Dropped A Suspicious File On The Machine Triggering Alert**. Click **Open Investigation Page**, as shown in Figure 1-76.

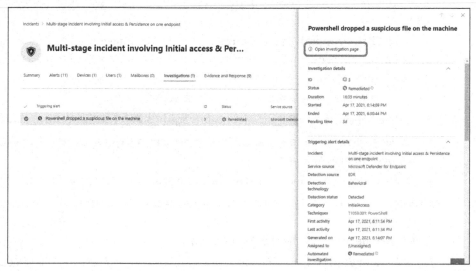

FIGURE 1-76 Open investigation page

38. You now see the **Investigation Summary** page shown in Figure 1-77.

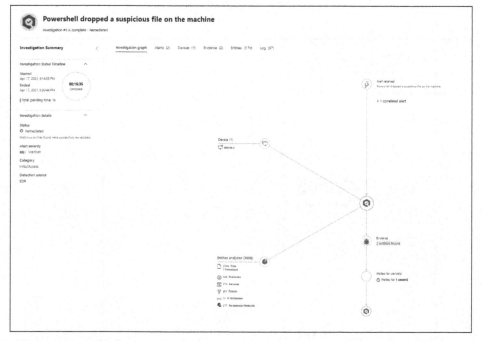

FIGURE 1-77 Investigation graph

39. The **Investigation Summary page** shows the investigation that was started automatically by the Automated Investigation self-healing technology in Defender for Endpoint. The **investigation graph** is best read in a counterclockwise direction, starting with the top-most element, **Alert Received**. The investigation graph shown here tells you the following things:

- **PowerShell Dropped A Suspicious File On The Machine** is the alert that triggered the investigation. Also, there is **one correlated alert**, which you can see by clicking the **Alerts** section above the **investigation graph**.

- One device is involved in the investigation: **WIN10-1**.

- To determine how to get the device healthy again, **3,698 Entities were analyzed**.

- Entities analyzed were composed of **files, processes, services, drivers, IP addresses**, and **persistence methods**.

- Based on the entities analyzed, **two entities were found to be malicious**.

Clicking each icon in the Investigation graph will take you to the respective sections above the graph.

40. Click the **Evidence** icon, which looks like a bug.

41. In the **Evidence** list, click the entity named `winatp-intro-backdoor.exe`. This will open the **File** fly-out menu shown in Figure 1-78.

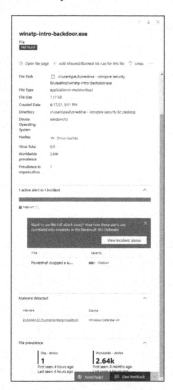

FIGURE 1-78 File menu

42. This fly-out page provides detailed information about this file, including file hashes, worldwide prevalence, file path, file size, and more. Click **Open File Page** at the top of the **File** fly-out menu.

43. On the **File Page**, you can see all the information Defender for Endpoint has on this file. You can also take the following actions:

   - **Stop And Quarantine File**   Stops this file if it is running on any endpoint and quarantines the file.

   - **Add Indicator**   Add this file's SHA2 to the file indicators list. Indicators are files, IP addresses, URLs, or code-signing certificates that you want to block or allow in your environment.

   - **Collect File / Download File**   Allows you to collect the file from an endpoint that has the file and download it from the portal. Either the **Collect File** or **Download File** option will be displayed, depending on whether the file is present in your subscription. If **Download File** is shown, more than likely, the file has been collected in the past and is present in your Defender for Endpoint tenant. If **Collect File** is shown, the file has not been collected and needs to be retrieved from an endpoint. Once the file is available for download, you can use **Download File**, which will prompt you for a password. The password will be used for the zip archive that the file is placed in before being downloaded to your machine.

   - **Consult a Threat Expert**   This option allows you to submit a question about this file to the Microsoft Threat Experts (MTE) service. For example, if you thought this file showed suspicious behavior but were not sure, selecting this option would send a request to an MTE team member. This is a service that must be purchased and is not covered on the exam.

   - **Action Center**   Allows you to see what actions have been performed on this file and the status of the action.

44. Click the **PowerShell Dropped A Suspicious File On The Machine** text at the top of the screen to return to the investigation shown in Figure 1-79.

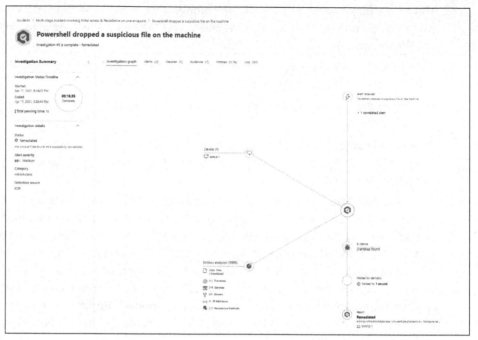

FIGURE 1-79   Investigation Summary

45. At the left under **Investigation Details**, you see that the **Status** is **Remediated**.

46. Earlier in this chapter, you learned about **remediation levels,** which are configurable on **device groups**. In this example, the device is configured for **fully automated remediation**, meaning any pending actions resulting from an investigation will automatically be approved. You can see the remediation level by clicking the **device icon** in the **investigation graph,** which takes you to the **Devices** tab shown in Figure 1-80.

FIGURE 1-80   Devices tab

47. In the list of devices, you see that WIN10-1.CONTOSO.COM has a **Remediation Level** of **Fully Automated**.

48. Because Automated Investigation retuned this device back to healthy by removing the threats, you can now close this incident.

49. Click the incident name **Multi-Stage Incident Involving Initial Access & Persistence On One Endpoint** at the top of the page. You can also access this incident using the **Incident** menu item under **Incidents & Alerts** on the far-left menu.

50. Once you are on the incident page for this incident, click the **Manage Incident** option in the upper-right portion of the screen. This will bring up the **Manage Incident** fly-out menu, as shown in Figure 1-81.

FIGURE 1-81 Manage Incident

51. Click the toggle switch next to **Resolve Incident**. This will change the status of the incident and all alerts in the incident to **Resolved**.

52. Select **True Alert** as the **Classification**.

53. Under **Determination**, you have the following options:

   - **APT**   Advanced Persistent Threat indicates this incident is related to an attack by a known actor.

   - **Malware**   Incident was caused by malware.

   - **Security Personnel**   A member of the security team triggered this incident on their own machine.

   - **Security Testing**   Indicates this incident was part of a security simulation. Choose this option.

   - **Unwanted Software**   The incident was caused by software that should not run on the machine.

   - **Other**   Select if this incident does not match any of the previous determination options.

> **IMPORTANT   DETERMINATION SETTING**
>
> The Determination setting will be applied to the incident and any linked alerts to the incident that do not already have a determination set on the individual alert.

54. Type comments in the **Comment** text box. Adding comments is optional, but it is helpful to document your findings while investigating the incident. Other security responders can see the findings and add additional information if applicable.

55. Once you complete your comment entry, click **Save**.

Congratulations, you have now triaged your first incident in Microsoft Defender for Endpoint!

Creating custom detections

While there are many built-in detections in Microsoft Defender for Endpoint, most security operations teams need the ability to create custom detections. There are three ways to generate custom detections:

- Generate custom indicators
- Generate custom detection rules using Advanced Hunting
- Create an alert API

> **MORE INFO   CREATING AN ALERT API**
>
> Typically, custom detection rules and custom indicators are used to create custom detections. Creating an alert API is not covered on the exam, though more information can be found at *https://aka.ms/sc200_mdealertapi*.

Custom detection rules using Advanced Hunting

Advanced Hunting is one of the most popular features in Microsoft Defender for Endpoint. It provides lightning-fast query response time against up to 30 days of data, even in environments with millions of endpoints onboarded. The query language you use to search your data in Advanced Hunting is called Kusto Query Language, or KQL. If you have used Azure services such as Log Analytics in the past, you already have some exposure to KQL. Advanced Hunting can be used for ad-hoc queries against your data, which is typically how custom detections start out.

> **MORE INFO   LOG ANALYTICS QUERIES**
>
> Microsoft hosts a GitHub repository that is filled with great queries to get you started: *https://GitHub.com/microsoft/Microsoft-365-Defender-Hunting-Queries.*

At this Advanced Hunting GitHub, there is a KQL query we can use to detect WMI deletions of shadow-copy snapshots. This is a technique usually seen in correlation with Ransomware. Shadow-copy snapshots are removed prior to encryption so that recovery using these snapshots is not possible. Here is the KQL query:

```
DeviceProcessEvents
| where FileName =~ "wmic.exe"
| where ProcessCommandLine has "shadowcopy" and ProcessCommandLine has "delete"
| project DeviceId, Timestamp, InitiatingProcessFileName, FileName,
ProcessCommandLine, InitiatingProcessIntegrityLevel, InitiatingProcessParentFileName
```

This query is explained by the following pseudocode:

```
"Check the DeviceProcessEvents table for event entries where the process file name is
like wmic.exe and where the process command line has the strings shadowcopy and delete.
Once this data is found, show the DeviceID, Timestamp, InitiatingProcessFileName,
FileName, ProcessCommandLine, InitiatingProcessIntegrityLevel, and
InitiatingProcessParentFileName."
```

Now that you understand what this query is doing, you will create a custom detection using this query and by following these steps:

1. Log in to *https://security.microsoft.com* as a member of the Azure Active Directory **Global Administrator** or **Security Administrator** roles or as a member of an Endpoint role with the **Manage Security Settings** permission.

2. In the menu on the left, click **Hunting** > **Advanced Hunting**.

3. By default, the **Get Started** section is shown on the right. You can go through the exercises or click the **Query** section to change to the query editor. On the left is the **schema** for advanced hunting, as shown in Figure 1-82.

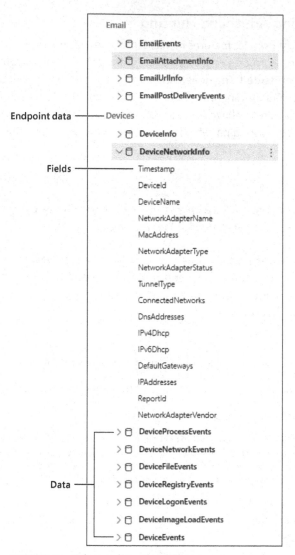

FIGURE 1-82 Advanced Hunting schema

The three dots next to each table opens the **schema reference** for that table. Hovering over the fields pops up a **description** for the field.

4. Type the following query into the query window. Note KQL is a **case-sensitive** language.

```
DeviceProcessEvents
| where FileName =~ "wmic.exe"
| where ProcessCommandLine has "shadowcopy" and ProcessCommandLine has "delete"
| project DeviceId, Timestamp, InitiatingProcessFileName, FileName,
ProcessCommandLine, InitiatingProcessIntegrityLevel,
InitiatingProcessParentFileName
```

Notice when you type, you are assisted by autocomplete.

5. To make sure the query syntax is error free, click **Run Query**.

    You probably will not get any results in your environment, which is okay. To create a custom detection, the query does not need to return results initially.

TIP DON'T QUERY TOO OFTEN

You do not want a query to return results too often because the custom detection will generate too many alerts.

---

6. Click the **Create Detection Rule** option in the upper-right corner of the query window, which displays the error shown in Figure 1-83.

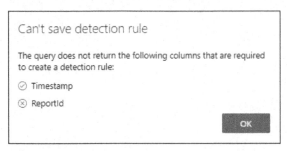

FIGURE 1-83 Error when creating a custom detection

7. This happened because we did not add the `ReportId` field to the `project` statement in the query, which is required to be in the returned fields for a custom detection. `Timestamp`, `ReportId`, and a field that represents a specific **device**, **user**, or **mailbox** are all required for custom detections.

8. Modify your query to add `ReportId` to the project line, as shown below:

```
DeviceProcessEvents
| where FileName =~ "wmic.exe"
| where ProcessCommandLine has "shadowcopy" and ProcessCommandLine has "delete"
| project ReportId, DeviceId, Timestamp, InitiatingProcessFileName, FileName,
ProcessCommandLine, InitiatingProcessIntegrityLevel,
InitiatingProcessParentFileName
```

9. Click **Run Query** to make sure you do not have syntax errors and then **click Create Detection Rule**.

10. The following fields are shown in the **Create Detection Rule wizard**, as well as in Figure 1-84.

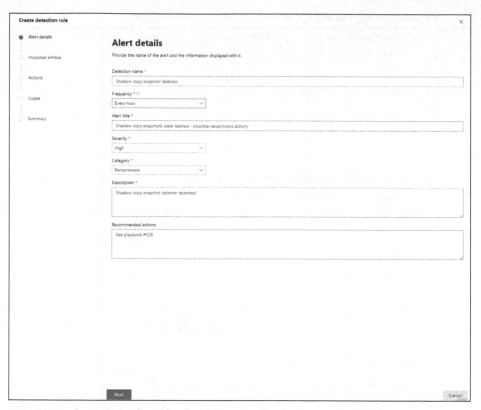

FIGURE 1-84 Create Detection Rule wizard, Alert Details

- **Detection Name** A name for the detection.
- **Frequency** This is how often the custom detection rule will run. The choices are **Every 24 Hours**, **Every 12 Hours**, **Every 3 Hours**, or **Every Hour**. The more often your custom detection rule runs, the smaller the window of time it will look back. In Figure 1-84, **Every Hour** has been chosen.
- **Alert Title** This is the title of the alert you will see in the alert view.
- **Severity** This is the severity of the alert. The choices are **High**, **Medium**, **Low**, and **Informational**. Choose **High** because this is ransomware-related and needs to be triaged as fast as possible.
- **Category** This is the type of activity that best matches this alert. Choose **Ransomware**.
- **Description** This is a description for the custom detection rule.
- **Recommended Actions** This instructs the incident responder regarding the steps to take for triaging and resolving this alert.

11. Click **Next** to advance to the **Impacted Entities** page shown in Figure 1-85.

FIGURE 1-85 Impacted Entities

12. Only the **Device** option will be available because the device info will be returned in this query. **Select the Device** option and select **DeviceId** from the drop-down menu. Click **Next** to open the **Actions** page shown in Figure 1-86.

FIGURE 1-86 Create Detection Rule, Actions

13. **From this screen,** you can trigger a response action on the device that triggers the custom detection. These actions are the same as covered previously. **Select Isolate Device** and make sure **Full** is selected because you do not want to allow Outlook, Skype, or Teams to have access while isolated. Then click **Next** to open the **Scope** page shown in Figure 1-87.

FIGURE 1-87 Scope for the custom detection rule

14. The **Scope** page lets you select which device group you want to target with the custom detection rule. Select **All Devices** and click **Next**.

15. The **Summary** page lists all the configuration settings made so far in the Create Detection Rule wizard. You can edit any of the settings from this screen. When the settings are configured as desired, click **Create** to create the custom detection rule.

To test the custom detection rule, follow these steps:

1. Run the following command on an onboarded endpoint using an elevated command prompt or PowerShell:

```
WMIC.exe shadowcopy delete /nointeractive
```

2. Wait for about 5 minutes for the data to reach the tenant.

3. Log in to *https://security.microsoft.com* as a member of the **Global Administrator** or **Security Administrator** Azure AD roles or as a member of an Endpoint role with the **Manage Security Settings** permission.

4. In the menu on the left, expand **Hunting** and click **Custom Detection Rules**.

5. You should see the custom detection rule you created in previous steps. Click the **bubble** next to the custom detection rule. A **fly-out menu** for the rule will appear, as shown in Figure 1-88:

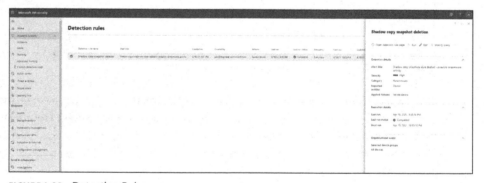

FIGURE 1-88 Detection Rules

6. In this fly-out menu, you can see the **Last Run** and **Next Run** of this custom detection rule. To see the full details of this rule, click **Open Detection Rule Page** to open the page shown in Figure 1-89.

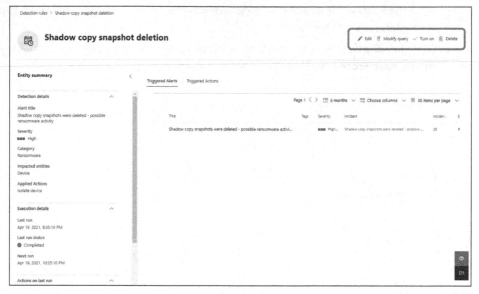

FIGURE 1-89 Click Run to manually run the custom detection rule.

7. On this page, you can fully manage the custom detection rule and see any **Triggered Alerts** and **Triggered Actions**. If you do not see a triggered alert and the **Last Run Time** field has not been populated, click **Run** in the top-right corner of the page.

8. If the data reached the tenant from the onboarded device, this should generate the custom detection alert shown in Figure 1-90.

FIGURE 1-90 Custom detection rule alert

9. Note the fields in the details on the right reflect the information provided when you created the custom detection rule.

10. Click the **ellipsis (…)** next to the **Device Name** at the top of the alert. You should see the **Release From Isolation** option at the bottom right (see Figure 1-91).

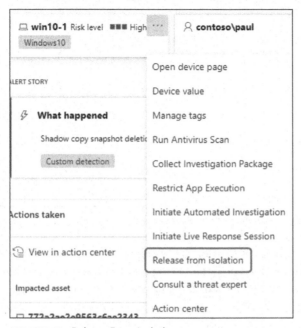

FIGURE 1-91 Release From Isolation

11. This indicates the machine is currently isolated because that was the action you specified to occur when activity on a device matched the custom detection rule question. Click **Release From Isolation**.

> **MORE INFO** **CREATE AND MANAGE CUSTOM DETECTION RULES**
>
> See the following article for more information on creating and managing custom detection rules: *https://aka.ms/sc200_m365customdetect*.

Custom indicators

Indicators are another way to generate custom alerts, as well as block activity based on files, IP addresses, URLs, domains, and certificates. While you could create custom detection rules for these types of indicator-based detections, custom indicators are a much better-suited tool for non-logic-based detections, and they have the additional benefit of being able to block the file.

You receive some Indicators of compromise (IOCs) from a threat intel feed, which contains an SHA256 hash. If this hash is seen in your environment, you want Microsoft Defender for

Endpoint to raise an alert. To accomplish this, you need to create a custom alert based on a file indicator by following these steps:

1. Log in to *https://security.microsoft.com* as a member of the **Global Administrator** or **Security Administrator** Azure Active Directory roles or as a member of an Endpoint role with the **Manage Security Settings** permission.

2. In the menu on the left, click **Settings**.

3. On the **Settings** page, click **Endpoints**.

4. On the **Endpoints settings** page under **Rules**, click **Indicators**.

5. Under **File Hashes**, click the **Add Item** option, which opens the **Add File Hash Indicator** menu shown in Figure 1-92.

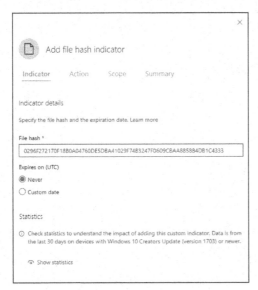

FIGURE 1-92   Add a file hash indicator.

6. On the **Add File Hash Indicator** fly-out menu on the **Indicator** page, in the **File Hash** text box, type the following SHA256 hash. (This hash is from a benign text file generated for the purposes of this book. You can generate your own text file and use the Get-FileHash PowerShell command to test it in your environment.)

   0296F272170F18B0A04760DE5DBA41029F74B3247F0609CBAA8858B4DB1C4333

7. Set **Expires On (UTC)** to **Never**, as previously shown in Figure 1-92, then click **Next** to advance to the **Action** page shown in Figure 1-93.

FIGURE 1-93 Add File Hash Indicator, Action tab

8. Select **Alert Only** and provide an **Alert Title, Alert Severity, Category, Recommend-ed Actions,** and **Description**. Notice these are all the same fields you set in custom detections rules. This is because we are configuring an alert to generate when this indi-cator is seen. Click **Next** to move to the **Scope** page shown in Figure 1-94.

FIGURE 1-94 Add File Hash Indicator, Scope tab

9. Use the **Scope** page to configure what **device group** this indicator and alert will target. Choose **All Devices In My Scope** and click Next.

10. The **Summary** page allows you to see all your choices. If everything looks good, click the **Save** button. The next time this file hash is needed on any onboarded endpoint, an alert will be raised with the previously entered information.

> **MORE INFO   CREATE INDICATORS**
>
> For more information about creating indicators, see *https://aka.ms/sc200_mdeioc*.

Managing risk through security recommendations and vulnerability management

Keeping up with vulnerabilities and risky security configurations is a daunting task. Traditionally, scanning-based vulnerability assessment tools seemed like they were doing good work. They would scan as many devices as the tool could reach over the network, assess the configuration weaknesses and vulnerabilities, and output a multipage report with all the required actions that an already overworked infrastructure administration team would need to fix. There are three major issues with this approach:

1. Offline devices are not scanned, resulting in blind spots in the report.

2. When the vulnerability or weakness on the device is remediated, it is a manual effort to update the report or would require another scan that is also subject to incomplete information caused by offline devices.

3. The list of weaknesses and vulnerabilities is typically a lengthy list with little prioritization. IT teams mitigate the high-ranked items, but those items do not necessarily represent true organizational risk.

One workaround to issues 1 and 2 above is to install an agent on the devices so they report their data, rather than being scanned remotely. This leads to other issues, such as broken or missing agents and lack of reporting when the device is not connected to the corporate network.

Threat and Vulnerability Management (TVM) in Microsoft Defender for Endpoint does not have these issues for the following reasons:

1. **There is no agent** The sensor is built into the Windows Operating System.

2. **There is no scanning** The Defender for Endpoint service that reports EDR data also reports these weaknesses and vulnerabilities on an ongoing basis.

3. **No corporate network required** Any time the device has access to the Internet, it can send data since the Defender for Endpoint service is in Azure.

4. **Vulnerabilities and configuration weaknesses are prioritized based on risk to the organization** When the risk of a vulnerability or configuration weakness raises, such as when a public exploit is posted that uses a vulnerability, the prioritization dynamically changes to ensure that you remediate the riskiest vulnerabilities and weaknesses in your environment.

> **MORE INFO** **THREAT AND VULNERABILITY MANAGEMENT**
>
> For more information about threat and vulnerability management, see
> *https://aka.ms/sc200_tvm*.

Threat & Vulnerability Dashboard

You need to have a quick and clear view of the weaknesses and vulnerabilities that are present across your organization. The Threat & Vulnerability Dashboard is a great way to get this comprehensive, high-level assessment. Follow these steps to familiarize yourself with the dashboard.

1. Log in to *https://security.microsoft.com* as a member of the **Global Administrator** or **Security Administrator** Azure Active Directory roles or as a member of an Endpoint role with the **View Data—Threat And Vulnerability Management** permission.

2. Under **Endpoints**, expand **Vulnerability Management** and click **Dashboard**.

3. The following tiles are shown in the dashboard shown in Figure 1-95.

   - **Exposure Score** This shows the amount of exposure affecting devices in your organization. Ideally, you want the score to be as low as possible.

   - **Top Security Recommendations** This is a list of actions you can take to lower your Exposure Score. They are ordered by **Impact**, which is the measure of the number of points by which your Exposure Score will be lowered by remediating that action

   - **Microsoft Secure Score For Devices** This rates the security posture of your environment based on **Application, OS, Network, Accounts,** and **Security Controls**. A higher percentage indicates a better security posture.

   - **Exposure Distribution** This shows the number of devices that are susceptible to attacks, which are ranked as **High, Medium,** and **Low**.

- **Remediation Activities** This is a list of activities to remediate vulnerabilities and configuration weaknesses.
- **Top Vulnerable Software** This is a list of software with vulnerabilities that is intelligently ranked on factors such as number of vulnerabilities, threats, and number of affected devices.
- **Top Exposed Devices** This is a list of devices with the most exposure that is intelligently ranked on factors such as number of vulnerabilities, threats, and security recommendations.

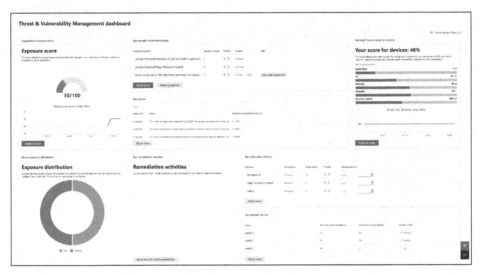

FIGURE 1-95 Threat & Vulnerability Management Dashboard

Remediation activities and exceptions

Now that you have your security recommendations ranked intelligently and dynamically, you need to assign remediation activities to the individual or teams responsible for patch management. The Threat & Vulnerability Management Dashboard tells you which actions to take first that will have the **greatest impact in lowering the risk** in your environment.

EXAM TIP

Be sure to know how to create a remediation activity and exceptions!

Follow these steps to create a remediation activity:

1. Log in to *https://security.microsoft.com* as a member of the **Global Administrator** or **Security Administrator** Azure Active Directory roles or as a member of an Endpoint role with the **Active Remediation Actions: Threat And Vulnerability Management—Exception Handling And Remediation Handling** role.

2. Under **Endpoints**, expand **Vulnerability Management** and click **Recommendations** to open the view shown in Figure 1-96.

FIGURE 1-96 Security recommendations

3. Just remediating the **Update Microsoft 10 (OS And Built-In Applications)** line item will result in the Exposure Score lowering by 30.65 points. One of the reasons this action will lower the score is because there is a verified, public exploit available for some of the vulnerabilities that these two devices are affected by.

4. You can tell if there is an exploit available for one or more of these vulnerabilities by looking at the icons under **Threats**. These threats indicate the following:

- **Threat insights** As shown in Figure 1-97, when this icon is red, there is a publicly available exploit for one or more vulnerabilities.

FIGURE 1-97 Threat insights icon

- **Breach insights** If this icon is red, there is an active alert attributed to the vulnerability, as shown in Figure 1-98.

FIGURE 1-98 Breach insights icon

5. Click **Update Microsoft Windows 10 (OS And Built-In Applications)** in the list of security recommendations.

6. Click **Request Remediation** to open the view shown in Figure 1-99.

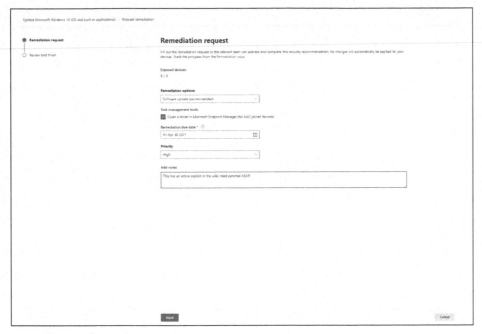

FIGURE 1-99 Remediation Request wizard

7. Select **Software Update (Recommended)** under **Remediation Options**.
8. Select the **Open A Ticket In Microsoft Endpoint Manager (For AAD Joined Devices)** check box.

> **TIP ENABLE MICROSOFT INTUNE CONNECTION**
>
> If you do not see the **Open A Ticket In Microsoft Endpoint Manager (For AAD Joined Devices) option,** you need to turn on the **Microsoft Intune Connection** in the **Endpoint Advanced Features** settings.

9. Select a **Remediation Due Date**.
10. Under **Priority**, select **High**.

11. Type some notes under **Add Notes** and click **Next** to open the **Review And Finish** screen shown in Figure 1-100.

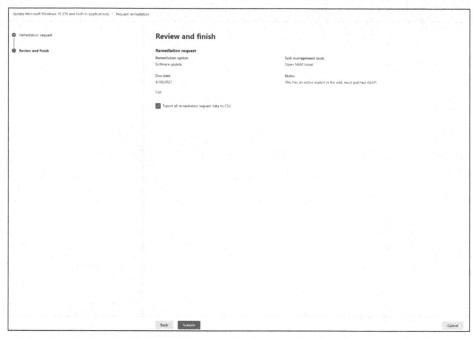

FIGURE 1-100 Review And Finish, Request remediation wizard

12. Select **Export All Remediation Request Data To CSV**. This creates a CSV file that you can provide with your change management request because it contains the remediation action and a list of the machines requiring the remediation.

13. Click **Submit**.

14. Once the remediation request is created, click **Done**.

Now that you have a remediation request created, you can track the request in the **Remediation** menu item under **Vulnerability Management**. Your patch management team should now see the remediation request in Microsoft Endpoint Manager under **Security Tasks**, as shown in Figure 1-101.

FIGURE 1-101 Security tasks in Microsoft Endpoint Manager

In some cases, you need to create an exception for security recommendations. For example, machines that do not support the hardware requirements for Credential Guard. Follow these steps to create an exception for these machines:

1. Log in to *https://security.microsoft.com* as a member of the **Global Administrator** or **Security Administrator** Azure Active Directory roles or as a member of an Endpoint role with the **Active Remediation Actions: Threat And Vulnerability Management—Exception Handling** And **Remediation Handling**.

2. In the menu on the left, under **Endpoints**, expand **Vulnerability Management** and click **Recommendations**.

3. In the **Search** option in the upper-right of the window, type **credential guard**. This should filter the security recommendation list as shown in Figure 1-102.

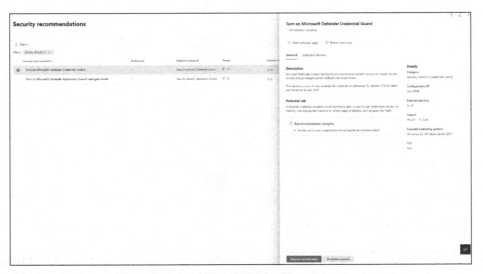

FIGURE 1-102   Turn on Microsoft Defender Credential Guard

4. Click the **Turn On Microsoft Defender Credential Guard** security recommendation. This will open a window with a description of the recommendation. Click the **Exception Options** button at the bottom of the window to open the **Create Exception** screen shown in Figure 1-103.

FIGURE 1-103 Create Exception

5. This screen allows you to set the **Exception Scope** to a device group. Under **Justification And Duration**, select **Planned Remediation (Grace)** to indicate that this is a temporary exception. The **Provide Justification Context** text box allows you to enter notes for the exception reason, which in this case is that because the hardware is old and does not support Credential Guard, it will be replaced. The **Exception Duration** allows you to set a fixed time length (30, 60, or 90 days), or you can select a custom date up to 1 year beyond the current date.

6. Once you select your options, click **Submit**.

7. When the Exception is created, click **Done**.

You now have an exception created for the **Turn On Microsoft Defender Credential Guard** security recommendation.

MORE INFO **CREATE AND VIEW EXCEPTIONS FOR SECURITY RECOMMENDATIONS**

For more information about managing exceptions, see *https://aka.ms/sc200_tvmexception*.

Skill 1-3: Detect, investigate, respond, and remediate identity threats

Your identity is composed of unique characteristics that other people and systems use to distinguish you from other people and objects. Most people think of Social Security Numbers or drivers licenses when you ask them what identity means to them. In security operations, an identity is a set of credentials that is used to identify a user or system and grant authorization and access to a system based on these credentials. When identities are compromised, the attacker effectively becomes the identity, using it to conceal themselves and gain unauthorized access to systems.

Identifying and responding to Azure Active Directory identity risks

In Azure Active Directory (AD) Identity Protection, there are two methods that can be used to detect attackers using stolen identities to access systems. These methods include:

- **User risk**   The user account shows a pattern of unusual usage.
- **Sign-in risk**   The user account signs in from a known suspicious IP address.

When an identity such as a user account shows signs of either of these conditions, protections can be put in place to ensure the user account is being used by the intended party. These protections can be put in place either automatically, such as forcing a multifactor authentication (MFA) challenge followed by a password reset, or by an administrator taking actions to secure the account through blocking a user account. Azure AD Identity Protection policies can be set to configure Azure Active Directory to respond and remediate appropriately to these identity threats.

In Skill 1-1, you saw that Contoso CFO Paul DePaul's credentials were phished using a fake log-in page. You need to determine if Paul's identity—his user account—was stolen using Azure AD Identity Protection and if so, remediate this threat and configure the appropriate policies to improve the protection of user accounts going forward. To do this, follow these steps:

1. Log in to *https://portal.azure.com* as a **Global Administrator** or **Security Administrator**.

2. Using the **Search** bar at the top of the portal, type **identity protection** and **click Azure AD Identity Protection** to open the **Identity Protection Overview** page shown in Figure 1-104.

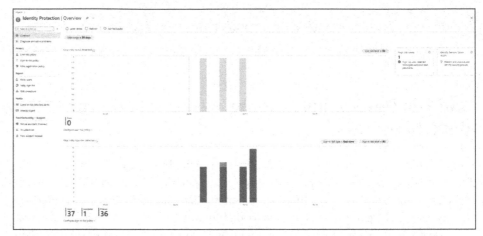

FIGURE 1-104 Azure AD Identity Protection Overview

3. You see there are risky users and sign-ins detected. Under the **Report** section on the left, click **Risky Users**, as shown in Figure 1-105.

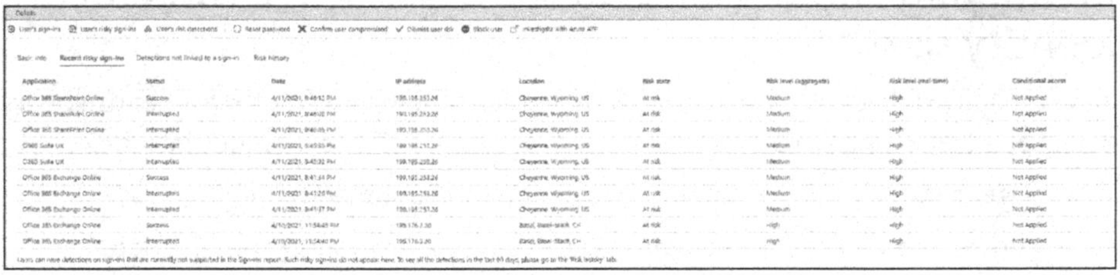

FIGURE 1-105 Recent Risky Sign-Ins

4. You see that there are several risky sign-ins for Paul DePaul. Clicking the first entry in the list and then clicking **Risk Info** in the lower pane brings up the view shown in Figure 1-106.

FIGURE 1-106 Risky Sign-Ins risk information

5. This **successful log-in** was from an **anonymous IP address**. Anonymous IPs are used by attackers to mask their real IP addresses so that they remain anonymous on the Internet.

6. In this example, clicking the **user's risk report** takes you to the **Paul DePaul—Risky Users** screen, which is shown in Figure 1-107.

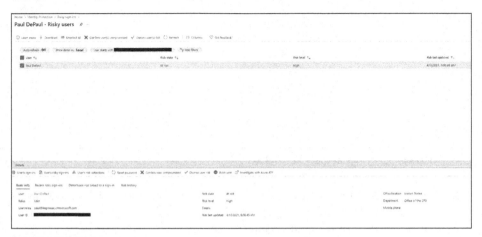

FIGURE 1-107 Risky users

7. You can take action based on the findings so far. Because it seems that Paul's account is compromised given the amount of risky sign-in events and his account's **Risk Level** is **High**, click **Block User** to prevent future sign-ins for Paul's account. Click **Confirm User Compromised**, which will signal back to Azure AD Identity Protection that this is a true-positive.

> **MORE INFO IDENTITY PROTECTION RISKS**
>
> For more information about identity protection risks, see *https://aka.ms/sc200_idrisks*.

Configuring users at risk alerts

You need to be alerted when a risky user or sign-in is detected. To be notified via email alerts when this type of risky activity occurs, follow these steps:

1. Log in to *https://portal.azure.com* as a **Global Administrator** or **Security Administrator**.

2. Using the **Search** bar at the top of the portal, type identity protection and **click Azure AD Identity Protection**.

3. Under **Notify**, click **Users At Risk Detected Alerts**, as shown in Figure 1-108.

FIGURE 1-108   Users At Risk Detected Alerts

4. Here, you can type email addresses to be notified when user's risk level reaches or exceeds **Low, Medium,** or **High levels**. You want to be alerted any time any risk is detected, so select **Low** and click **Save**.

5. **Weekly Digest** is a weekly email containing risky sign-ins, users, and links to the related reports to users you specify. Configure the users you for whom you want to receive the weekly digest and click **Save**.

> **MORE INFO**   **AZURE AD IDENTITY PROTECTION NOTIFICATIONS**
>
> For more information about configuring these notifications, see *https://aka.ms/ sc200_idpnotify*.

Configuring multifactor authentication and risk policies

To improve your defenses against identity compromise such as what happened to Paul's user account, you can configure policies to make it harder for attackers to use compromised accounts if they have the username and password for the account. A multifactor authentication (MFA) registration policy allows you to add a third form of authentication in addition to the username and password required when a user logs in. In the previous example with Paul's account, the attacker had the username and password and could log in. Once MFA is added to Paul's account, when Azure AD Identity Protection detects a risky sign-in for Paul, Azure AD could then challenge him to use a third form of authentication, such as a rotating cipher on his cell phone, before granting him access.

To require users to register for MFA, follow these steps to set an MFA registration policy:

1. Log in to *https://portal.azure.com* as a **Global Administrator** or **Security Administrator**.

2. Using the **Search** bar at the top of the portal, type **identity protection** and **click Azure AD Identity Protection**.

3. Under **Protect**, click **MFA Registration Policy**, as shown in Figure 1-109.

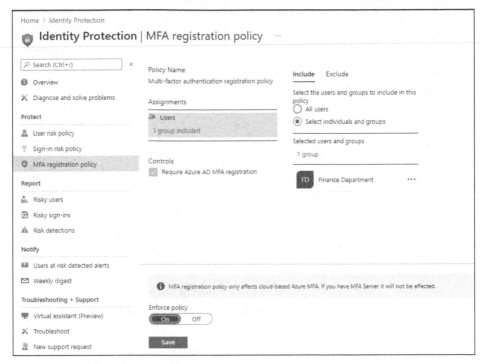

FIGURE 1-109 MFA registration policy

4. Under **Assignments**, choose the **users or groups** to target for this policy. In this example, the **finance department** that Paul is a member of is targeted.

5. Under **Enforce Policy**, click to activate the policy, and then click **Save**.

Now that an MFA registration policy is configured, you can configure an MFA challenge if Azure AD Identity Protection suspects a sign-in is risky. Follow these steps to configure a sign-in risk policy.

1. Log in to *https://portal.azure.com* as a **Global Administrator** or **Security Administrator**.

2. Using the **Search** bar at the top of the portal, type **identity protection** and **click Azure AD Identity Protection**.

3. Under **Protect**, click **Sign-In Risk Policy**, as shown in Figure 1-110.

4. Under **Users**, select the desired users or groups. In this example, we have chosen the finance department.

5. Under **Sign-In Risk**, specify the risk level that will trigger the policy. Select **Low And Above** to trigger an alert on any indication that the sign-in is risky.

FIGURE 1-110 Sign-In Risk Policy

6. Under **Controls**, select **Allow Access**, select **Require Multi-Factor Authentication**, and click **Done**.

7. Click the **Enforce Policy slider to the On position**, and then click **Save**.

Next, you configure a user risk policy that will take action when a user is marked as being at risk. Follow these steps:

1. Log in to *https://portal.azure.com* as a **Global Administrator** or **Security Administrator**.

2. Using the **Search** bar at the top of the portal, type **identity protection** and **click Azure AD Identity Protection**.

3. Under **Protect**, click **User Risk Policy**, as shown in Figure 1-111.

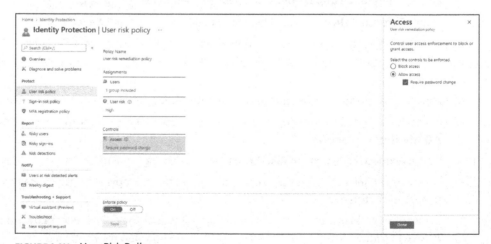

FIGURE 1-111 User Risk Policy

4. Under **Users**, select the desired users or groups. In this example, we have chosen the finance department.

5. Under **User Risk**, specify the risk level that will trigger the policy. Select **High** to trigger on users who are marked as high risk.

6. Under **Controls**, select **Allow Access**, select the **Require Password Change** box, and click **Done**.

7. Click the **Enforce Policy** slider to toggle it **On**, and then click **Save**.

> **MORE INFO**   **IDENTITY PROTECTION POLICIES**
>
> For more information about configuring Identity Protection policies, see *https://aka.ms/ sc200_idppol*.

Identifying and responding to Active Directory Domain Services threats using Microsoft Defender for Identity

Microsoft Defender for Identity helps you detect and investigate malicious activity involving identities in Active Directory. Using various signals like network traffic and events from domain controllers, Defender for Identity can detect and investigate techniques in the following stages of the MITRE ATT&CK framework:

- Reconnaissance
- Credential access
- Discovery
- Lateral movement
- Exfiltration
- Command and control
- Defense evasion
- Persistence

To begin monitoring your Active Directory environment, follow this process:

1. First, you need to create your Microsoft Defender for Identity instance.

2. Once the instance is created, you then configure a user account or, preferably, a group Managed Service Account (gMSA) so that Defender for Identity can look up objects in Active Directory.

3. Lastly, you install the Microsoft Defender for Identity sensor on each of your domain controllers.

4. Each sensor gathers network traffic and events from your domain controllers to detect malicious activity and generate alerts.

> **MORE INFO**   **QUICKSTART FOR MICROSOFT DEFENDER FOR IDENTITY**
>
> For a quick start guide on setting up Defender for Identity, see *https://aka.ms/sc200_setupmdi*.

Investigating an alert in Microsoft Defender for Identity

An example of a technique in the reconnaissance stage is when an attacker explores Server Message Block (SMB) sessions from a server, such as a file server or domain controller, to find user accounts and the IP addresses they originate from. This allows the attacker to map out what accounts they need to compromise to gain access to the systems with those IP addresses. The User And IP Address Reconnaissance (SMB) alert in the Defender for Identity portal shows this attack. You will use this alert to train your security operations team on how to triage alerts in the Microsoft Defender for Identity portal.

> **MORE INFO   GENERATING A SIMILAR ATTACK**
>
> To generate a similar alert in your environment, follow the lab guide here: *https://aka.ms/ sc200_mdiplaybook*.

Follow these steps to triage this alert:

1. Log in to the **Microsoft Defender for Identity portal** at *https://portal.atp.azure.com* as a member of the **Global Administrator or Security Administrator Azure AD role**. You can also log in as a lower-privileged user if they are a member of the **Azure ATP (instance name) Administrators**, **Azure ATP (Instance Name) Users**, or **Azure ATP (Instance Name) Viewers** Azure AD groups. This opens the **Timeline** view shown in Figure 1-112.

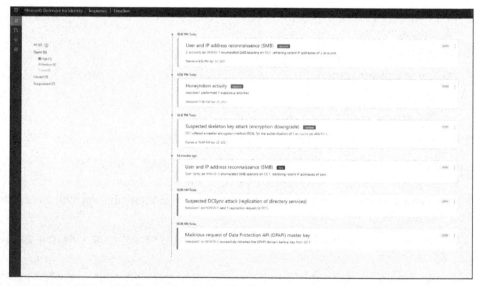

FIGURE 1-112   Microsoft Defender for Identity Timeline

2. The **Timeline** shows alerts generated by Defender for Identity in chronological order. Click the **User And IP Address Reconnaissance (SMB)** alert to open the alert shown in Figure 1-113.

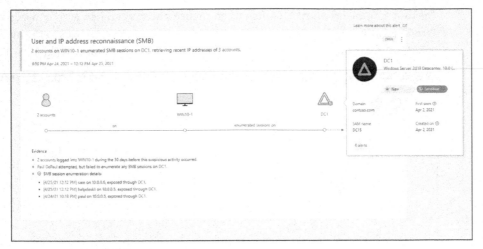

FIGURE 1-113 Alert detail

3. The alert tells you that **two different accounts** from WIN10-1 enumerated **SMB sessions** on the domain controller named DC1. Hovering the mouse over DC1 shows the **operating system**, when the machine was **first seen**, and the domain it is a member of. Also, you can see that it is marked as a **Sensitive** object because it is a **domain controller**.

4. Under **Evidence**, you can see the **accounts** and **IP addresses** that were exposed because of this enumeration, which can help you in your investigation into suspicious activities involving these accounts.

5. You can also search for a user account and see details about the alert. In the **Search box** located in the upper-right portion of the screen, type **helpdesk1** and press **Enter** to bring up the **helpdesk1** user page shown in Figure 1-114.

FIGURE 1-114 User account timeline

6. The user account **helpdesk1** has **five open security alerts** and is logged into **two different computers**. Also, you can access a timeline view of the **activities** performed by helpdesk1. Click **Directory Data** on the left to display the view shown in Figure 1-115.

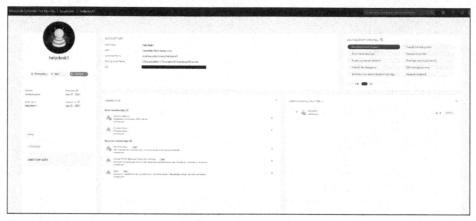

FIGURE 1-115   User Directory Data

7. This view shows information from Active Directory about the user, such as **group memberships**, **account info**, and **user account control features**, such as **Password Never Expires**. Note this account is also marked **Sensitive** because it is a member of a sensitive group, **Domain Admins And Administrators**.

8. Note the **profile picture** of helpdesk1 is a **bee.** This is because helpdesk1 is configured as a **Honeytoken** account, as shown in Figure 1-116.

FIGURE 1-116   Honeytoken configuration

9. An account can be configured as **Honeytoken** account so that an **alert** will generate when the user account **authenticates** to **Active Directory**. This can serve as a **trap** for attackers to signal they are in your environment.

> **MORE INFO   MANAGE SENSITIVE OR HONEYTOKEN ACCOUNTS**
>
> More information about sensitive and honeytoken accounts can be found here: *https://aka.ms/sc200_mdihoney.*

Using Microsoft Cloud App Security to identify and respond to threats in Software as a Service

While Software as a Service (SaaS) provided faster time-to-value because of its quick implementation times for users, SaaS also introduced new challenges for security operations and data loss prevention teams in terms of monitoring and application control. The use of SaaS applications such as Office 365, Dropbox, and others allow users to share files and interact with people outside their organizations more easily than ever before. The need for security operations teams and data loss prevention officers to monitor and control this type of activity is what birthed the Cloud App Security Broker (CASB) market. CASB products, such as Microsoft Cloud App Security (MCAS), allow security operations and data loss prevention teams to:

- Discover what cloud applications are used in the environment.

- Apply conditional access to sanctioned cloud applications for session control, such as allowing files to be downloaded only to corporate-owned assets.

- Use policies to control what data is shared from the cloud application and with whom it is shared.

- Detect anomalies and threats associated with cloud application sign-ins and activities.

Configure threat detection policies in MCAS

MCAS has several threat-detection policies for discovering and alerting on suspicious and malicious activities occurring in cloud applications. One of the built-in anomaly detection policies is the Impossible Travel Policy. The Impossible Travel Policy raises an alert when a user performs actions in a cloud application from two physical locations during a time interval that is shorter than the time it would take someone to travel between these two locations.

Let's say you suspect that there are anomalous user log-in activities occurring in your environment, such as user accounts being used from disparate locations. Follow these steps to examine the Impossible Travel Policy that can detect these threats:

1. Log in to *https://portal.cloudappsecurity.com* as a member of the **Global Administrator or Security Administrator Azure AD role**s.

2. Under **Control**, click **Policies**.
3. Click the **Threat Detection** tab at the top of the main page.

4. Scroll down and click **Impossible Travel Policy** to open the **Edit Anomaly Detection Policy** page shown in Figure 1-117.

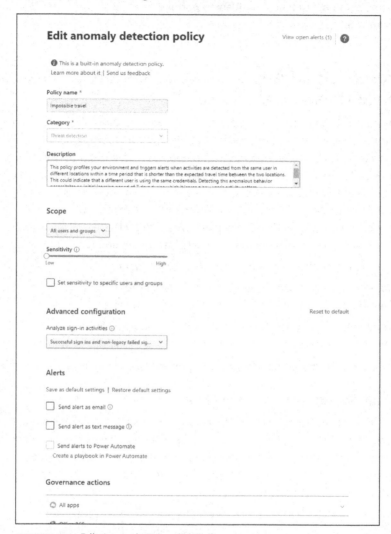

FIGURE 1-117   Edit Anomaly Detection Policy

5. In the **Edit Anomaly Detection Policy** page for the Impossible Travel Policy, you can target specific users or groups for the policy and adjust the **Sensitivity** of the policy. For example, if most of your users travel frequently, you can set the **Sensitivity** to **Low**. However, because your finance department users do not travel and the group contains users with access to sensitive data, you need the policy to be more sensitive for those users.

6. Find the **Scope** section of the policy page shown in Figure 1-118.

FIGURE 1-118 Impossible Travel Policy Scope

7. Select **Set Sensitivity To Specific Users And Groups**.

8. Under **Filters**, select **User Groups Equals Finance Department**.

9. Slide the **Sensitivity bar** under the filter to **High**. This will increase the sensitivity for **finance department** users for this policy.

10. You can configure **Alerts** from this policy to be sent via email or text message. Because you are using Microsoft 365 Defender, these alerts will appear in the Microsoft 365 Security portal (*https://security.microsoft.com*), so there is no need to configure an Alert here.

11. Scroll down to see the **Governance Actions** shown in Figure 1-119.

FIGURE 1-119 Governance Actions

12. You can select actions to apply to all cloud apps or to specific actions for specific cloud apps when the policy is matched by an activity. Under **Office 365**, **select the Confirm User Compromised** option. This will flag the user to be challenged for MFA, and if successful, the user will be required to change their password per your sign-in and user risk policy settings defined in Skill 1-2.

13. Once finished, click **Update** to save your changes to the policy.

> **NOTE** **SEVEN-DAY LEARNING PERIOD**
>
> The Impossible Travel Policy has a learning period of seven days to minimize benign true positives as much as possible.

Respond to alerts in MCAS

When policies are matched, alerts will be generated for investigation and response. You configured the Impossible Travel Threat detection policy, so now you will investigate the generated alerts. Follow these steps to investigate an Impossible travel alert:

1. Log in to *https://portal.cloudappsecurity.com* as a member of the **Global Administrator or Security Administrator Azure AD role**s.

2. Click the **Alerts** option in the menu on the left.

3. At the top of the **Alerts** page, click the **Category Filter** drop-down menu and select **Threat Detection**.

4. Click the **Impossible Travel Activity** alert to open the alerts shown in Figure 1-120.

FIGURE 1-120 Impossible Travel Activity alerts

5. The alert indicates that **Paul DePaul** had activities originating from the **Netherlands** and **Russia** within a **4-minute period**, which is what triggered the alert. A subset of the activities performed using Paul's account are shown in the Activity Log sections. All activities can be seen by clicking the **Investigate In Activity Log** option.

EXAM TIP

You must enable **File Monitoring** in the MCAS settings under **Information Protection** to see file activity store in cloud apps.

---

6. Click the drop-down menu next to **Resolution Options**, as shown in Figure 1-121.

FIGURE 1-121 Resolution options

7. Because it appears that Paul's account is compromised, click **Confirm User Compromised**.

8. Click **Confirm User Compromised** again on the confirmation pop-up window.

9. Because you have taken steps to mitigate this alert, click the **Close Alert** button shown in Figure 1-122.

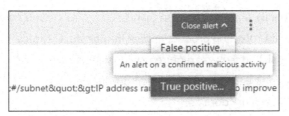

FIGURE 1-122 Close Alert

10. Click **True Positive**.

11. The **Close Alert As True Positive** pop-up window offers these options: **Comment**, **Send Feedback**, and **Opt-In To Share Your Email Address**. The latter option allows the MCAS development team to contact you for more information if required.

> *MORE INFO* **MANAGE ALERTS**
>
> For more information on managing alerts in MCAS, see *https://aka.ms/sc200_mcasalertmgmt*.

> *MORE INFO* **DETECT SUSPICIOUS USER ACTIVITY WITH UEBA**
>
> For a full tutorial on managing IP address rangers and tuning anomaly detection policies in MCAS, see *https://aka.ms/sc200_mcasalerttune*.

Skill 1-4: Manage cross-domain investigations in the Microsoft 365 Defender Security portal

In the previous skills, you investigated alerts generated in each of the Microsoft threat protection products and the risk domains they cover (see Figure 1-123).

Product	Risk domain
Microsoft Defender for Office 365	Email and Office documents
Microsoft Defender for Endpoint	Devices
Microsoft Defender for Identity	Identities
Microsoft Cloud App Security	Cloud applications

FIGURE 1-123 Microsoft threat protection products

Each of these products are best-in-market for the risk domains they cover. Unfortunately, attackers do not operate in silos. They move to whatever risk domain they need to achieve their end goals. Investigation is especially challenging for security operations teams for the following reasons:

- Alerts are investigated individually, and there are too many alerts to triage and manage.
- Alerts generated by each threat protection product appear in separate consoles.
- Each console has a different look and feel and requires a wide variety of skill sets.
- Automated self-healing is siloed to each threat protection product.
- Data searches are done within each risk domain.

Microsoft 365 Defender addresses these challenges with the following design principles:

- **Single-incident model** Machine Learning runs across alerts generated by each threat protection product and places them into incidents. This helps the incident responder track an attacker as they move through risk domains.

- **Portal consolidation**   Each of the threat protection products is consolidating into the Microsoft 365 Security portal at *https://security.microsoft.com.*
- **Automated self-healing**   Automated self-healing now spans across email and device risk domains.
- **Advanced hunting unified schema**   One schema to rule all the threat domains.

Examine a cross-domain incident

Contoso Corporation recently experienced a security incident on April 11, 2021, which involved a high-ranking finance officer named Paul DePaul and the CEO Bob Smith. Figure 1-124 is a flow diagram of the attack.

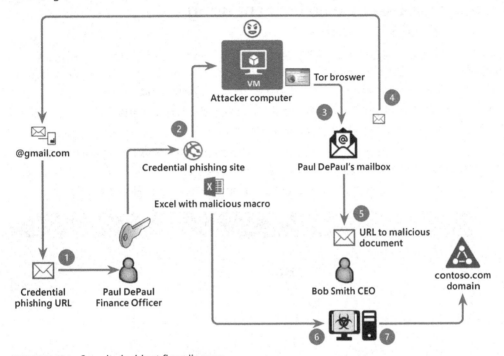

FIGURE 1-124   Security incident flow diagram

Following are the steps of the attack shown in Figure 1-124:

1. The attacker sends an email to Paul DePaul, a high-ranking finance officer at Contoso Corporation. In the email is a URL to a credential phishing site, and the email appears to come from Bob Smith, the CEO of Contoso Corporation.

2. Paul clicks the link and enters his username and password into the website, which means the attacker now has Paul's credentials.

3. The attacker uses a Tor browser to anonymously access Paul's mailbox.

4. The attacker sets up an email forwarding rule to send emails received by Paul from Bob Smith to the attacker's email.

5. The attacker emails Bob Smith using Paul's mailbox. The email contains a URL to a malicious, macro-enabled Excel document hosted on a web server.

6. Bob opens the Excel document thinking it is from Paul. He runs the macro, which sets up a command-and-control channel back to the attacker's computer.

7. The attacker begins to run commands to explore Contoso's Active Directory domain.

This attack spans the risk domains of email, identity, and device, which makes it time consuming to piece together using individual alerts and possibly involving separate teams at Contoso. Because the attacker is already on a device inside Contoso, the security operation team needs to work quickly to mitigate the threat.

Manage a cross-domain incident using Microsoft 365 Defender

Microsoft 365 Defender uses a single incident model that aggregates alerts from Microsoft Defender for Office 365, Defender for Endpoint, Defender for Identity, and MCAS. Data from each of these solutions is also aggregated to provide a unified hunting experience.

You need to triage the incident in Microsoft 365 Defender, stop the attacker, and remediate the threat. Follow these steps to mitigate this incident:

1. Log in to *https://security.microsoft.com* as a member of the **Global Administrator** or **Security Administrator** Azure Active Directory roles.

2. On the **Home** screen, the **Threat Analytics card** is shown (see Figure 1-125).

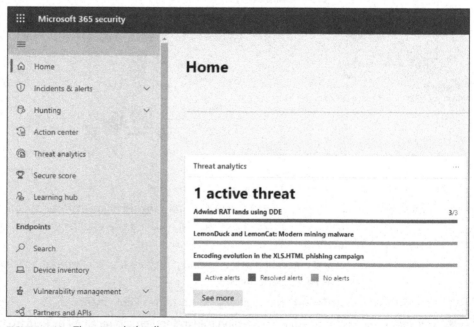

FIGURE 1-125 Threat analytics tile

3. The **Threat Analytics** card indicates there is **1 active threat**: **Adwind RAT lands using DDE**. Click the **red bar** to open the **Threat Analytics Report** shown in Figure 1-126.

FIGURE 1-126 Threat analytics report

4. **Threat analytics** is a collection of threat intelligence reports written by threat research-ers at Microsoft. Data from Microsoft 365 Defender is integrated into these reports to indicate the degree to which your organization is from the described threat. The report also shows ways to mitigate these risks.

5. Under **Related Incidents**, you see that there are **three active alerts** in **one active incident**. Click **View All Related Incidents**.

6. Click the **Incident** listed as **Related Incidents** to open the incident view shown in Figure 1-127.

7. The incident that was linked to the Threat Analytics reports is titled **Multi-Stage Inci-dent Involving Initial Access & Discovery On One Endpoint Reported By Multiple Sources**. This name is generated by machine learning that aggregated all the alerts from the alert sources. You see that there are **16/16 Active Alerts** that fall within **four MITRE ATT&CK tactics**. This indicates that of the 16 alerts in this incident, 16 of them are not resolved. You also see that there is **one impacted device**, **two impacted users**, and **one impacted mailbox**.

FIGURE 1-127 Incident page

8. To mitigate the threat as fast as possible, you need to isolate the affected device and prevent the involved user accounts from logging in. Click the **Devices** section to bring up the **Devices** tab shown in Figure 1-128.

FIGURE 1-128 Devices tab

9. In this example, click the **bubble** next to the **win10-2 device**, and then click **Isolate Device**. In the isolation confirmation pop-up window, enter comments into the Comments field. It is mandatory that you add comments so that other incident responders working in the console know why the device has been isolated. Once you enter your comments, click **Confirm**.

10. Click the **Users** section to open the **Users** tab shown in Figure 1-129.

FIGURE 1-129 Suspend User

11. Click the **Paul user object** as shown in Figure 1-129, click the **ellipsis (...)** to display additional actions and click **Suspend User**. Click **Suspend User** on the confirmation pop-up window. **Repeat** these steps for the **Bob user object located under Paul**. This will prevent Paul and Bob from logging in, but it also will keep the attacker from logging in as Paul or Bob.

Now that the threat is mitigated, you need to investigate the attack to understand how it developed. Follow these steps to investigate how the attack happened:

1. Click **Manage Incident** in the upper-right part of the screen. Click **Assign To Me** and then click **Save**. Next, click the **Alerts** section to bring up the alert view shown in Figure 1-130.

FIGURE 1-130 Alerts view in an incident

2. In the **Service Source** column, multiple sources are shown. Click the **bubble** next to the **Impossible Travel Activity** alert to display further details about this alert, as shown in Figure 1-131.

3. This alert indicates that **Paul DePaul** traveled from the **Netherlands** to **Russia** within **4 minutes**.

FIGURE 1-131 Impossible Travel Activity alert

4. In the **Alerts** list, click the **bubble** next to **Creation Of Forwarding/Redirect Rule**, and then click **Open Alert Page**, as shown in Figure 1-132.

FIGURE 1-132 Inbox mail forwarding rule

5. In this alert, you see that a **new rule** was created in **Paul's mailbox**. The **Parameters** text box shows that the rule forwards emails to a gmail.com account when the email is from Bob.

6. Return to the **Alerts** page of the **incident**.

7. Click the **bubble** next to one of the **Suspicious PowerShell Command-Line** alerts and click **Open Alert Page**, as shown in Figure 1-133.

FIGURE 1-133 Suspicious PowerShell Command Line alert

8. At the top of the alert page are the entities that the alert applies to—the device **win10-2** and user **CONTOSO\bob**. Under **Alert Story** is the process tree where the rest of the alerts in this incident are shown. Because there are multiple alerts pertaining to EXCEL.EXE, Defender for Endpoint **taints this process (marks it as untrustworthy)**, which means all subprocesses and their associated alerts are shown. This prevents the incident responder from needing to click every alert in the incident.

9. The document that more than likely contained the malicious macro is named quote3245.xlsm. The .XLSM extension indicates that it is an Excel file with a macro. Because Excel opened this file and is a child process of msedge.exe—which is a subprocess of OUTLOOK.EXE—this tells you that the file was downloaded from a URL in an email. You can use **Advanced Hunting** to find this email and the URL.

10. Click **Hunting** in the menu on the far left and click **Advanced Hunting**.

11. Use this query:

```
let badfile = "quote3245.xlsm";

EmailUrlInfo

| where Timestamp between (datetime(2021-04-11T20:00:00) .. datetime(2021-04-
13T00:00:00)) and Url has badfile

| join EmailEvents on NetworkMessageId

| project Timestamp, NetworkMessageId, Url, SenderFromAddress,
RecipientEmailAddress
```

The query is broken down like so:

- It sets the variable `badfile` to `quote3245.xlsm`.
- It then searches the `EmailUrlInfo` table for `quote3245.xlsm` as a partial match in the `Url` field records.
- Next, it joins the `EmailEvents` table on the results, keying off the `NetworkMessageId`.
- You need the `join` to expose the additional fields in the email—the `SenderFromAddress` and `RecepientEmailAddress`.

12. Click **Run Query**.

13. The results are shown in Figure 1-134.

FIGURE 1-134 Advanced hunting query editor

14. You can see the full **URL** from which the file was downloaded, as well as the **sender (Paul)** and the **recipient (Bob)**. The attacker used Paul's compromised mailbox to send the email to Bob to increase the chances of Bob clicking the link and opening the document because it came from Paul, not a Gmail account.

15. Copy the `NetworkMessageId` by right-clicking the value and choosing **Copy Value To Clipboard**. We need it to remove the email from Bob's mailbox.

16. In the menu on the far left, under **Email & Collaboration**, click **Explorer**.

17. Change the **View** drop-down menu to **All Email**. In the query field selector, select **Network Message ID**, click in the text box next to **Network Message ID**, and press

Ctrl+V to paste in the `NetworkMessageId` you copied in the previous step. Change the date range to before and after April 11, 2020 to only search email around April 11, 2020 and click the **Refresh** button.

18. As shown in Figure 1-135, the search found the email that was sent from Paul to Bob with the malicious URL.

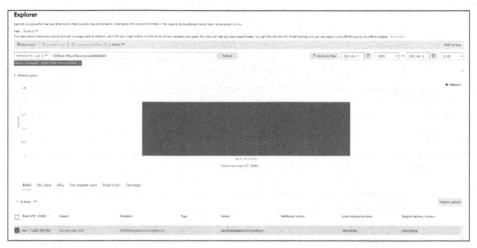

FIGURE 1-135 Email and collaboration explorer query tool

19. The bar chart in Figure 1-135 shows the number of recipients for this email that were returned in this search and the date and time they were received. Below the bar chart are the email details. In the email details area, click the **check box** to select the email, as shown in Figure 1-135.

20. Click the **Actions drop-down menu** shown in Figure 1-136.

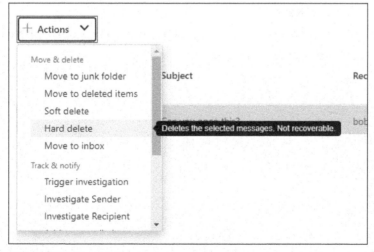

FIGURE 1-136 Email Actions

21. Click **Hard Delete**, which will remove the email from Bob's mailbox **permanently**.

Now that you removed the email, you need to ensure the URL is blocked from Endpoints by using URL indicators. Follow these steps to add a URL indicator:

1. On the far-left menu under **Endpoints**, click **Search**.

2. Select **URL** in the drop-down menu, type the domain you want to search for, and press **Enter**. If there are multiple URLs that match your search, you will need to click the correct URL. If there is only one match for your search, a page like the one shown in Figure 1-137 will be shown.

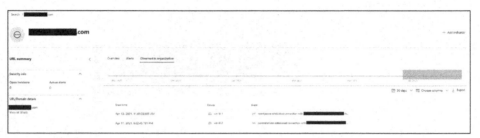

FIGURE 1-137 URL page

3. The **URL page** allows you to see what machines had network communications with the URL. There are two machines in Contoso that accessed the URL that delivered the malicious Excel document, so you need to block this domain.

4. Click **Add Indicator** in the upper-right portion of this screen to open the **Add URL/Domain Indicator** wizard.

5. Under **Expires On (UTC)**, select **Never**, and then click **Next** to advance to the **Action** tab shown in Figure 1-138.

6. Under **Response Action,** select **Alert And Block**, type details for the **Alert** in the **Description** field, and click **Next**.

7. On the **Scope** tab, under **Device Groups**, click **All Devices In My Scope**; click **Next**.

8. To add the indicator, click **Save** on the **Summary** page.

FIGURE 1-138 Add URL/Domain Indicator

To ensure the malicious document `quote3245.xlsm` is not allowed to be opened on any endpoint in Contoso, use these steps to add a file indicator:

1. On the far-left menu, under **Endpoints**, click **Search**.

2. Select **File** from the drop-down menu and type the file name **quote3245.xlsm**; press **Enter** to search.

3. The file page for `quote3245.xlsm` opens, as shown in Figure 1-139.

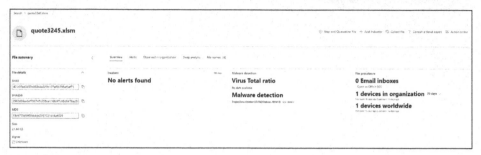

FIGURE 1-139 File page

4. You can see on which devices the file was seen. In the upper-right part of the screen, click **Add Indicator**.

5. In the **Add File Hash Indicator** wizard, select **Never from the options under Expires On (UTC)**. Click **Next** to advance to the **Action page** shown in Figure 1-140.

FIGURE 1-140 Add file hash indicator

6. On the **Action** tab, configure the **Response Action** to **Alert And Block**, type details for the **Alert**, and click **Next**.

7. On the **Scope** page, click **All Devices In My Scope** and click **Next**.

8. Click **Save** on the **Summary** page to add the file hash indicator.

Now that all the entities from the incident are cleaned up, you should now close the incident. Follow these steps to close the incident:

1. On the far-left menu, under **Incidents & Alerts**, click **Incidents** and locate the incident named **Multi-Stage Incident Involving Initial Access & Discovery On One Endpoint Reported By Multiple Sources.**

2. In the upper-right portion of the incident page, click **Manage Incident** to open the **Manage Incident fly**-out menu shown in Figure 1-141.

FIGURE 1-141 Manage Incident

3. Click the **Resolve Incident** toggle, and under **Classification**, select **True Alert**.

4. Under **Determination, choose Malware**, and click **Save**.

> **MORE INFO** **TRACK AND RESPOND TO EMERGING THREATS WITH THREAT ANALYTICS**
>
> To learn more about Threat Analytics, see *https://aka.ms/sc200_ta*.

> **MORE INFO** **THE UNIFIED MICROSOFT 365 SECURITY CENTER OVERVIEW**
>
> To learn more about the Microsoft 365 Security portal, see *https://aka.ms/sc200_m365secoverview*.

Thought experiment

In this thought experiment, demonstrate your skills and knowledge of the topics covered in this chapter. You can find answers to this thought experiment in the next section.

Securing Contoso Corporation from modern threats

You are a senior member of the security operations team at Contoso Corporation, a company that writes software for autonomous cars. Executives at the company report they have received an increasing amount of spear phishing emails that appear to come from board of director members. Most of these spear phishing emails contain URLs pointing to websites that mimic Office 365 log-in pages. Unfortunately, the security team at Contoso is overwhelmed by the number of alerts coming from endpoints, so they have not been able to give the spear phishing issue enough attention.

To make matters worse, the tier 1 security operators report they had access to Microsoft Defender for Endpoint data last week, but after you enabled the roles feature in Defender for Endpoint, they no longer have access to the Endpoint data.

MCAS is also generating many Impossible Travel Alerts, which started around the time Contoso switched its VPN provider to another company overseas.

1. What configuration changes could you make in Microsoft Defender for Office 365 to mitigate the spear phishing issue?

2. What could you do to help the security operations team keep up with Endpoint alerts?

3. Why did the tier 1 security operations team lose access to Defender for Endpoint data after roles were enabled in Defender for Endpoint? How can you fix this issue?

4. What can you do to tune the MCAS impossible travel alerts to reduce the number of benign true positives?

Thought experiment answers

This section contains the solution to the thought experiment. Each answer explains why the answer choice is correct.

1. You can configure anti-phishing policies and add the email addresses of the board of directors to the users to protect. You can also configure a Safe Links policy to address the credential phishing URLs. Both changes are made in Microsoft Defender for Office 365.

2. You can configure device groups in Microsoft Defender for Endpoint to Full—Remediate Threats Automatically and enable an advanced feature, Automatically Resolve Alerts. This will enable the Automated Investigation self-healing feature in Microsoft Defender for Endpoint to investigate new alerts, remediate found threats, and automatically close alerts. This would reduce the workload of the security team.

3. The tier 1 security operations team was given access to the Microsoft Defender for Endpoint data through membership in the Azure AD role **Security Readers**. When Roles are enabled in Defender for Endpoint, **Security Readers** lose access to the portal. To resolve this issue, the tier 1 team's security group should be assigned a role with the permission to view data for security operations data.

4. Add the VPN IP network ranges to the known IP addresses configuration in MCAS. This will exclude the VPN IP range from impossible travel detections and reduce the benign true positives.

Chapter Summary

- Safe Links, Safe Attachments, and anti-phishing policies in Microsoft Defender for Office 365 can help protect users from malicious links, attachments, and impersonated emails, respectively.

- Attack Simulation Training can help educate your users on how to spot phishing and other malicious document content.

- Microsoft Defender for Endpoint not only helps you protect, detect, and respond to endpoint threats, it can also recommend security settings and report vulnerable software in your environment that pose the highest risk of exploitation.

- The automated investigation self-healing feature can reduce the workload of your security operations team, so they can concentrate on proactive hunting and improving protection.

- Azure Active Directory Identity Protection can detect risky sign-ins and user accounts at risk of being compromised. Multifactor authentication and requiring a password change can be invoked to protect these accounts.

- Microsoft Cloud App Security allows you to discover the cloud applications you users access. It can also alert you to unusual and malicious activity based on user behavior patterns.
- Microsoft Defender for Identity can detect reconnaissance and user account compromise in Active Directory Domain Services environments.
- Microsoft 365 Defender improves the efficiency and effectiveness of your security operations teams by providing a single portal for Microsoft threat protection products, a single incident model, intelligent Automated Investigation self-healing, and a combined schema for Advanced Hunting and custom detections.

CHAPTER 2

Mitigate threats using Azure Defender

One critical component of any Security Operations Center (SOC) is the quality of the alert that is received from a given data source. The quality of the alert can be measured by the relevance of the information contained in the alert, how that alert reflects into the threat vectors of a cloud workload, and how these indications can help security operation analysts to investigate and respond to that alert. Azure Defender has different plans that offer threat detections for specific workloads, based on analytics that were created specifically for the threat vector of the workload's type.

To mitigate threats using Azure Defender you must be able to design, configure, and manage the different types of Azure Defender plans, manage rules, and understand how to investigate and automate response.

Skills covered in this chapter:

- Design and configure an Azure Defender implementation
- Plan and implement the use of data connectors for ingestion of data in Azure Defender
- Manage Azure Defender alert rules
- Configure automation and remediation
- Investigate Azure Defender alerts and incidents

Skill 2-1: Design and configure an Azure Defender implementation

Before implementing Azure Defender it is important to understand the different design considerations that will directly affect how you configure the solution based on the scenario's requirements. This section of the chapter covers the skills necessary to design and configure Azure Defender implementation according to the SC-200 exam outline.

Plan and configure Azure Defender settings, including selecting target subscriptions and workspace

When planning to use Azure Defender, you must understand the requirements for the type of plan that you want to implement. If you are planning the implementation of Azure Defender for Servers, Azure Defender for Kubernetes, or Azure Defender for SQL Server on Machines, you also need to consider the requirement to deploy the Log Analytics (LA) Agent to the machines. By doing so, you will need to select the workspace to which the agent will send the information.

Other Azure Defender plans that are based on other Azure Platform as a Service (PaaS) offerings don't require a workspace configuration in the beginning. This includes plans such as Azure Defender for Key Vault, Azure Defender for App Service, Azure Defender for Resource Manager, Azure Defender for Storage, Azure Defender for Containers Registries, Azure Defender for SQL database, and Azure Defender for DNS. You will only need to configure a workspace for these Azure Defender plans if you consider utilizing the *continuous export* capability in Azure Security Center. This feature is often used in the following scenarios:

- When the organization wants to store all alerts that are triggered by all Azure Defender plans in the workspace because. By default, only VM-based alerts are stored in the workspace.
- When the organization wants to store all security recommendations or regulatory compliance information in the workspace.
- When the organization needs to send the alerts to a security information and event management (SIEM) via Azure Event Hub.

When you first activate Azure Security Center, the auto-provisioning feature is not enabled. However, if you want to ensure that all VMs are automatically configured to receive the LA agent and send the data to the correct workspace, you should enable this option. When auto-provisioning is enabled, and the **Connect Azure VMs To The Default Workspace(s) Created By Security Center** option is selected, Security Center will automatically create and manage a new workspace. Security Center creates a new resource group and a workspace (called default workspace) in the same geolocation of the VM and connects the agent to that workspace. The naming conventions for the default workspace and resource group are shown below:

- **Workspace** `DefaultWorkspace-[subscription-ID]-[geo]`
- **Resource Group** `DefaultResourceGroup-[geo]`

The fact that a default workspace is created according to the geolocation of the VM is an advantage if your design requirements dictates that you need to ensure that the data sent from the VM is stored in the same region as the VM's location. Table 2-1 shows where the workspace will reside according to the VM's location:

TABLE 2-1 VM and workspace locations

VM Location	Workspace Location
United States and Brazil	United States
Canada	Canada
Europe	Europe
United Kingdom	United Kingdom
East Asia and Southeast Asia	Asia
Korea	Korea
India	India
Japan	Japan
China	China
Australia	Australia

If your organization is already utilizing a Log Analytics workspace and it wants to leverage the same workspace for Security Center, you should select the **Connect Azure VMs To A Different Workspace** option and specify the workspace, which can be any workspace across all selected subscriptions within the same tenant.

The general best practice for workspace creation is to keep it as minimal as possible, which is not the case when you configure Security Center to manage the workspaces. When reading a scenario in the SC-200 exam, take into consideration the business requirements as well as the technical requirements. These requirements will lead you to select one of these two options:

- You could use the default workspace, which can create a lot of workspaces according to the regions where the company's VMs reside
- You could take a more centralized approach where all VMs across all subscriptions will have to send data to a single workspace.

> **IMPORTANT** **BEST PRACTICES**
>
> If you plan to use the same workspace for Azure Sentinel and Azure Security Center, make sure to read the best practices highlighted in this post: *http://aka.ms/ascbooklawbp*.

The actual steps to configure auto-provisioning and specify the workspace are provided later in this chapter.

Configure Azure Defender roles

Security Center uses Role-Cased Access Control (RBAC) based in Azure. By default, there are two roles in Security Center: **Security Reader** and **Security Admin**. The **Security Reader** role should be assigned to all users that need read access only to the dashboard. For example, Security Operations personnel that needs to monitor, and respond to security alerts, should be assigned the **Security Reader** role. It is important to mention that the assignment of this role is done in the Azure level, under the resource group that Security Center is monitoring, and using **Access Control (IAM)**, as shown in Figure 2-1.

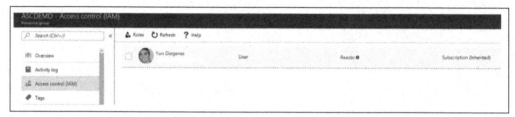

FIGURE 2-1 Access control in Azure

Workload owners usually need to manage a particular cloud workload and its related resources. Besides that, the workload owner is responsible for implementing and maintaining protections in accordance with company security policy. **Security Admin** role should be assigned for users that need to manage Security Center configuration.

Only subscription **Owners/Contributors** and **Security Admins** can edit a security policy. Only subscription and resource group Owners and Contributors can apply security recommendations for a resource. To enable Azure Defender, you need **Security Admin** or **Subscription Owner** privilege. To learn more about Role-Based Access Control (RBAC) in Azure, visit *http://aka.ms/azurerbac*.

Custom roles

There will be some scenarios where the organization may want to provide a more granular privilege for some users instead of granting access to the entire **Security Admin** access role. Consider an organization called Contoso that needs to provide privilege to security opera-tion analysts to simply visualize and create alert-suppression rules. In this case, the **Security Admin** role provides more privileges than what is necessary. For scenarios like this, you can create a custom role in Azure and assign write privilege to this operation: `Microsoft.Security/alertsSuppressionRules/write`.

> **MORE INFO** **CREATING CUSTOM ROLES**
>
> To create custom roles, see *http://aka.ms/SC200_CustomRole*.

Another common scenario is when an organization needs to create a custom role to allow users to configure or edit the just-in-time (JIT) VM access. You need a set of privileges to work with JIT; these privileges will vary according to the type of operation that you need to perform or that you want to allow a user to perform. You can be very granular about this permission assignment by using these guidelines:

To configure or edit a JIT policy for a VM, you need to assign these actions to the role:

- On the scope of a subscription or resource group that is associated with the VM: `Microsoft.Security/locations/jitNetworkAccessPolicies/write`.

- On the scope of a subscription or resource group of VM: `Microsoft.Compute/virtualMachines/write`.

To request access to a VM, you need to assign these actions to the user:

- On the scope of a subscription or resource group that is associated with the VM: `Microsoft.Security/locations/jitNetworkAccessPolicies/initiate/action`.

- On the scope of a subscription or resource group that is associated with the VM: `Microsoft.Security/locations/jitNetworkAccessPolicies/*/read`.

- On the scope of a subscription or resource group or VM: `Microsoft.Compute/virtualMachines/read`.

- On the scope of a subscription or resource group or VM: `Microsoft.Network/networkInterfaces/*/read`.

On the scope of a subscription, resource group, or VM that you need to read JIT policies, assign these actions to the user:

- `Microsoft.Security/locations/jitNetworkAccessPolicies/read`

- `Microsoft.Security/locations/jitNetworkAccessPolicies/initiate/action`

- `Microsoft.Security/policies/read`

- `Microsoft.Security/pricings/read`

- `Microsoft.Compute/virtualMachines/read`

- `Microsoft.Network/*/read`

Also, if you need to see the JIT NSG policy from the VM—Networking blade, you need to add the following policies:

- `Microsoft.Network/networkSecurityGroups/read`

- `Microsoft.Network/networkSecurityGroups/defaultSecurityRules/read`

- `Microsoft.Network/networkSecurityGroups/securityRules/read`

While the permissions above can be utilized to apply the principle of least privilege, keep in mind that you will need to merge some permissions if you are accessing via the Azure portal. For example, to configure or edit a JIT policy for a VM, you will need the privileges given and the privileges to read JIT policies.

Configure data retention policies

Azure Defender provides 500 MB per node, per day of free allowance for the data allocated in the Log Analytics workspace against the following subsets of security data types:

- WindowsEvent
- SecurityAlert
- SecurityBaseline
- SecurityBaselineSummary
- SecurityDetection
- SecurityEvent
- WindowsFirewall
- MaliciousIPCommunication
- LinuxAuditLog
- SysmonEvent
- ProtectionStatus

Update and UpdateSummary data types can be used when the Update Management solution is not running on the workspace or when solution targeting is enabled.

If the workspace is in the legacy *Per Node* pricing tier, the Azure Defender and Log Analytics allocations are combined and applied jointly to all billable ingested data. When you configure Azure Defender to utilize a workspace, the data will be stored there is going to be available for 30 days by default. However, you can configure data retention at the workspace level up to 730 days (2 years) for all workspaces unless they are using the legacy *free* tier (for example, when using Azure Security Center without upgrading to Azure Defender).

> **IMPORTANT AZURE MONITOR PRICING**
>
> When you choose to extend your data retention for the workspace used by Azure Defender, extra charges will be applied as per Log Analytics workspace pricing. If the same workspace is shared with Azure Sentinel, you get 90 days of data retention included. Visit the Azure Monitor pricing page for more information about the current pricing: *https://azure.microsoft.com/en-us/pricing/details/monitor/*.

Depending on the scenario that you are addressing, you might need to extend the data retention to more than 30 days. Make sure to always review the business and technical requirements of the scenario for hints about data retention. Once you determine the data retention goal, follow the steps below to configure data retention in Log Analytics workspace:

1. Navigate to the Azure portal by opening *https://portal.azure.com*.
2. In the search bar, type **log ana**, and under **Services**, click **Log Analytics Workspaces**.
3. In the **Log Analytics Workspaces** dashboard, click the workspace for which you want to configure data retention.

4. In the left navigation pane, in the **General** section, click **Usage And Estimated Costs.** The **Usage And Estimated Costs** page appears, as shown in Figure 2-2.

FIGURE 2-2   Log Analytics workspace usage and cost

5. Click the **Data Retention** button, and the **Data Retention** blade appears, as shown in Figure 2-3.

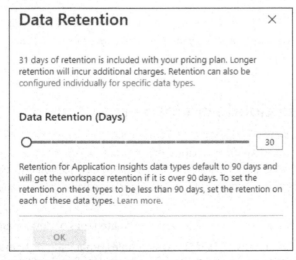

FIGURE 2-3   Configuring data retention for the Log Analytics workspace

6. You can use the **Data Retention (Days)** slider to increase the number of days that you want to retain the data. Once you finish, click the **OK** button to commit the changes.

You can also utilize an Azure Resource Manager (ARM) template to configure data retention by using the `retentionInDays` parameter. The advantage of using an ARM template for this operation is that you can apply in scale, and you can also customize other parameters. For example, if the scenario requires that you set the data retention to 30 days and trigger an immediate purge of older data, you can do that by using the `immediatePurgeDataOn30Days` parameter, which eliminates the grace period. This configuration could also be useful for compliance-related scenarios where immediate data removal is mandatory.

While the extension of the data retention policy for the entire workspace is usually the most common scenario, there are some situations that you might need to change the data retention based on a specific data type. Retention settings for individual data types are available from 4 to 730 days (except for workspaces in the legacy free tier). These settings will override the workspace-level default retention. You will also need to use ARM to change this setting. In the example below, the data retention for the `SecurityEvent` data type is being changed to 550 days:

```
PUT /subscriptions/00000000-0000-0000-0000-00000000000/resourceGroups/
MyResourceGroupName/providers/Microsoft.OperationalInsights/workspaces/MyWorkspaceName/
Tables/SecurityEvent?api-version=2017-04-26-preview
    {
        "properties":
        {
            "retentionInDays": 550
        }
    }
```

EXAM TIP

When evaluating a scenario in the SC-200 exam, look for business requirements that lead to cost savings on data. Changing data retention only in certain data types can be used to reduce overall costs for data retention.

Assess and recommend cloud workload protection

As enterprises start their journeys to the cloud, they will face many challenges as they adapt their on-premises tools to a cloud-based model. In a cloud environment where there are different workloads to manage, it becomes imperative to have ongoing verification and corrective actions to ensure that the security posture of those workloads is always at the highest possible quality.

Security Center has a variety of capabilities that can be used in two categories of cloud solutions:

■ **Cloud Security Posture Management (CSPM)** This enables organizations to assess their cloud infrastructure to ensure compliance with industry regulations and identify security vulnerabilities in their cloud workloads.

- **Cloud Workload Protection Platform (CWPP)**   This enables organizations to assess their cloud workload risks and detect threats against their servers (IaaS), containers, databases (PaaS), and storage. It also allows organizations to identity faulty configurations and remediate those with security best-practice configurations. To use the CWPP capabilities, you need to upgrade to Azure Defender.

With an Azure subscription, you can activate the free tier of Security Center, which monitors compute, network, storage, and application resources in Azure. It also provides security policy, security assessment, security recommendations, and the ability to connect with other security partner solutions.

Even organizations that are getting started with Infrastructure as a Service (IaaS) in Azure can benefit from this free service because it will improve their security postures. When you upgrade your Security Center subscription from the free tier to Azure Defender, the Azure Defender for Servers will be automatically enabled. With this plan, the following features will be available:

- Security event collection and advanced search
- Network Map
- Just-in-time VM Access
- Adaptive application controls
- Regulatory compliance reports
- File integrity monitoring
- Network Security Group (NSG) hardening
- Security alerts
- Threat protection for Azure VMs, non-Azure VMs, and PaaS services
- Integration with Microsoft Defender for Endpoint (MDE)
- Integration with Microsoft Cloud App Security (MCAS)
- Multi-cloud support for Amazon Web Services (AWS) and Google Cloud Platform (GCP)
- Vulnerability assessment integration with Qualys

Another advantage of upgrading to Azure Defender is that it allows you to monitor on-premises resources and VMs hosted by other cloud providers. You achieve this by onboarding your machine using Azure Arc and then installing the Log Analytics agent on the target machine.

Assessment and recommendations

Security Center will identify resources (compute, network, storage, identity, and application) that need security recommendations and will automatically suggest changes. You can see all recommendations in a single place, which is available under **General** > **Recommendations**. There, you can see security controls, as shown in Figure 2-4.

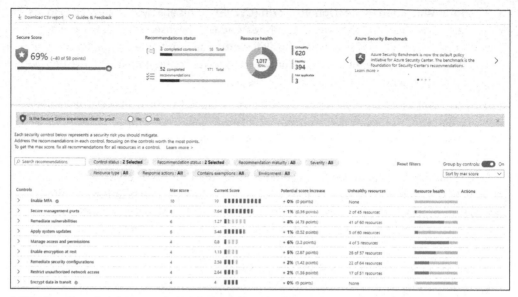

FIGURE 2-4 Security recommendations in Azure Security Center

During this initial assessment, Azure Security Center will also identify which workloads are available in the subscription. Also, it will suggest enabling the different Azure Defender plans for cloud workload protection. All plans will be part of the Azure Defender security control, as shown in Figure 2-5.

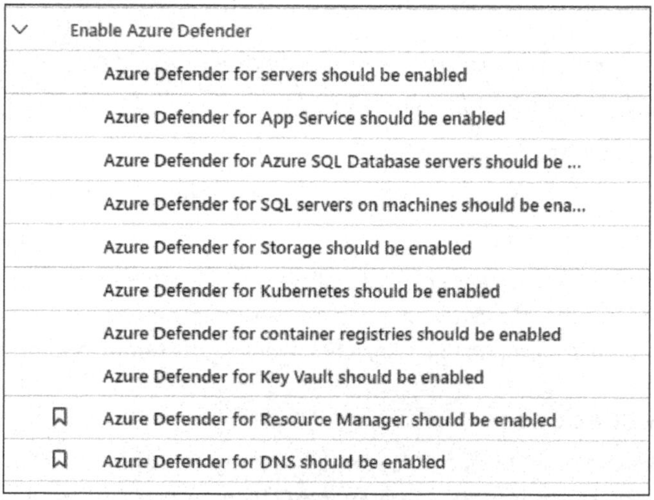

Enable Azure Defender
Azure Defender for servers should be enabled
Azure Defender for App Service should be enabled
Azure Defender for Azure SQL Database servers should be ...
Azure Defender for SQL servers on machines should be ena...
Azure Defender for Storage should be enabled
Azure Defender for Kubernetes should be enabled
Azure Defender for container registries should be enabled
Azure Defender for Key Vault should be enabled
Azure Defender for Resource Manager should be enabled
Azure Defender for DNS should be enabled

FIGURE 2-5 Enable Azure Defender security control

Enabling Azure Defender

To enable Azure Defender, you can click each recommendation and follow the remediation steps, go to the **Price & Settings** option in the left navigation pane, select the subscription, and select the plans you want to utilize. To review the pricing selection, click the **Price & Settings** option in the left navigation pane, and under **Management**, click the subscription on which you want to enable Azure Defender. The **Azure Defender** plans page will appear, as shown in Figure 2-6.

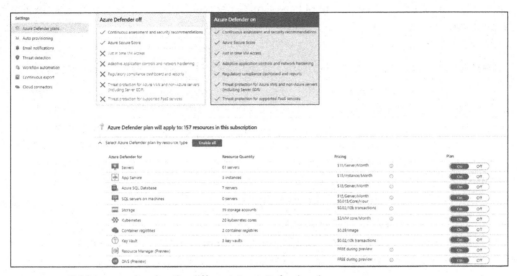

FIGURE 2-6 Pricing page showing the different Azure Defender plans

On this page, you can change the toggle to **ON** or **OFF**, where **ON** means that the Azure Defender plan is enabled on the selected subscription. While most of the Azure Defender plans can only be enabled on the subscription level, there are a couple that can be enabled individually:

- Azure Defender for SQL (Azure SQL Database)
- Azure Defender for Storage (Storage)

In both cases, you can toggle these to the **OFF** setting on this page, and you can go to each Azure SQL database or each Azure Storage account and enable Azure Defender from there. You might do this if the business requirement is to save cost by only enabling Azure Defender for SQL or Azure Defender for Storage on a company's most critical assets, rather than enabling them for the entire subscription.

Make sure to analyze the business requirements that will guide you when deciding whether to disable it at the subscription level and enable it on each resource. If you need to enable Azure Defender in scale, you can also use ARM Templates or Azure Policy.

Skill 2-2: Plan and implement the use of data connectors for ingestion of data sources in Azure Defender

When you upgrade from Azure Security Center to Azure Defender, you can start monitoring the security posture of different cloud providers, including Amazon Web Service (AWS) and Google Cloud Platform (GCP). Ingesting data from these platforms is a mandatory step when you need to have visibility across different workloads located in multiple cloud providers. This section covers the skills necessary to plan and implement the use of data connectors for ingestion of data sources in Azure Defender according to the SC-200 exam outline.

Identify data sources to be ingested for Azure Defender

Azure Defender supports the integration of partner security solutions, such as vulnerability assessment by Qualys and Rapid7. It can also integrate with the Microsoft Azure Web Application Firewall on the Azure Application Gateway. The advantage of using this integration varies according to the solution. For vulnerability assessment, the agent can be provisioned using the license you already have for the product (Qualys or Rapid7). Follow these steps to access the **Security Solutions** dashboard:

1. Navigate to the Azure portal by opening *https://portal.azure.com*.

2. In the search bar, type **security,** and under **Services,** click **Security Center.**

3. In Security Center main dashboard, in the **Management** section, click **Security Solutions.** The **Security Solutions** page appears, as shown in Figure 2-7.

FIGURE 2-7 Security Solutions page with the connected solutions and available data sources

The **Connected Solutions** section is populated according to the solutions that were already deployed. The deployment of the solution will vary according to the vendor. For vulnerability assessment, you will deploy the agent based on the Azure Security Center recommendation indicating that your machine is missing a vulnerability assessment. The **Add Data Source** section of this page allows you to:

- **Onboard a non-Azure machine**   In this scenario, you will need to select the workspace in which the Log Analytics (LA) agent will report to, Then you will need to obtain the workspace ID and key, deploy the agent to the server, and configure it to use the workspace ID and key based on your workspace's selection.

- **Connect to a SIEM platform**   In this scenario, you need to configure an Azure Event Hub, stream the data from Azure Defender to this Event Hub, and configure the SIEM to obtain the info from the Event Hub using a SIEM connector. The SIEM connector will vary according to the supported vendor (Splunk, ArcSight, QRadar, or Palo Alto). Keep in mind that you don't need to use an Event Hub if you are connecting Azure Defender with Azure Sentinel. In this case, you just need to use the Azure Defender connector in Azure Sentinel.

- **Azure Web Application Firewall (WAF)**   In this scenario, the goal is to surface the Azure WAF logs in the Azure Defender Security Alerts Dashboard. Note that this integration only works for WAF v1.

Configure automated onboarding for Azure resources and data collection

PaaS-related resources in Azure don't require an agent to work, which means that as long as you have the Azure Defender plan enabled on the subscription level, the subsequential resources will automatically have Azure Defender enabled on them. For example, if the technical requirement is to have Azure Defender for Storage enabled on all existing and new storage accounts, you just need to enable Azure Defender for Storage at the subscription level.

As mentioned earlier in this chapter, when dealing with Azure VMs (IaaS scenario), you will need to install the LA Agent. For Azure VMs, this agent can be auto-provisioned based on the auto-provisioning settings that were configured at the subscription level. To change these settings, follow these steps:

1. Open **Azure portal** and sign in with a user who has **Security Admin** privileges.
2. In the left navigation menu, click **Security Center**.
3. In the Security Center's left navigation menu, under **Management**, click the **Pricing & Settings** option.
4. Click the subscription for which you want to review the auto-provisioning settings.
5. In the **Settings** section on the left, click **Auto Provisioning**. The **Auto Provisioning** settings appear, as shown in Figure 2-8.

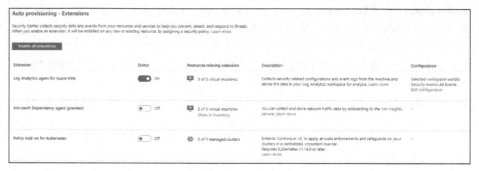

FIGURE 2-8 Auto Provisioning settings in Security Center

6. In the **Configuration** section for the **Log Analytics Agent For Azure VMs**, click **Edit Configuration**.

7. In the **Extension Deployment Configuration** blade shown in Figure 2-9, the default setting, **Connect Azure VMs To The Default Workspace(s) Created By Security Center**, allows Security Center to manage the workspace. Use this option if you can select another workspace to be used by Security Center. This is the preferred option when you have multiple subscriptions and want to centralize the workspace.

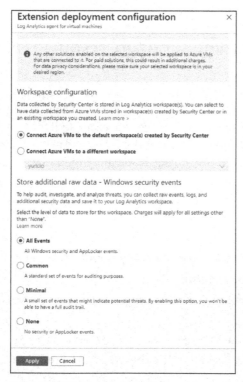

FIGURE 2-9 Options to control the workspace and data collection

In the **Store Additional Raw Data** section, you can configure the level of data collection granularity for Windows systems. Each setting will determine the type of events that will be collected. If you are using a Group Policy Object (GPO) to configure your servers where the agent will be installed, we recommended that you enable the `Process Creation Event 4688` audit policy and the `CommandLine` field inside event 4688. Audit Process Creation determines whether the operating system generates audit events when a process is created (starts). Information includes the name of the program or the user who created the process. Following is a summary of what each option collects:

- **All Events**   If you select this option, all security events will be stored in your workspace.
- **Common**   When you select this option, only a subset of events will be stored in your workspace. Microsoft considers these events—including login and logout events—to provide sufficient detail to represent a reasonable audit trail. Other events, such as Kerberos operations, security group changes, and more, are included based on industry consensus as to what constitutes a full audit trail.
- **Minimal**   Choosing this setting results in the storage of fewer events than the **Common** setting, although we aren't sure how many fewer events or what types of events are omitted. Microsoft worked with customers to ensure that this configuration surfaces enough events that successful breaches are detected and that important low-volume events are recorded. However, logout events aren't recorded, so it doesn't support a full user audit trail.
- **None**   This option disables security event storage.

To enable data collection for Adaptive Application Controls, Security Center configures a local AppLocker policy in Audit mode to allow all applications. This will cause AppLocker to generate events that are then collected and stored in your workspace. It is important to note that this policy will not be configured on any machines on which there is already a configured AppLocker policy. To collect Windows Filtering Platform Event ID 5156, you need to enable the Audit Filtering Platform Connection: `Auditpol /set /subcategory:"Filtering Platform Connection" /Success:Enable`.

Connect on-premises computers

As explained previously, VMs that are in Azure will be provisioned automatically, which means that the monitoring agent will be automatically installed. If you need to onboard on-premises computers, you will need to install the agent manually. Follow the steps below to onboard non-Azure computers or VMs:

1. Open **Azure portal** and sign in with a user who has **Security Admin** privileges.

2. In the left navigation menu, click **Security Center**.

3. In the Security Center's left navigation menu, under **General**, click the **Getting Started** option and click the **Get Started** tab.

4. Under **Add Non-Azure Computers**, click the **Configure** button, as shown in Figure 2-10.

FIGURE 2-10 Option to onboard non-Azure computers

5. In the **Add New Non-Azure Computers** blade, select the workspace in which you want to store the data from these computers, and before onboarding any computer, make sure to click **Upgrade** to upgrade the Workspace to Azure Defender, as shown in Figure 2-11.

FIGURE 2-11 Upgrading the workspace to Azure Defender

6. If the **Upgrade** button did not change to **+ Add Servers**, click the **Refresh** button, and you should see the **+ Add Servers** button, as shown in Figure 2-12. Click **Add Servers** to proceed.

FIGURE 2-12 Adding servers to the workspace

7. Once you click the **+ Add Servers** button, the **Agents Management** page appears, as shown in Figure 2-13.

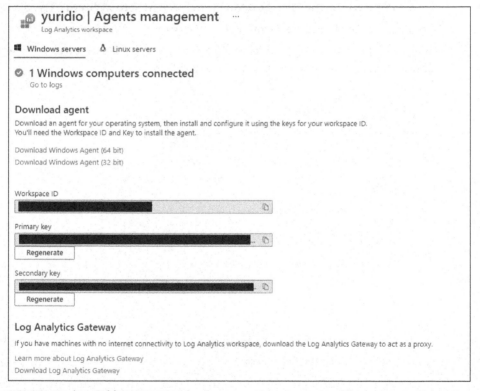

FIGURE 2-13 Agents Management

8. On this page, click the appropriate Windows agent (64-bit or 32-bit version). If you are installing the agent on a Linux operating system, click the **Linux Servers** tab and follow the instructions from there. Make sure to copy the **Workspace ID** and **Primary Key** values to the clipboard; you will need those values when installing the agent on the target system.

9. When you finish downloading it, you can close the Security Center dashboard (close your browser) and copy the agent installation file to a shared network location where the client can access it.

For this example, the agent installation will be done on an on-premises Windows Server 2016 computer, though the same set of procedures apply to a non-Azure VM located in a different cloud provider. Log in on the target system and follow the steps below to perform the installation:

1. Double-click in the MMASetup-AMD64.exe file, and if the **Open File—Security Warning** dialog appears, click **Run**.

2. If the **User Access Control** dialog appears, click **Yes**.

3. On the **Welcome To The Microsoft Monitoring Agent Setup Wizard** page, click **Next**.

4. Read the **Microsoft License Terms** and click **I Agree**.

5. In the **Destination Folder** page, leave the default selection and click **Next**. The **Agent Setup Options** page appears, as shown in Figure 2-14.

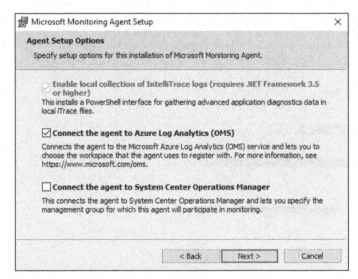

FIGURE 2-14 Selecting the target service

6. Select **Connect The Agent To Azure Log Analytics (OMS)**, as shown in Figure 2-14, and click **Next**. The **Azure Log Analytics** page appears, as shown in Figure 2-15.

7. On this page, you need to enter the **Workspace ID** and **Workspace Key** that were obtained in step 8 of the previous procedure. Notice that the primary key should be entered in the **Workspace Key** field. If this computer is behind a proxy server, you need to click the **Advanced** button and provide the Proxy URL and authentication if needed. Once you finish filling in these options, click **Next**.

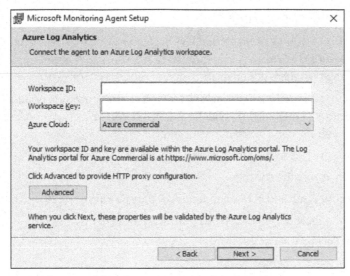

FIGURE 2-15   Providing the workspace ID and primary key

8. On the **Microsoft Update** page, select **Use Microsoft Update For Updates (Recommended)** and click **Next**.

9. On the **Ready To Install** page, review the summary field and click **Install**.

10. The **Installing The Microsoft Monitoring Agent** page appears, and the installation proceeds.

11. Once the installation is finished, the **Microsoft Monitoring Agent Configuration Completed Successfully** page appears. Click **Finish**.

You can also perform this installation using the command-line interface (CLI). Use the following code:

```
MMASetup-AMD64.exe /Q:A /R:N /C:"setup.exe /qn ADD_OPINSIGHTS_WORKSPACE=1 OPINSIGHTS_
WORKSPACE_AZURE_CLOUD_TYPE=0 OPINSIGHTS_WORKSPACE_ID=<yourworkspaceID> OPINSIGHTS_
WORKSPACE_KEY=<yourworkspaceprimarykey> AcceptEndUserLicenseAgreement=1"
```

Most of the parameters that you saw in the agent installation are self-explanatory. The only one that isn't immediately obvious is the OPINSIGHTS_WORKSPACE_AZURE_CLOUD_TYPE parameter, which is the cloud environment specification. The default is 0, which represents the Azure commercial cloud. You should only use 1 if you are installing the agent in an Azure government cloud.

It can take some time for this new non-Azure computer to appear in Security Center. If you want to validate the connectivity between this computer and the workspace, you can use the TestCloudConnection tool. On the target computer, open the command prompt and navigate to the \Program Files\Microsoft Monitoring Agent\Agent *folder*. From there, execute the TestCloudConnection.exe command, and if the connectivity is working properly, you should see all tests followed by this message: Connectivity test passed for all hosts for workspace id <workspace id>.

Connect AWS cloud resources

For Azure Defender to connect with AWS, the target AWS account must have AWS Security Hub enabled on it. AWS Security Hub has a cost associated to it, which varies according to the number of accounts and regions where it is enabled.

Once the AWS connector is operational, you will start seeing security recommendations for AWS appearing in the Security Center Recommendations Dashboard. However, before configuring the AWS connector, you will need to: do the following:

1. Configure AWS Security Hub in the target account:

   - Enable AWS Config with the console.

   - Enable AWS Security Hub and confirm that there is data flowing to it.

2. Configure AWS authentication, which can be by creating these roles:

   - An IAM role for Security Center

   - An AWS user for Security Center

3. Regardless of the authentication method you selected previously, make sure that this role/user has the following permissions policies:

   - SecurityAudit

   - AmazonSSMAutomationRole

   - AWSSecurityHubReadOnlyAccess

4. When configuring the Account ID in AWS, make sure to use this Microsoft Account ID: 158177204117.

With those steps in place, you are ready to configure the Cloud Connector. If you also want to onboard servers that are in AWS, you will need to ensure that the following three tasks are done before configuring the cloud connector in Azure Defender:

1. Install the AWS Systems Manager on your Servers (EC2 instance) that reside in AWS. For instructions, see *http://aka.ms/ascbookaws*.

2. Configure this Server (EC2 Instance) to use Azure Arc. For instructions, see *http://aka.ms/ascbookarc*.

3. In Azure, make sure to create a service principal that will be used for Azure Arc. To configure that service principal, follow the steps from this article: *http://aka.ms/ascbookspn*.

Now that all prerequisites are fulfilled, you can follow the steps below to start the configuration of the AWS connector in Security Center:

1. Open **Azure portal** and sign in with a user who has ownership privileges in the subscription.

2. In the left navigation menu, click **Security Center**.

3. In the Security Center's left navigation menu, under **Management**, click the **Cloud Connectors** option and click the **Connect AWS Account** button. The **Connect AWS Account** page appears, as shown in Figure 2-16.

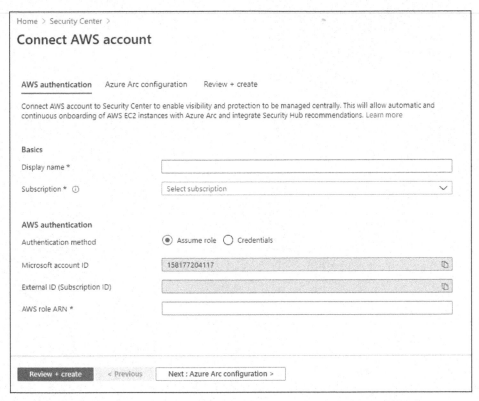

FIGURE 2-16 Connect AWS Account

4. In the **Basics** section, type a **Display Name** for the connector and select the appropriate **Subscription** from the drop-down menu.

5. In the **AWS Authentication** section, use the appropriate method (**Assume Role** if you created a role or **Credentials** if you created a user). Assuming that you created a role, the **AWS Role ARN** must be provided. This number is located in the summary of the role you created in AWS. Click the **Next: Azure Arc Configuration** button, and the **Azure Arc Configuration** tab appears, as shown in Figure 2-17.

Connect AWS account

AWS authentication   **Azure Arc configuration**   Review + create

The following configurations are used to onboard AWS EC2 instances from the AWS account to Azure Arc. This will only apply for EC2 instances with supported OS and have SSM agent installed. Learn more

Project details

Select the resource group where you want the onboarded AWS EC2 instances to be managed within Azure.

Subscription ⓘ | Free Trial ⌄

Resource group * ⓘ | ⌄

Region * ⓘ | East US ⌄

Authentication

An account with the permission to onboard the non-Azure machines to Azure is required. Please create a Service Principal following these instructions

Service principal client ID * ⓘ

Service principal client secret * ⓘ

Proxy server

If your environment requires a proxy server in order to be connected to the internet, specify the proxy server information.

Proxy server url

[Review + create]   [< Previous]   [Next : Review + create >]

FIGURE 2-17 Configuring Azure Arc settings

6. Select the **Resource Group** and **Region**.

7. In the **Authentication** section, you need to provide the **Service Principal Client ID** and the **Service Principal Client Secret**.

8. Click the **Review + Create** button and complete this operation.

9. Once you finish, you will see the connector, as shown in Figure 2-18.

Display name	Environment	Account / Org ID	Subscription	Status
ContosoAWS	AWS	648032645484	Free Trial	Valid

+ Add AWS account   + Add GCP account   ⟳ Refresh

Subscriptions **All**   Providers **All**

FIGURE 2-18 AWS connector configured

After some time, you will be able to see recommendations for your AWS account. In the search box, you can type **AWS**, and you will see all AWS-related recommendations, as shown in Figure 2-19.

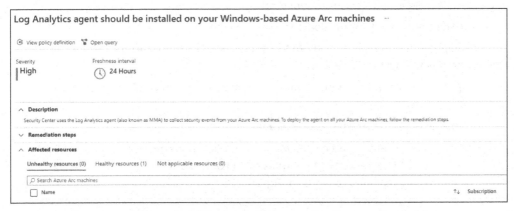

FIGURE 2-19   AWS-related recommendations

At this point, your Azure Arc machines will be discovered, but you still need to install the Log Analytics agent on those machines. There is a specific recommendation for that, as shown in Figure 2-20.

Log Analytics agent should be installed on your Windows-based Azure Arc machines   ...

⊕ View policy definition   ⌕ Open query

Severity   Freshness interval
| High   🕐 24 Hours

∧ **Description**
Security Center uses the Log Analytics agent (also known as MMA) to collect security events from your Azure Arc machines. To deploy the agent on all your Azure Arc machines, follow the remediation steps.

∨ **Remediation steps**

∧ **Affected resources**

Unhealthy resources (0)   Healthy resources (1)   Not applicable resources (0)

⌕ Search Azure Arc machines

☐ Name   ↑↓   Subscription

FIGURE 2-20   Recommendation to install the Log Analytics agent on the Azure Arc machine

You can leverage the **Quick Fix** feature to deploy the agent to this Azure Arc machine quickly. You just need to select the server and click the **Remediate** button. As mentioned in the freshness interval description, it might take 24 hours for this remediation to take effect.

Connect GCP cloud resources

For Azure Defender to connect with GCP, the target GCP account must have Google Security Command Center. Google Security Command Center has two pricing tiers: Standard (free) and Premium (paid). The free tier includes 12 recommendations, and the premium tier includes about 120 recommendations.

When connecting your GCP accounts to specific Azure subscriptions, you need to take into consideration the Google Cloud resource hierarchy. Based on this hierarchy, you can

- Connect your GCP accounts to ASC at the organization level
- Connect multiple organizations to one Azure subscription
- Connect multiple organizations to multiple Azure subscriptions

> **IMPORTANT** **ALL PROJECTS ADDED**
>
> **When you connect an organization, all projects within that organization are added to Security Center.**

Now that you understand the prerequisites, you will need to prepare the settings on GCP prior to deploy the GCP Connector in Azure Defender. Perform the following operations in GCP:

- Configure GCP Security Command Center.
- Enable Security Health Analytics.
- Enable GCP Security Command Center API.
- Create a dedicated service account for the security configuration integration.
- Create a private key for the dedicated service account.

With all prerequisites fulfilled, you can follow the steps below to start the configuration of the GCP connector in Azure Defender:

1. Open **Azure portal** and sign in with a user who has ownership privileges in the subscription.
2. In the left navigation menu, click **Security Center**.
3. In the Security Center's left navigation menu, under **Management**, click the **Cloud Connectors** option and click the **Add AWS account** button. The **Connect AWS Account** page appears, as shown in Figure 2-21.

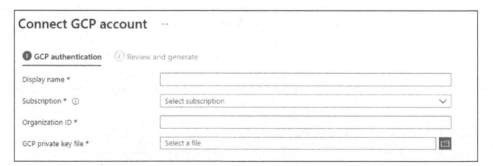

FIGURE 2-21   Connect GCP Account

4. In the **Display Name** field, type a name for this connector.
5. In the **Subscription** drop-down menu, select the Azure subscription that you want to connect with (where the GCP recommendations will appear).

6. In the **Organization ID** field, type your GCP organization ID.

7. In the **GCP Private Key File** field, browse to the JSON file you created in GCP.

8. Click **Next: Review And Generate**, and in the **Review And Generate** tab, commit the changes.

The security recommendations for your GCP resources will appear in the Security Center Recommendations Dashboard and in the regulatory compliance dashboard between 5 and 10 minutes after the onboard process is completed. To view only the GCP recommendations, you can also change the **Environment** filter in the security Recommendations Dashboard to filter for **GCP** only, as shown in Figure 2-22.

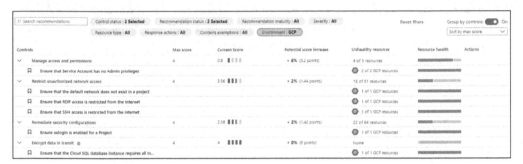

FIGURE 2-22 GCP recommendations

At this point, the onboarding process for VMs located in GCP is similar to AWS. The only difference is that in AWS, the auto-discovery of VMs happens as part of the connector's configuration (Arc parameters); in GCP, you will have to onboard manually (install Azure Arc on each VM and the LA agent).

EXAM TIP

When studying for the SC-200 exam, make sure you know the exact order of operations that must be done in AWS and GCP before going to Azure Defender to configure the connectors.

Skill 2-3: Manage Azure Defender alert rules

For the Security Operations Center (SOC) to be effective, it needs to have high-level, quality data to be analyzed. For some workloads, the ingestion of raw data is desirable. However, over time, SOC Analysts became too busy rationalizing the raw data to identify indications of compromise. When using Azure Defender, you will take advantage of a high-level, quality alert that already provides the needed information about an attack and how to respond to it. This section of the chapter covers the skills necessary to manage Azure Defender alert rules according to the Exam SC-200 outline.

Validate alert configuration

Azure Defender uses advanced security analytics and machine-learning technologies to evaluate events across the entire cloud fabric. The security analytics include data from multiple sources, including Microsoft products and services, the Microsoft Digital Crimes Unit (DCU), the Microsoft Security Response Center (MSRC), and external feeds. This is the core of Azure Defender threat detection, and on top of that, there will be different mechanisms of detection according to the workload.

With the continuous change in the threat landscape for different workloads, using a generic threat detection that will cover "some scenarios" is not sufficient. For this reason, Azure Defender has threat detections that are specific for each supported Azure service. You can enable Azure Defender according to the scenarios for which you want to have threat detection. At the time this book was written, the following options were available:

- Azure Defender for Servers
- Azure Defender for App Service
- Azure Defender for SQL Database
- Azure Defender for SQL on machines
- Azure Defender for Storage
- Azure Defender for Azure Kubernetes (AKS)
- Azure Defender for Azure Container Registries (ACR)
- Azure Defender for Key Vault
- Azure Defender for Resource Manager
- Azure Defender for DNS

Each one of those options can be enabled separately, and you have 30 days free to try those detections. There is not much configuration for alerts, and you don't need to create custom rules or enable specific options. You only need to enable the Azure Defender plan, and at that point, you might receive an alert if suspicious activity is detected.

The number of security alerts you see in the Security Alerts Dashboard can vary depending on the number of resources that you are monitoring with Azure Defender and the business itself. Some organizations receive more attacks than others, which means they have more security alerts. You can validate the alert using the **Create Sample Alerts** feature. Follow the procedures below to do that:

1. Open **Azure portal** and sign in with a user who has **Security Admin** privileges.
2. In the left navigation menu, click **Security Center**.
3. In the Security Center's left navigation menu, under **General**, click the **Security Alerts** option.

4. In the top-right corner, click **Create Sample Alerts** option. The **Create Sample Alerts (Preview)** blade appears, as shown in Figure 2-23.

Create sample alerts (Preview)   ✕

Try Azure Defender alerts by creating sample alerts from our different Azure Defender plans. Learn more >>

Subscriptions

Free Trial   ⌄

Azure Defender plans

6 selected   ⌄

Create sample alerts

FIGURE 2-23   Create Sample Alerts

5. In the **Subscriptions** drop-down menu, select the subscription for which you want to generate the sample alert.

6. Click the **Azure Defender plans** drop-down menu, click **Select All** to uncheck all plans, and select only **Virtual Machines**.

7. Click the **Create Sample Alerts** button to generate the sample alerts.

After a few minutes, you will see six sample alerts appear in the Security Alert Dashboard, as shown in Figure 2-24.

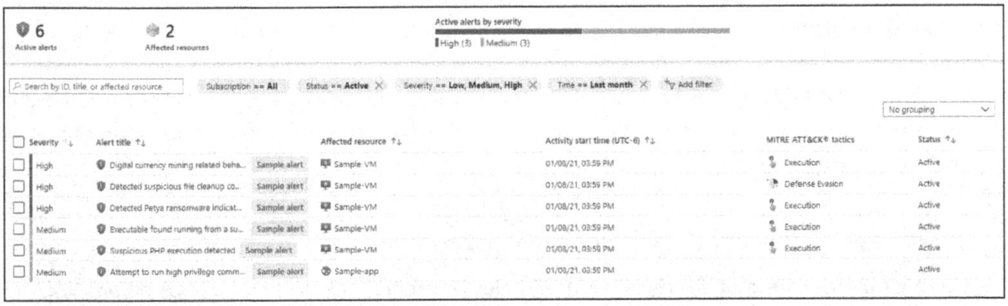

FIGURE 2-24   Security Alert Dashboard with the sample alerts for VMs

By default, the Security Alert Dashboard presents the alerts indexed by severity, but you can use the filtering options to change the severities that you want to see. You can also filter by:

- **Subscription**   If you have multiple subscriptions selected, you can customize which subscriptions you want to see alerts from.

- **Status**   By default, only **Active** is selected. Also, you can change it to see alerts that were dismissed.

- **Time** Allows you to configure the timeline of the alerts that you can see (up to the three last months).
- **Add Filter** Allows you to add more filters that are not visible by default.

In addition to the filters, you can also use the search box to search for alert ID, alert title, or affected resource. Once you find the alert that you want, you can click it, and the alert details page appears, as shown in Figure 2-25.

FIGURE 2-25 Alert details page

This initial page allows you to review the alert's details and change the status from **Active** to **Dismissed**. You also have a graphical representation of where the alerts fit into the Mitre ATT&CK Tactics framework.

> ***MORE INFO*** **MITRE ATT&CK TACTICS FRAMEWORK**
>
> You can obtain more information about this framework at *https://attack.mitre.org/versions/v7/.*

After reviewing the alert's details, you can obtain more granular information accessing the alert's full page. To do that, click the **View Full Details** button, which will make the full alert page appear, as shown in Figure 2-26.

FIGURE 2-26 Alert details page

The right part of the full alert page shows more details that are relevant for the alert. In the bottom part of the page is the **Related Entities section**, which enumerates the relevant entities (Related Entities, including Account, File, Host, Host Logon Session, and Process) that were used during this attack. Keep in mind that the related entities will vary according to the alert type and whether those entities were used. Although the example shown in Figure 2-26 is from a sample alert, the fields shown in this alert type are the same ones that you would see in a real live alert.

Another important option on this page is the **Take Action** tab, which contains relevant information to mitigate the threat highlighted in this alert, the recommendations that could be remediated to prevent future attacks, the option to trigger a Logic App automation, and the option to create a suppression rule. Figure 2-27 shows an example of the content of this tab.

FIGURE 2-27 Take Action tab with the available options for an alert

Set up email notifications

When high-fidelity alerts are triggered, you might want to notify the right people about those alerts to ensure you give the right level of visibility and awareness. By configuring the email notifications option in Azure Security Center, you will be able to establish who should be notified and what they should be notified about by selecting the alert's severity. This option is natively available in Azure Security Center, which means you don't have to upgrade to Azure Defender to use this feature.

It is important to emphasize that Security Center limits the volume of outgoing mails. This is an important step to avoid email fatigue to the recipients. This limitation is applied for each subscription based on the alert's severity as shown below:

- **High-severity alert**   Maximum of one email per 6 hours (4 emails per day)
- **Medium-severity alert**   Maximum of one email per 12 hours (2 emails per day)
- **Low-severity alert**   Maximum of 1 email per 24 hours

You can configure the alert severity about which you want to be notified. Follow the steps below to configure the email notifications in Azure Security Center:

1. Open **Azure portal** and sign in with a user who has **Security Admin** privileges.
2. In the left navigation menu, click **Security Center**.
3. In the Security Center's left navigation menu, under **Management**, click the **Pricing & Settings** option.
4. Click the subscription for which you want to change this setting.

5. On the **Azure Defender Plans** page, under **Settings** on the left, click **Email Notifica-tions**. The **Email Notifications** page appears, as shown in Figure 2-28.

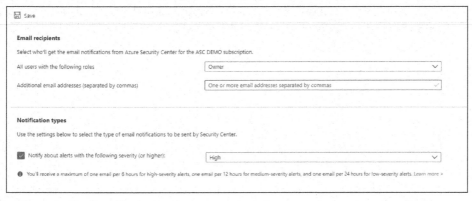

FIGURE 2-28 Email notifications options

6. In the **Email Recipients** section, click the **All Users With The Following Roles** drop-down menu and select the user role that you want to notify via email. The available options are **Owner**, **AccountAdmin**, **ServiceAdmin**, and **Contributor**. You can select more than one role.

7. In the **Additional Email Addresses** field, you can add other email addresses that you also want to notify.

8. In the **Notification Types** section, you have the option to select the alert severity in the **Notify About Alerts With The Following Severity (Or Higher)** drop-down menu.

9. Once you finish the configuration, click the **Save** button to commit the changes.

Create and manage alert suppression rules

There are some scenarios in which you might want to dismiss an alert because you consider a false positive for your environment. A typical scenario is when organizations are going through a *pentest* (penetration test) exercise conducted by their red team, there are some alerts that start getting triggered, and they want to suppress it to avoid noise and alert pollution. For those scenarios, you can leverage the alert suppression feature. To create or delete an alert suppression rule, you need to have **Security Admin** or an **Owner** privileges. To view alert suppression rules, you need to have **Security Reader** or **Reader** privileges.

Before configuring the alert suppression, you should identify the exact alert that you want to suppress and for how long the suppression rule should be active. Is important to establish an expiration date for the rule because you don't want to be blind to this alert forever. Usually, those suppression scenarios are happening for a reason, and for the most part, these reasons are happening because of a temporary circumstance. Follow the steps below to configure an alert suppression rule:

1. Open **Azure portal** and sign in with a user who has **Security Admin** privileges.

2. In the left navigation menu, click **Security Center**.

3. In the Security Center's left navigation, under **General**, click the **Security Alerts** option.

4. In the Security Alerts Dashboard, click the **Suppression Rules** option, and the **Suppression Rules** page appears, as shown in Figure 2-29.

FIGURE 2-29 Suppression Rules page

5. Click the **Create New Suppression Rule** option, and the **New Suppression Rule** blade appears, as shown in Figure 2-30.

FIGURE 2-30 New Suppression Rule

6. In the **Rule Conditions** section, click the **Subscription** drop-down menu and select the subscription to which you want to apply this rule.

7. Under **Alerts**, select **Custom**, and in the drop-down menu, select the alert that you want to suppress. For this example, select the **Suspicious PHP Execution Detected** *sample alert*.

8. Under the **Entities** option, you can make the suppression more granular by choosing specific fields from the alert that should match with the rule to be suppressed. You can click the plus sign button (**+**) to add multiple entities. Just keep in mind that when you do that, the suppression rule will only apply if *both* conditions are true. In other words, there is an AND between each entity field. For this example, leave this selection as is.

9. In the **Rule Details** section, under **Rule Name**, type a name for this rule. (The rule name cannot have any spaces.) For this example, type **PHPSuppression**.

10. Under **State**, leave the default option, which is **Enabled**.

11. Under **Reason**, you can select the most appropriate option in the drop-down menu. For this example, select **Other**, and under **Comment**, type **suppression for red team exercise**.

12. Under **Rule Expiration**, configure the rule for two months from the day that you are configuring.

13. To validate the rule, click the **Simulate** button, and you will see the result right under the **Test Your Rule** option.

14. Click the **Apply** button to commit the change and create the rule; the rule appears in the **Suppression Rules** page, as shown in Figure 2-31.

Rule Name	Subscription Name	Rule Last Modified	Expiration Date	Rule State
PHPSuppression	Visual Studio Ultimate with MSDN	01/09/21, 11:19 AM	07/08/21, 11:39 AM	Enabled

FIGURE 2-31 Suppression rule created

The next time this alert is triggered, it will be automatically suppressed. It is important to mention that suppressed alerts are still available for you to see. You just need to change the filter in the Security Alerts Dashboard to see alerts that were *dismissed*. If you are using the **Continuous Export** feature to export all alerts to the Log Analytics workspace, the suppressed alerts will also be available in the workspace. You just need to run a query to list all dismissed alerts.

Skill 2-4: Configure automation and remediation

Automation is a very important component for any SOC to operate at an optimal level. Automating response for alerts can save time and reduce the likelihood that a threat actor will continue infiltrating the environment and perform more malicious actions. This section covers the skills necessary to configure automation and remediation based on the Exam SC-200 outline.

Configure automated response in Azure Security Center

Azure Security Center utilizes the workflow automation feature to expedite an automated response for recommendations and alerts. Response for recommendations is more applicable to the cloud security posture management scenario. Response for alerts is more applicable to a cloud workload protection platform scenario, which is the scenario that SOC Analysts will be primarily working on.

Workflow automation leverages Azure Logic Apps as the automation engine, and within the Logic App, you have almost unlimited possibilities to automate processes. To create a workflow automation, you need **Security Admin** role privileges or have **Owner** privileges on the resource group. In addition to that, you also you also must have **write** permissions on the target resource. Prior to creating the workflow automation, you need to create a Logic App that will be used by the automation. To work with Azure Logic Apps workflows, you must also have **Logic App Contributor** permissions to create or modify an existing Logic App.

To enable automation, the workflow automation feature brings additional trigger types to Logic Apps, which are:

- The **When An Azure Security Center Recommendation Is Created Or Triggered** trigger will start a Logic App Playbook in the following conditions:
    - A resource has been added to a recommendation as a result of an ASC assessment.
    - A resource status has changed within a recommendation as a result of an ASC assessment, where the resource status can be healthy, unhealthy, or not applicable.
    - A Logic App is manually triggered from a recommendation within ASC.
- The **When An Azure Security Center Alert Is Created Or Triggered** trigger will start a Logic App Playbook in the following conditions:
    - An alert is created in Azure Defender.
    - From an alert, the Logic App is manually triggered.

The first trigger type will help you to create several types of automation artifacts. For example, you could let the Logic App create a ServiceNow ticket if a new alert is created and notify the incident response team about this new alert. You could also auto-remediate or quarantine resources if they are part of an alert. Every time Azure Security Center triggers the Logic App, it will send a lot of information that you can use for further steps, including

- Name of the assessment as a GUID
- Assessment ID
- The recommendation's display name
- Metadata information for the recommendation, including a description, remediation steps, and severity
- Resource details, including the resource ID
- Status code (healthy, unhealthy, or not applicable)
- A deep link to the assessment result in the recommendations blade

This information can then be used within the Logic App, either for storing it or for notifying someone, but it also can be used to retrieve further information from other APIs, such as the different Azure Security Center REST API providers.

If you want to auto-remediate a resource, the information about the resource and the assessment/recommendation helps you determine the next steps. To create a workflow automation, follow these steps below:

1. Open the **Azure portal** and sign in with a user who has **Security Admin** privileges.

2. In the left navigation pane, click **Security Center**.

3. In the left navigation pane, in the **Management** section, select **Workflow Automation**, and then click + **Add Workflow Automation**. The **Add Workflow Automation** blade appears, as shown in Figure 2-32.

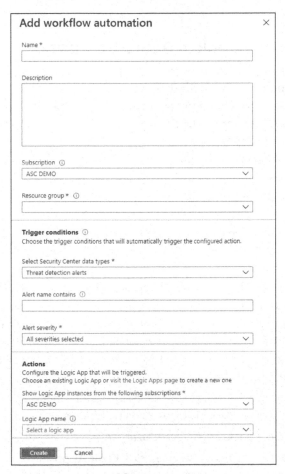

FIGURE 2-32 Add Workflow Automation

4. Enter a **Name**, and select the **Subscription** and **Resource Group** in which you want to store the workflow configuration.

5. From the **Select Security Center Data Types** drop-down menu, you can choose **Threat Detection Alerts** or **Security Center Recommendation**. This will determine the trigger type upon which the workflow will react. Notice that the blade will change depending on your selection. For this example, select **Threat Detection Alerts**.

6. Under the **Alert Name Condition**, type the name of the alert, which is based on the Azure Defender plan that will trigger the alert.

7. From the **Alert Severity** drop-down menu, select the severity of the alert that you want to automate the response.

8. Under **Actions**, select the subscription from which you are going to retrieve the Logic Apps, In the **Logic App Name** drop-down menu, select the Logic App that will have the automation that you previously created.

9. Click the **Create** button.

Design and configure a playbook in Azure Defender

Playbooks are collections of procedures that can be run from Azure Defender in response to an alert. Although the term *playbook* doesn't appear in the dashboard, it is a term that is commonly used by security professionals when referring to a collection of instructions that can help automate and orchestrate a response to an incident. Playbooks in Azure Defender are based on workflows built into Azure Logic Apps.

When planning the implementation of playbooks for Azure Defender, you need to design your solution based on the business and technical requirements. For example, if the technical requirement is to automatically run a playbook if a particular alert is triggered, you will need to use the workflow automation feature. Suppose the requirement is to allow security operations analysts to manually execute a playbook when they are reviewing the alerts. In that case, you don't need to use the workflow automation, but you need to create the playbook in Logic Apps and make it available to be used on-demand.

Before starting the Logic App creation, you need to determine what you want to accomplish. That's why it is so important to first establish the workflow of actions and then validate the actions with the team. Only after that can you start the implementation. For this example, the goal is to send an email to the incident response team with the details about an alert and the remediation steps. The security analyst who is going to triage the events will trigger this Logic App once they identify an alert that needs escalation.

The steps to configure the workflow automation are the same as explained in the previous section. Follow the steps below to configure a new playbook using Logic Apps:

1. Navigate to the Azure portal by opening *https://portal.azure.com*.

2. In the search bar, type **logic apps**, and under **Services**, click **Logic Apps**.

3. On the Logic Apps page, click the **+ Add** button; the **Create A Logic App** page appears, as shown in Figure 2-33.

FIGURE 2-33   Options to create a new Logic App automation

4. In the **Project Details** section, select the subscription that will host the Logic App and the resource group.

5. In the **Instance Details** section, type a name for the Logic App and select the region. Optionally, you could also associate this Logic App with an existing integration service and push the Logic App runtime events to a Log Analytics workspace. For this example, leave the default selection and click the **Review + Create** button.

6. Click the **Create** button to finish the configuration.

7. The **Microsoft.Empty Workflow** page appears. Click the **Go To Resource** button, and the Logic Apps Designer page appears, as shown in Figure 2-34.

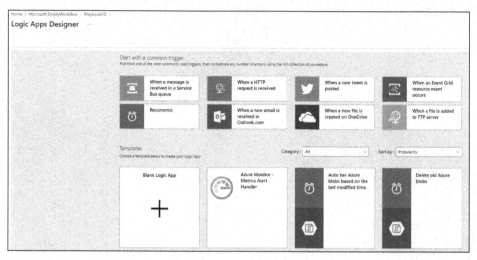

FIGURE 2-34 Logic Apps Designer main page

8. On this page, you can either select one of the templates available or create a new one from scratch. For this example, click the **Blank Logic App** tile, and the **Logic Apps Designer** page appears, as shown in Figure 2-35.

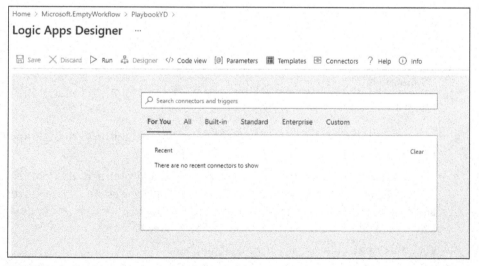

FIGURE 2-35 Starting a new Logic App from scratch

9. In the **Search Connectors And Triggers** field, type **Security Center**. You will see the connectors available under **All** and the options to activate the connector under **Triggers**, as shown in Figure 2-36.

FIGURE 2-36   Selecting the trigger for the workflow

10. Because the intent here is to create a playbook of actions that will be used for an alert, select the **When An Azure Security Center Alert Is Created Or Triggered** option under **Triggers**. The **+ New Step** page shown in Figure 2-37 appears.

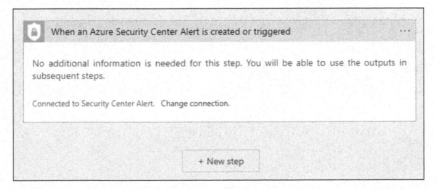

FIGURE 2-37   Selecting a new step for the workflow

11. Click the **+ New Step** button, and on the **Choose An Operation** page, click the **All** tab, as shown in Figure 2-38.

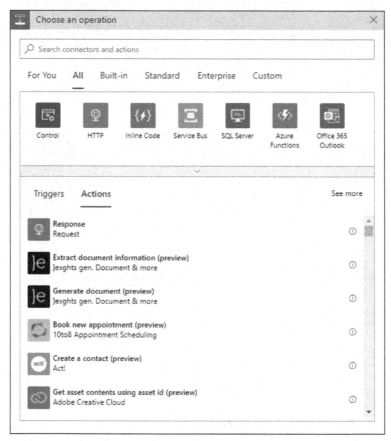

FIGURE 2-38 Selecting a built-in connector

12. Under **All**, click the **Office 365 Outlook** icon; under **Actions**, click the **Send An Email (V2)** option. The **Send An Email (V2)** dialog box will appear, as shown in Figure 2-39.

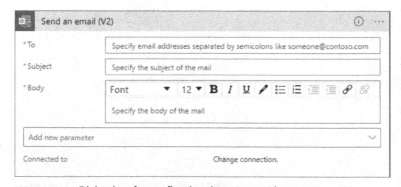

FIGURE 2-39 Dialog box for configuring the automated message

13. In the **To** field, type the email for the incident response team.

14. In the **Subject** field, type the subject for this automated email.

15. In the **Body** field, click in the **Specify The Body Of The Mail** area, and the dynamic content floating menu appears. This menu allows you to add fields from the Azure Defender alert to the email message. Figure 2-40 shows an example of how the fields can be inserted in the body of the email.

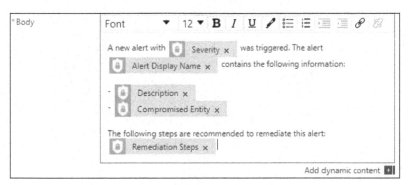

FIGURE 2-40   Dynamic content inserted in the body of the email

16. Click the **Save** button.

Now that the Logic App is created, you can choose to link this Logic App to a workflow automation or for the automation to trigger manually from the alert itself. To trigger from the alert, open the **Security Alerts Dashboard**, select the alert you want to triage, and click the **Take Action** button. From there, you can click the **Trigger Logic App** button in the **Trigger Automated Response** section, as shown in Figure 2-41.

FIGURE 2-41   Manually triggering an existing Logic App

Remediate incidents by using Azure Defender recommendations

Although alerts are based on actions that have already taken place, you can always learn from them and ensure that you implement the necessary steps to remediate and prevent them from happening again.

When an alert is triggered, you will have a substantial amount of information to rationalize to better understand what happened in that situation. By reviewing the alert, you will be able to answer five main questions that are important for your investigation. The questions are shown in the alert blade, as shown in Figure 2-42.

FIGURE 2-42 Answers to the major investigation's questions

It is important to emphasize that not all alerts will have the same level of information; it really depends on the type of threat and the analytics for that threat. As you can see in Figure 2-42, there is a tab called **Take Action**, which has important information that will help you to know what needs to be done. The information in this tab will also vary according to the alert and the current conditions of the environment because Azure Defender will look at relevant security recommendations that were not remediated and could have contributed for this scenario to occur. See Figure 2-43.

On this page, you can follow the steps under **Mitigate The Threat** to take reactive actions to remediate this alert. Keep in mind that these are initial suggestions to mitigate, but depending on the environment and the stage of the attack, other actions might need to be performed in addition to those steps.

An Azure Defender alert also creates this important correlation between the attacked resource and the security recommendations that are open for that resource. This helps create a link between the incident response team (reactive work) and the cloud security posture management team (proactive work).

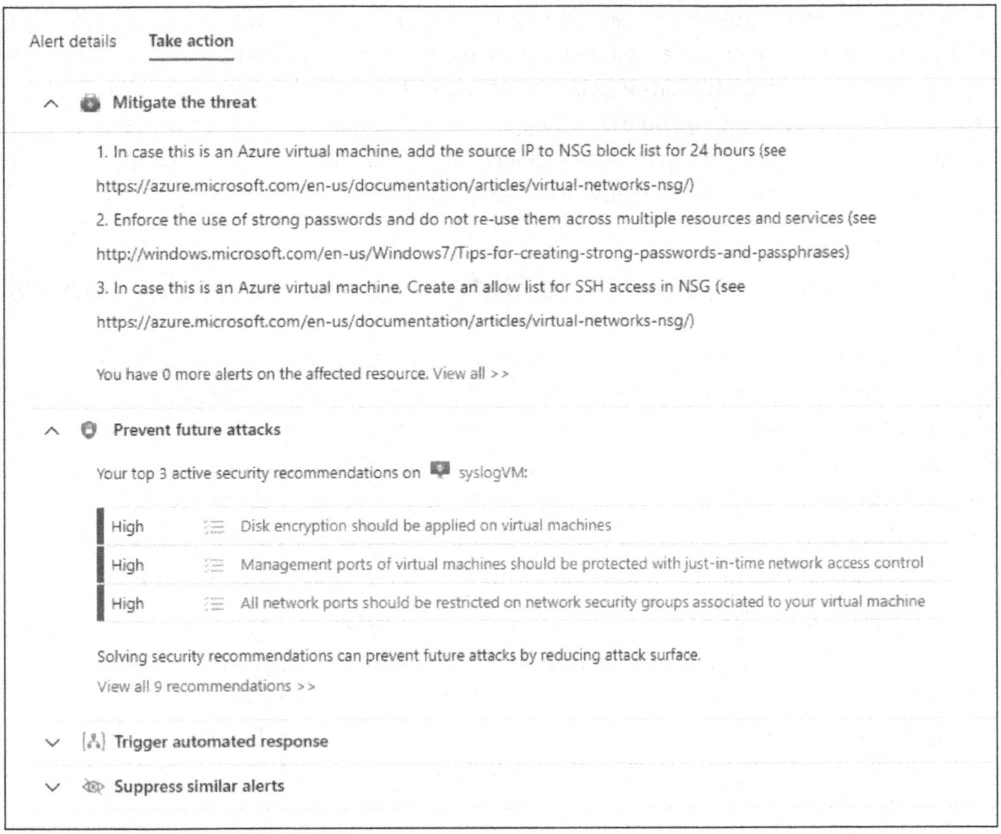

FIGURE 2-43 Take Action tab with the mitigation and prevention steps

Create an automatic response using an Azure Resource Manager template

The workflow automation feature that was covered earlier in this chapter can also be automated to be deployed in scale using this Azure policy: `Deploy Workflow Automation for Azure Security Center alerts` (policy ID: f1525828-9a90-4fcf-be48-268cdd02361e). One advantage of using this Azure policy to deploy workflow automation is that you can assign this policy to the management group level, which means all your subscriptions under the management group will inherit this automation.

Also, you can also use an Azure Resource Manager template (ARM template) to create a workflow automation that triggers a Logic App when specific security alerts are received by Azure Defender.

> **MORE INFO   ARM TEMPLATE SAMPLE**
>
> You can view an ARM template sample for this deployment at *http://aka.ms/SC200_WFARM*.

The technical requirements for a scenario dictate whether you are going to use an ARM Template to deploy a workflow automation. If you need to deploy in scale and at the beginning of the pipeline for all subscriptions in your tenant, the ARM template is a good choice because it can be fully deployed with a single click. Keep in mind that the template assumes that you already have your Logic App created and that it is functional. That's why it is imperative that you correctly design your response prior to creating any type of automation.

Skill 2-5: Investigate Azure Defender alerts and incidents

For security analysts, it is imperative to have access to the right information in order to optimize the time of response. For this reason, is important to have analytics that were created according to the workload that you are monitoring. Azure Defender provides high-quality alerts that can be utilized during different types of investigations. This section of the chapter covers the skills necessary to investigate Azure Defender alerts and incidents according to the Exam SC-200 outline.

Describe alert types for Azure workloads

The types of alerts that Azure Defender triggers will depend on the Azure Defender plans that are enabled on your subscription. The analytics will be specific for the threat vector of each workload, and you can use the information available on the alert to further investigate this issue. The sections that follow will cover the available alert types in Azure Defender according to the plan.

Azure Defender for Servers (Windows)

Azure Defender for Servers detection in Windows looks at Windows Security events, and once it finds something suspicious, it triggers an alert. For example, if you execute the following command in a VM that is monitored by Azure Defender for Server, it will be considered a suspicious activity:

```
powershell -nop -exec bypass -EncodedCommand "cABvAHcAZQByAHMAaAB1AGwAbAAgAC0AYwBv
AG0AbQBhAG4AZAAgACIAJgAgAHsAIABpAHcAcgAgAGgAdAB0AHAAcwA6AC8ALwBkAG8AdwBuAGwAbwBhAGQAL
gBzAHkAcwBpAG4AdAB1AHIAbgBhAGwAcwAuAGMAbwBtAC8AZgBpAGwAZQBzAC8AUwB5AHMAbQBvBvAG4ALgB6AGk
AcAAgAC0ATwB1AHQARgBpAGwAZQAgAGMAOgBcAHQAZQBtAHAAAXABzAHYAYwBoAG8Acw
B0AC4AZQB4AGUAIAB9ACIA"
```

PowerShell is a very powerful tool, and as you can see at the MITRE ATT&CK site (*https://attack.mitre.org/techniques/T1086/*), PowerShell has been used in many attack campaigns. When Azure Defender for Servers detects the PowerShell execution with the encoding command, it raises an alert for what the user is trying to hide. In this case, the command below downloads the `sysmon.zip` file from the `SysInternals` website and saves it in the `C:\temp` folder with the `svhost.exe` name:

```
powershell -command "& { iwr https://download.sysinternals.com/files/Sysmon.zip -OutFile
c:\temp\svchost.exe }"
```

PowerShell encoding to download malware from command and control is a common malicious pattern, so Azure Defender for Server will raise an alert.

MORE INFO   **DEFENDER FOR SERVERS (WINDOWS) ALERTS**

You can see the list of all alerts that can be generated by Azure Defender for Servers (Windows) at *http://aka.ms/sc200_azdefwindows*.

Azure Defender for Servers (Linux)

When Linux detection was first released, AuditD had to be installed in the Linux operating system. While AuditD provides a great amount of info that can be used to detect threats, not all Linux distros will have AuditD installed by default. For this reason, the latest change in behavior for Linux detections was to bake into the LA agent the necessary elements that will collect relevant data.

MORE INFO   **DEFENDER FOR SERVERS (LINUX) ALERTS**

You can see the list of all alerts that can be generated by Azure Defender for Servers (Linux) at *http://aka.ms/sc200_azdeflinux*.

Azure Defender for Kubernetes

Azure Defender for Kubernetes provides two layers of protection to enhance the level of detection. The first layer is in the host level (operating system), which is covered by the threat detections for Linux and is available as part of the Azure Defender for Server. Keep in mind that to have this layer of detection, you need to install the Log Analytics Agent for Linux on the Kubernetes nodes.

The second layer is the AKS cluster-level threat detection, which is covered by Azure Defender for Kubernetes (agentless solution). This threat detection is based on continuous analysis of Kubernetes' audit logs. Figure 2-44 shows an example of an alert that can be generated based on the Kubernetes log analysis done by Azure Defender for Kubernetes.

MORE INFO   **DEFENDER FOR AKS ALERTS**

You can see the list of all alerts that can be generated by Azure Defender for AKS at *https://aka.ms/azdforaks*.

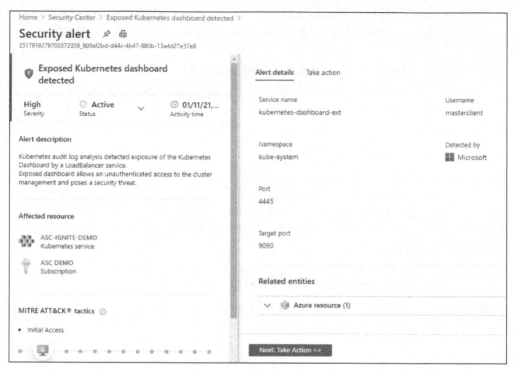

FIGURE 2-44 Alert generated by Azure Defender for Kubernetes

Azure Defender for App Service

Azure App Service is a service for hosting web applications, REST APIs, and mobile back ends. It enables you to develop in many languages, such as .NET, .NET Core, Java, Ruby, Node.js, PHP, or Python. Applications run and scale on both Windows and Linux.

Azure Defender leverages the scale of the cloud to identify attacks on App Service applications while focusing on emerging attacks while attackers are in the reconnaissance phase. While in the reconnaissance phase, attackers are scanning multiple Azure websites to identify vulnerabilities. Figure 2-45 shows an example of an alert generated by Azure Defender for App Service.

> **MORE INFO** **DEFENDER FOR APP SERVICE ALERTS**
>
> You can see the list of all alerts that can be generated by Azure Defender for App Service at *https://aka.ms/sc200_azdefappservice*.

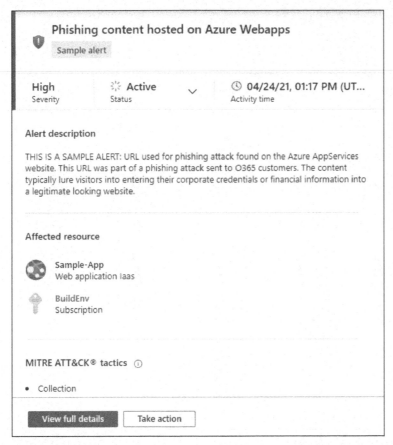

Phishing content hosted on Azure Webapps

Sample alert

High	⚙ Active ⌄	◷ 04/24/21, 01:17 PM (UT...
Severity	Status	Activity time

Alert description

THIS IS A SAMPLE ALERT: URL used for phishing attack found on the Azure AppServices website. This URL was part of a phishing attack sent to O365 customers. The content typically lure visitors into entering their corporate credentials or financial information into a legitimate looking website.

Affected resource

Sample-App
Web application Iaas

BuildEnv
Subscription

MITRE ATT&CK® tactics ⓘ

• Collection

[View full details] [Take action]

FIGURE 2-45 Alert generated by Azure Defender for App Service

Azure Defender for Storage

Azure Defender for Storage can be enabled for data stored in Azure Blob, Azure Files, and Azure Data Lakes Storage (ADLS) Gen2. You can enable Azure Defender for Storage on the subscription level, just like any other plan, and you can also enable it only on the storage accounts that you want to protect.

Alerts generated by Azure Defender for Storage can occur when there are suspicious access patterns, such as an access from a Tor exit node. Another scenario that an alert can be triggered is when there are suspicious activities in the storage account, such as an unusual change of access permission. Figure 2-46 has a sample alert for Azure Defender for Storage:

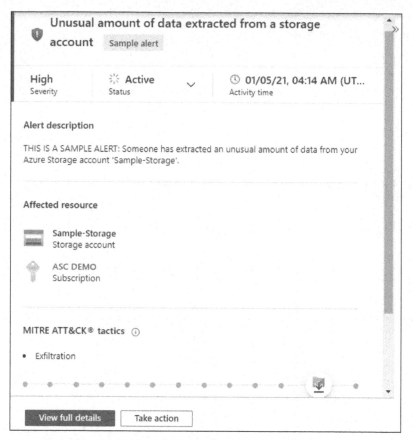

FIGURE 2-46 Sample alert for Azure Defender for Storage

In 2020, the hash reputation analysis for Storage, which is a major addition to Azure Defender for Storage was released. To add an extra layer of security, Azure Defender for Storage analyzes files that are uploaded using hash reputation, which leverages Microsoft Threat Intelligence. It is very important to emphasize that this is not an antimalware scan for storage. Instead, this feature inspects the storage logs and compares the hashes of newly uploaded files with information about known viruses, trojans, spyware, and ransomware.

> **MORE INFO   DEFENDER FOR STORAGE ALERTS**
>
> You can see the list of all alerts that can be generated by Azure Defender for Storage at *https://aka.ms/sc200_azdefstorage*.

Azure Defender for SQL

Azure Defender for SQL is a protection plan that helps you to mitigate potential database vulnerabilities and detect anomalous activities that may indicate threats against your databases. Azure Defender for SQL has evolved over the years and currently has two major plans:

- **Azure Defender for Azure SQL database servers** Includes Azure SQL Database, Azure SQL Managed Instance, and Dedicated SQL pool in Azure Synapse

- **Azure Defender for SQL servers on machines** Includes SQL Server running on VMs in Azure, on-premises, or in another cloud provider

Azure Defender for SQL provides threat detects for anomalous activities indicating unusual and potentially harmful attempts to access or exploit databases. Figure 2-47 has an example of an alert triggered by this plan.

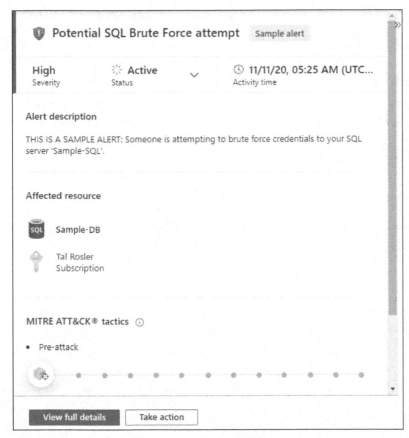

FIGURE 2-47 Sample alert for Azure Defender for SQL

The Azure Defender for Azure SQL database servers can be easily enabled on the subscription level or in an Azure SQL database that you want; no agent is required. However, to use the Azure Defender for SQL servers on machines, you need to enable the plan on the subscription level, and you must onboard the server, which means provisioning the Log Analytics agent on SQL Server. If your VMs are in Azure, you just need to use the auto-provisioning option in Azure Security Center to automatically onboard the Log Analytics Agent to your Azure VMs.

Another recent scenario is the integration with Azure Arc, which allows a deeper integration across different scenarios. It is recommended that you use Azure Arc for your SQL Servers on-premises or in different cloud providers (AWS and GCP), and once they are fully onboarded, you can deploy the Log Analytics Agent.

> **MORE INFO   DEFENDER FOR SQL ALERTS**
>
> You can see the list of all alerts that can be generated by Azure Defender for SQL at *https://aka.ms/sc200_azdsql*.

Azure Defender for Key Vault

Azure Defender for Key Vault uses machine learning to detects unusual and potentially harmful attempts to access or exploit Key Vault accounts. Unlike Azure Defender for Storage, the only option to enable Azure Defender for Key Vault is to enable it on the entire subscription. Figure 2-48 shows an Azure Defender for Key Vault sample alert.

FIGURE 2-48   Azure Defender for Key Vault sample alert

MORE INFO   **DEFENDER FOR KEY VAULT ALERTS**

You can see the list of all alerts that can be generated by Azure Defender for Key Vault at *http://aka.ms/AzDefKeyVaultAlerts*.

Azure Defender for Resource Manager

The Azure Resource Manager (ARM) is the deployment and management service for Azure. ARM provides a management layer that allows you to create, update, and delete resources in your Azure account. These operations can be done via Azure portal, PowerShell, Azure CLI, REST APIs, and client SDKs.

Threat actors who are targeting ARM will most likely use toolkits such as Microbust to discover weak configurations and to perform post-exploitation actions, such as credential dumping. Azure Defender for Resource Manager uses advanced security analytics to detect threats and trigger an alert when a suspicious activity happens.

Besides the detection of the Microbust toolkit, Azure Defender for Resource Manager can also detect suspicious resource management operations, which include suspicious IP addresses, the action of disabling the antimalware, and the execution of suspicious scripts in virtual machine extensions. It can also detect lateral movement from the Azure management layer to the Azure resources data plane. Figure 2-49 shows an example of this alert: **Antimalware File Exclusion In Your Virtual Machine**.

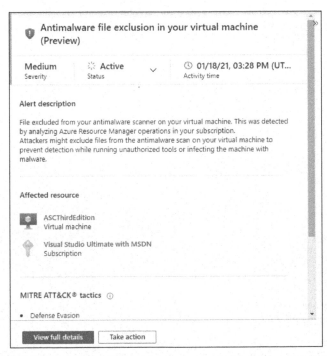

FIGURE 2-49   Antimalware file exclusion performed at the resource manager layer

Azure Defender for DNS

Azure Defender for DNS can identify DNS phishing attacks by analyzing DNS transactions and identifying requests for a possible phishing domain. Such activity is frequently performed by threat actors to harvest credentials and move them to remote services. This activity is usually followed by exploitation of any credentials on the legitimate service. Also, Azure Defender for DNS can identify the following:

- DNS tunneling, which can be used to exfiltrate data from your Azure resources
- Malware communicating with a command-and-control server
- Communication with malicious domains for phishing or cryptomining
- Communication with malicious DNS resolvers

Figure 2-50 shows an example of a suspicious activity detected by Azure Defender for DNS, based on an analysis of DNS transactions.

FIGURE 2-50 Suspicious DNS activity triggered the Azure Defender for DNS alert

MORE INFO **DEFENDER FOR DNS ALERTS**

You can see the list of all alerts that can be generated by Azure Defender for Resource Manager at *http://aka.ms/ASCBookAzDefDNSAlerts*.

Manage security alerts

Security operations analysts who are going to triage the alerts and take actions to remediate need to be familiar with Azure Defender Security Alerts Dashboard. Using the Security Alerts Dashboard, security operation analysts can create filters to narrow down the information that is most interesting to them at that moment.

To access the Security Alerts Dashboard and view the alerts, you just need **Security Reader** privilege. If you need to dismiss an alert, you will need **Security Admin** privileges. Follow the steps below to access the Security Alerts Dashboard:

1. Open **Azure portal** and sign in with a user who has **Security Admin** privileges.

2. In the left navigation menu, click **Security Center**.

3. In the **Security Center's left** navigation menu, under **General**, click the **Security Alerts** option. The Security Alerts Dashboard appears, as shown in Figure 2-51.

FIGURE 2-51 Security Alerts Dashboard

4. If you have multiple subscriptions selected in your portal, you can change the **Subscription** filter to visualize only the necessary alerts.

5. You can also filter by the following fields:

    ■ **Status**   You can visualize all active alerts or alerts that were dismissed.

    ■ **Severity**   To focus only on the severity that you need to investigate, you can also filter by the alert's severity.

    ■ **Time**   If you need to investigate an alert that occurred in a specific time frame, you can filter by time, which is based on days or months.

- **Alert Name** If you want to investigate a particular alert that took place across multiple resources, you can also filter by the alert name.

- **Affected Resource** Sometimes, you need to investigate the resource that was attacked to see if there are multiple alerts associated with that resource. This filter can be used for that.

- **Resource Type** Because there are many resource types in Azure, you might have scenarios where you need to investigate all alerts that occurred for a particular resource type. For example, you can use this filter if you want to see all alerts for resource type equals to Storage.

- **MITRE ATT&CK Tactics** You can use this filter if you need to identify all alerts that were triggered and identified as part of a particular phase of the MITRE ATT&CK framework. For example, you need to know all attacks that occurred during the execution phase of the MITRE framework.

- **Tags** You can use this filter if you need to identify all alerts that were triggered to resources that have a specific tag.

- **Owner** You can use this filter if you need to identify alerts that were triggered on resources that belong to a specific owner.

6. Once you finish configuring the filter, you will see only the information you need. At this point, you just need to open the alert by clicking it. The alert preview page appears, as shown in Figure 2-52.

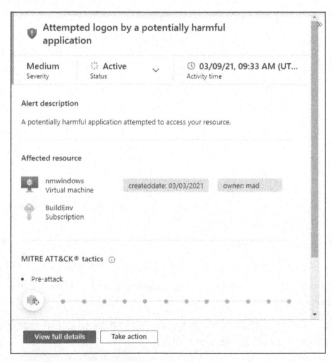

FIGURE 2-52 Alert preview page

7. To visualize all the details about the alert, click the **View Full Details** button, and the full alert page appears, as shown in Figure 2-53.

FIGURE 2-53 Full Security Alert visualization

8. On this page, you can explore all the alert's details and the related entities. In the **Take Action** tab, you can see remediation options, and you can trigger playbooks created via Logic App, as shown previously in this chapter.

Once you obtain all information you need from this page, you can close it and go back to the Security Alerts Dashboard.

Manage security incidents

Azure Defender has a type of alert called a security incident, which is raised in the console whenever the system identifies multiple alerts that, when correlated with each other, indicate that those alerts belong to the same attack. A security incident uses the fusion capability to correlate the alerts that appear to be related to each other.

Figure 2-54 shows an example of what such an attack campaign might look like and what alerts might be raised at the various stages of a cyberkill chain. The figure shows a highly sim-plified version of the cyberkill chain outlined earlier to make it easier to understand how fusion alerts work.

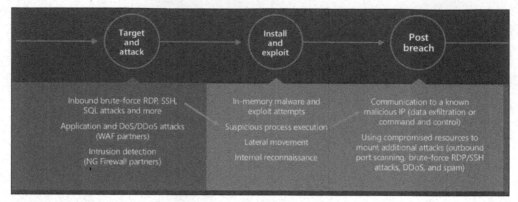

FIGURE 2-54 Azure Defender detections across the cyberkill chain

Following is the sequencing shown in Figure 2-54:

1. **Target and attack** In this phase, Azure Defender detects what appears to be a brute-force attack against the Remote Desktop Protocol (RDP) server on a VM. This determination is made by comparing a baseline of RDP connections to the VM and the current rate of RDP login attempts, along with other factors related to RDP logins.

2. **Install and exploit** Here, Azure Defender detects the execution of a suspicious process on the VM. This suspicious process could be predefined (known-bad malware), or it could be a process that wasn't executed on the machine during previous baselines and is therefore unrecognized. (For example, maybe the process is launched by software recently installed by the admin.) You'll have to correlate this event with other events to find out.

3. **Post breach** At this point, Azure Defender has detected what appears to be a communication channel established between the VM and a known-malicious IP address (probably flagged by a threat-intelligence feed). There's a very good chance that this is bad, but there is still a chance that it isn't. For example, maybe a security researcher or a red-team member working for the customer connected to the address on purpose. Yes, a connection to a known-bad IP address is serious, but it doesn't guarantee that the VM has been compromised.

Each phase of the cyberkill chain taken by itself indicates that something bad may be happening—but cannot offer you complete certainty. However, when you correlate these findings, you can be almost 100 percent sure that the VM has been compromised by a brute-force RDP attack, that the attacker has installed and run new malware on the machine, and that the malware is communicating with a command-and-control server (likely identified by a threat-intelligence feed).

In the Security Alert Dashboard, you can create a filter to visualize only Security Incidents that were detected, as shown in Figure 2-55.

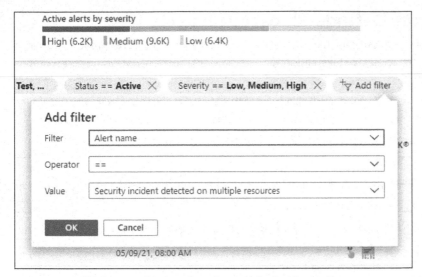

FIGURE 2-55 Filtering security alerts based on security incident only

After applying this filter, you will see only security incidents, which have a different icon (three connected dots), as shown in Figure 2-56.

FIGURE 2-56 Security incidents in Azure Defender

When you click a security incident and visualize the full details, you will see multiple alerts associated with the incident, as shown in Figure 2-57.

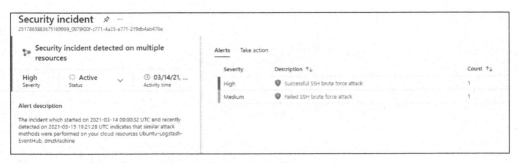

FIGURE 2-57 Multiple alerts associated with a security incident

Analyze Azure Defender threat intelligence

As you could see throughout this chapter, when Azure Defender identifies a threat, it triggers a security alert, which contains detailed information regarding the event, including suggestions for remediation.

For some alerts, Azure Defender will also provide threat intelligence reports to facilitate your investigation. These reports contain information about the detected threats, which includes:

- Attacker's identity or associations (if this information is available)
- Attacker's objectives
- Current and historical attack campaigns (if this information is available)
- Attacker's tactics, tools, and procedures
- Associated indicators of compromise (IoC) such as URLs and file hashes
- Victimology, which is the industry and geographic prevalence to assist you in determining if your Azure resources are at risk
- Mitigation and remediation information

Keep in mind that this information is not always available for all types of alerts. It's only available for the alerts that Azure Defender can correlate with Microsoft Threat Intelligence. The alert shown in Figure 2-58 shows an example of an alert that contains a threat intelligence report.

FIGURE 2-58   Alert with enrichment from a threat intelligence report

In the **Alert Details** tab, there is a link for the report, which in this case is called **Report: Shadow Copy Delete**. By clicking this hyperlink, you can download the PDF that contains the detailed information about this threat, as shown in Figure 2-59.

Microsoft
THREAT
INTELLIGENCE

Threat summary:
Shadow Copy Delete

MSTI-TS-Shadow-Copy-Delete

FIGURE 2-59   Threat intelligence report

Respond to Azure Defender Key Vault alerts

As you could see throughout this chapter, Azure Defender alerts are rich in details and information that can assist you when responding to alert and helping you take corrective actions to remediate the issue. The SC-200 exam's outline explicitly calls out the process of responding to an alert generated by Azure Defender for Key Vault. Although it has some unique steps, the majority of the approach is applicable to most of the other alerts.

Azure Defender for Key Vault alerts are unique because every alert includes an Object Identifier (Object ID), the User Principal Name (UPN), or the IP Address of the suspicious resource. It is important to highlight that the availability of this information can also vary according to the type of access that occurred. If your Key Vault was accessed by an application, then you will not see the associated UPN. If the traffic originated from outside Azure, then you won't see an Object ID. With that in mind, we can summarize the response process for an Azure Key Vault alert in the following steps:

- Contact
- Mitigation
- Impact
- Take action

Contact

In this step. you need to verify where the traffic is coming from; in other words, did the traffic originate from within your Azure tenant? Verify if you have Key Vault Firewall enabled. If you do, it's likely that granted access to the user or application is what triggered the alert.

If you can identify the source of the traffic as coming from your own tenant, then contact the user or application owner. If you are unable to verify the source of the traffic, skip to the next step.

Mitigation

In this step, you have the assumption that the access shouldn't have been authorized because you couldn't determine the source of the traffic in the previous step. If the traffic came from an unrecognized IP Address, make sure to:

- Enable the Azure Key Vault firewall (if you haven't done so already).
- Configure the firewall to allow only trusted resources and virtual networks.

However, if the source of the alert was an unauthorized application or suspicious user, make sure to configure the Key Vault's access policy settings to remove the corresponding security principal or restrict the operations the security principal can perform.

If the source of the alert has an Azure Active Directory role in your tenant, you should start by contacting your administrator and then determine whether you need to reduce or revoke Azure Active Directory permissions.

Impact

Once the impact of the attack has been mitigated, you need to investigate the secrets in your Key Vault that were affected. In this step, you will need to do the following:

- Review the triggered alert.
- Review the list of the secrets that were accessed and the timestamp.
- If you have Key Vault diagnostic logs enabled, review the previous operations for the corresponding caller IP, user principal, or object ID.

Take action

At this point, you already compiled a list of the secrets, keys, and certificates that were accessed by the suspicious user or application. Your next immediate action is to rotate those objects.

Ensure that affected secrets are disabled or deleted from your Key Vault. If the credentials were used for a specific application, you will need to contact the administrator of the application and ask them to audit their environment for any uses of the compromised credentials because they were compromised. If the compromised credentials were used, the application owner should identify the information that was accessed to mitigate the impact.

Manage user data discovered during an investigation

When the General Data Protection Regulation (GDPR) was created, it was very important to Security Center to provide mechanisms to delete personal data from the service in order to allow organizations to support their obligations under GDPR. To comply with that, you need to understand which information can be accessed and which role is required to access this information.

The first important aspect of an investigation when you need to be compliant with GDPR is the capability to search and identify personal data. A user who utilizes Security Center can view their personal data through Azure portal. It is important to mention that Security Center only stores security contact details, such as email addresses and phone numbers.

Another configuration that can be used to visualize an IP address is the list of allowed IP configurations using the just-in-time (JIT) VM access feature in Azure Defender. To access the just-in-time policies, the user needs to be assigned to the **Reader**, **Owner**, **Contributor**, or **Account Administrator** roles. To update or delete just-in-time policies, the user needs to be assigned to the **Owner**, **Contributor**, or **Account Administrator** roles.

IP address can also be included in some security alerts provided by Azure Defender, as well as the attacker's details. To view security alerts, the user needs to be assigned to the **Reader**, **Owner**, **Contributor**, or **Account Administrator** roles. Keep in mind that alerts can't be deleted, regardless of the role you have.

It is important to mention that the personal data found in the Security Center contact feature doesn't need to be classified. There, you will only see one or multiple email addresses that are saved by Security Center. The same recommendation is true for the IP addresses and port numbers found in the just-in-time feature in Azure Defender.

To access the security contact data, the user needs to be assigned the **Reader**, **Owner**, **Contributor**, or **Account Administrator** roles. Only the **Reader** role will not allow you to update or delete the contact information in Security Center.

Thought experiment

In this thought experiment, demonstrate your skills and knowledge of the topics covered in this chapter. You can find answers to this thought experiment in the next section.

Monitoring security at Tailwind Traders

You are one of the Azure administrators for Tailwind Traders, an online general store that specializes in a variety of products that are used around the home. Tailwind Traders has been using the Azure Security Center free tier and is enabling Azure Defender plans according to their needs.

As a part of your duties for Tailwind Traders, you need to work with the security operations center (SOC) to ensure that you have threat detection for the different workloads available in your cloud deployment in Azure. Tailwind Traders has five Azure Storage accounts that are utilized by the sales team. The sales team uses these storage accounts primarily to store files. One technical requirement established by the IT security team is that all files that are uploaded by the sales team must be flagged if they are considered compromised files, and upon detection, an email must be sent to the incident response (IR) team to start the investigation.

Another technical requirement established by Tailwind Traders' IT security team is to ensure that Servers (Windows or Linux) running in Azure or on-premises are fully monitored in Azure, including threat detection and vulnerability assessment.

Tailwind Traders' SOC Team wants to avoid alert fatigue. They need to ensure that the alerts that are considered false positives for their environment are not going to appear in the dashboard for the next six months when they plan to reevaluate their strategy to triage alerts. With this information in mind, answer the following questions:

1. Which Azure Defender plans do you need to enable?

2. Which feature will allow Tailwind Traders' SOC team to avoid alert fatigue?

3. How to ensure the IR Team will receive an email once a compromised file is uploaded to the storage?

4. Is it possible to enable storage protection just for some storage accounts?

Thought experiment answers

This section contains the solution to the thought experiment. Each answer explains why the answer choice is correct.

1. Based on this scenario, you will need to enable Azure Defender for Servers and Azure Defender for Storage.

2. Alert suppression rules.

3. You will need to create a Logic App to send email to IR and from Azure Security Center configure the Workflow Automation feature to trigger the Logic App once an alert generated by Azure Defender for Storage is triggered based on the hash reputation of the file that was uploaded.

4. Yes, they can disable Azure Defender for Storage on the subscription level and enable it only on the storage accounts they want.

Chapter Summary

- Azure Defender plans that are based on other Azure Platform as a Service (PaaS) offerings don't require a workspace configuration in the beginning. These include Azure Defender for Key Vault, Azure Defender for App Service, Azure Defender for Resource Manager, Azure Defender for Storage, Azure Defender for Containers Registries, Azure Defender for SQL database, and Azure Defender for DNS.

- By default, there are two roles in Security Center: **Security Reader** and **Security Admin**. The **Security Reader** role should be assigned to all users who only need read access to the dashboard. The **Security Admin** role should be assigned for users who need to manage the Security Center configuration. If you need a more granular control, you can create a custom role.

- Data retention policy can be configured using Azure Resource Manager (ARM) templates by using the `retentionInDays` parameter.

- Vulnerability assessment in Azure Defender is done using the built-in integration with Qualys, but you can also bring your own license key to deploy Qualys or Rapid7 solutions.

- To connect non-Azure machines from a different cloud provider, you need to install Azure Arc and then install the LA Agent.

- You need to upgrade to Azure Defender to use the AWS and GCP Connector and start ingesting information from those platforms.

- You can create sample alerts for all alerts that are in GA.

- To create or delete an alert suppression rule, you need to be **Security Admin** or **Owner**. To view alert suppression rules, you need to be **Security Reader** or **Reader**.

- To configure an automated response in Azure Security Center, you need to create a Logic App with the workflow of actions that will be executed and configure the workflow automation feature in Azure Security Center.

- For some alerts, Azure Defender will also provide threat intelligence reports to facilitate your investigation. These reports contain information about the detected threats.

CHAPTER 3

Mitigate threats using Azure Sentinel

Azure Sentinel is a cloud-based SIEM (security information and event management) solution. SIEM solutions have been in existence for a number of years, and their key purpose is to collect and correlate events across an organization's IT environment to detect anomalous activities that might be indicative of a security breach. These alerts can then be dealt with by a security operations center (SOC) team to investigate, respond, and mitigate the issue that the SIEM has alerted on. Having an effective SIEM is critical to any organization's security operations; you might have heard the phrase "that's out of scope... said no attacker ever." The fact is that attackers will use any vulnerable assets they find in an IT environment to move laterally to find objects of value (data, computer power, and the like), so an organization simply cannot afford to have blind spots in their monitoring. Individual security tools might pick up one aspect of an attack (such as initial access through a vulnerable endpoint), but this alert by itself won't allow an SOC to understand the full scope of the attack and respond appropriately. A SIEM allows security operations analysts to correlate events in the wider IT environment and understand the seriousness of a breach.

In this chapter you'll learn about designing an Azure Sentinel workspace, ingesting data sources into Azure Sentinel, managing analytics rules, configuring automation, using workbooks, and hunting for threats using Azure Sentinel.

Skills covered in this chapter:

- Design and configure an Azure Sentinel workspace
- Plan and implement the use of data connectors for the ingestion of data sources into Azure Sentinel
- Manage Azure Sentinel analytics rules
- Configure Security Orchestration, Automation, and Response (SOAR) in Azure Sentinel
- Manage Azure Sentinel incidents
- Use Azure Sentinel workbooks to analyze and interpret data
- Hunt for threats using the Azure Sentinel portal

Skill 3-1: Design and configure an Azure Sentinel workspace

This objective deals with designing and configuring an Azure Sentinel workspace. Because Azure Sentinel is a SaaS (Software as a Service) solution, much of the core configuration is taken care of for you by Microsoft, but—as with any SaaS—certain aspects of configuration that still need to be implemented by each individual organization using the service.

Plan an Azure Sentinel workspace

Azure Sentinel is an enrichment layer that sits on top of a Log Analytics workspace. You cannot use Azure Sentinel without first having a Log Analytics workspace created in your Azure tenant. Log Analytics is where all logs that are ingested into Azure Sentinel are stored. There are several aspects of design and architecture to consider before creating your Log Analytics workspace(s) for Azure Sentinel.

First, you must consider the number of workspaces. Where possible, it is recommended that you use one central security workspace. However, there are times when this might not be possible. The main reasons for requiring a multi-workspace deployment are as follows:

- If logs need to be kept in a certain jurisdiction for compliance or regulatory requirements for a global organization
- To reduce Azure region networking egress costs
- For subsidiary organizations that run their own security operations

> **NOTE** Remember that Log Analytics and Azure Sentinel have a one-to-one relationship. If you choose to have multiple Log Analytics workspaces in your deployment, you will, in turn, have multiple Azure Sentinel instances. This chapter will cover management of multi-workspace incidents later.

If you require multiple workspaces, this will take one of two forms:

- **Cross-tenant scenario**   Where multiple Azure tenants each have Azure Sentinel workspaces that need to be centrally managed
- **Cross-workspace scenario**   Where there are multiple workspaces in one Azure tenant that need to be centrally managed

Azure Sentinel can support scenarios where multiple Azure tenants are involved by using Azure Lighthouse, which is an Azure service that allows cross-tenant management, with the MSSP managing the customer's Azure Sentinel workspace. This architecture can also be used for organizations that have subsidiaries who have their own separate Azure tenants. Figure 3-1 shows how Azure Lighthouse can be used to manage Azure Sentinel workspaces in different Azure tenancies.

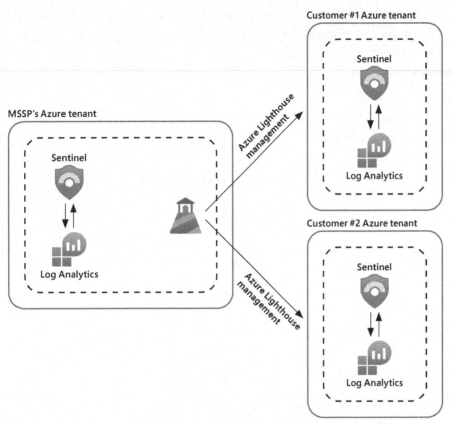

FIGURE 3-1 Managing Azure Sentinel workspaces across different Azure tenancies using Azure Lighthouse

There are many advantages to using Azure Lighthouse if your organization chooses to outsource their security operations. Here are a few:

- **All data stays in the end customer's Azure tenant**   Data is not stored in your MSSP's Azure tenant and is not mixed with other customer data. This preserves data sovereignty and allows for straightforward offboarding should the need arise.

- **MSSPs only have access to the Azure resource(s) that the end customer grants them**   This is unlike traditional delegated access in on-premises environments where a third-party service provider might have had access to the whole IT environment, even when only a specific application is needed.

- **MSSPs get consolidated views of all the customer workspaces they manage**   They don't have to log in to each Azure Sentinel workspace separately, which is inefficient and not scalable.

> *MORE INFO* **RUNNING AZURE SENTINEL USING AZURE LIGHTHOUSE**
>
> You can learn more about running Azure Sentinel with Azure Lighthouse here:
> *https://aka.ms/azsentinelmssp.*

Aside from Azure Lighthouse, there are several features in Log Analytics and Azure Sentinel that allow for investigation of incidents across workspaces in the same Azure tenant, as shown in Figure 3-2 and discussed in detail later in this chapter:

- Cross-workspace queries
- Cross-workspace analytics rules
- Cross-workspace hunting queries
- Cross-workspace workbooks

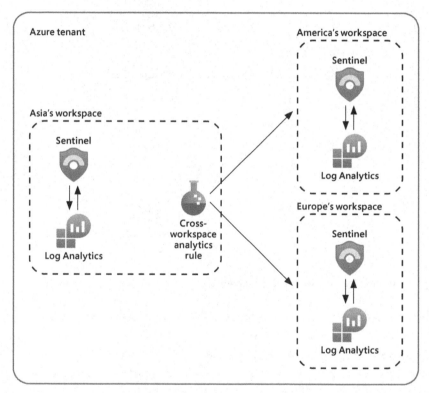

FIGURE 3-2 Cross-workspace analytics rules in the same Azure tenant

Other aspects of Azure Sentinel design to consider are as follows:

- **Azure tenant placement** A Log Analytics workspace is an Azure resource, and like with any Azure resource, consideration needs to take place for where this will sit. You will need to define a subscription, resource group, and region. It is recommended that the Log Analytics workspace that you are going to set up Azure Sentinel on top of is placed in a separate resource group for simplicity in configuring RBAC (more detail later). You may choose to place the workspace in an existing Azure Subscription or in a separate one.

- **Commitment tiers** If you plan to ingest more than 100GB per day into your Azure Sentinel workspace, it is worthwhile looking at commitment tiers that give you a discount on ingestion compared to pay-as-you-go pricing. Note that even if you don't ingest data up to your commitment tier allotment, you will be charged for it anyway if you change commitment tiers. Commitment tiers need to be configured at both the Log Analytics and Azure Sentinel level.

> **MORE INFO** **AZURE SENTINEL COMMITMENT TIERS**
>
> You can learn more about Azure Sentinel commitment tiers here: *https://azure.microsoft. com/pricing/details/azure-sentinel/.*

After you have decided on the number of workspaces and how they will fit into your Azure tenancy, you can enable Log Analytics workspace(s) and subsequently Azure Sentinel by performing the following steps:

1. Navigate to the Azure portal by opening *https://portal.azure.com.*

2. In the **Search** bar, type **Sentinel**, and under **Services**, click **Azure Sentinel Workspace**. The **Azure Sentinel** page appears, as shown in Figure 3-3.

FIGURE 3-3 Creating a new Log Analytics workspace

3. Click **Create**. The **Add Azure Sentinel To A Workspace** page appears.

4. Click **Create A New Workspace**.

5. The **Create Log Analytics Workspace** page appears, as shown in Figure 3-4.

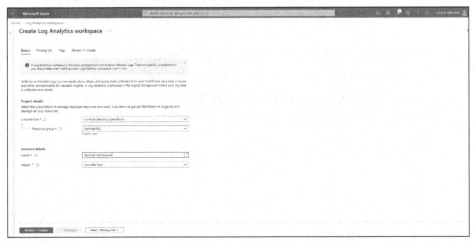

FIGURE 3-4 Create Log Analytics Workspace page

6. Configure the **Subscription**, **Resource Group**, and **Region** for your Log Analytics workspace.

7. Select **Pricing Tier**, add **Tags** (if required), and then select **Create**. Wait for your Log Analytics workspace to be provisioned.

8. In the Azure portal, search for **Azure Sentinel** and select **Add** on the Azure Sentinel page. The **Add Azure Sentinel To A Workspace** page appears, as shown in Figure 3-5.

FIGURE 3-5   Add Azure Sentinel To A Workspace

9. Select the Log Analytics workspace on which you want to activate Azure Sentinel.

Configure Azure Sentinel roles

As with other Azure resources, Azure Sentinel comes with several built-in Azure roles that you can assign to users who need to access your workspace. Remember to adhere to the principle of least privilege and always assign the absolute lowest level of privilege that a user requires to complete their role. Following are the built-in rules:

- **Azure Sentinel Reader**   Can view data, incidents, workbooks, and other Azure Sentinel resources.

- **Azure Sentinel Responder**   In addition to the permissions granted by an Azure Sentinel Reader role, the Azure Sentinel Responder role allows for managing of incidents.

- **Azure Sentinel Contributor**   In addition to the permissions that Reader and Responder roles have, Azure Sentinel Contributor can create and edit workbooks, analytics rules, and other Azure Sentinel resources.

To assign an Azure Sentinel role to a user, perform the following steps:

1. Navigate to the Azure portal by opening *https://portal.azure.com*.

2. In the **Search** bar, type **Resource Groups**, and under **Services**, click **Resource Groups**. The **Resource Groups** page appears, as shown in Figure 3-6.

FIGURE 3-6 The Resource Groups page in the Azure portal

3. Select the resource group that your Azure Sentinel workspace is associated with. The resource group's overview page appears.

4. From the **resource group** overview page, select the **Access Control (IAM)** page, which is shown in Figure 3-7.

FIGURE 3-7 Access Control (IAM) for a resource group

5. On the **Access Control (IAM)** page, select **Add role assignment**, as shown in Figure 3-8.

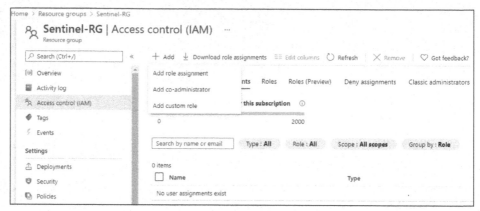

FIGURE 3-8   Adding a role assignment for a user

6. The **Add Role Assignment** blade appears, as shown in Figure 3-9.

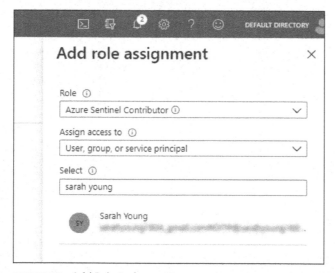

FIGURE 3-9   Add Role Assignment

7. On the **Add Role Assignment** blade, search for the Azure Sentinel role you want to assign, and in Azure AD, search for the user who you want to assign the role to.

8. Select **Save** to add this assignment.

> **NOTE**   The steps above detail how to assign Azure Sentinel permissions to a user based on the resource group. It is also possible to follow these steps and assign the role at the subscription or management group level that the workspace is in and the resource group will subsequently inherit this permission. However, best practice dictates that roles should be added at the resource group level, not at the subscription level or management group level.

Design Azure Sentinel data storage

Earlier in this chapter we explained that Azure Sentinel's data store is Log Analytics, which itself is a part of the wider Azure Monitor platform. As the name suggests, Azure Monitor is a suite of services in the Azure platform that assist with monitoring.

TIP When reading Microsoft documentation, you might find that some Log Analytics and Sentinel documentation refers to Azure Monitor. Remember, Log Analytics, and therefore Azure Sentinel, is a part of the Azure Monitor platform; this isn't a typo or a mistake in the documentation.

Log Analytics is an immutable log store that uses different tables to store the logs that it ingests in rows. What this means is that after data has been ingested into a Log Analytics workspace, it cannot be changed or amended and will only be removed from the workspace when the log reaches its retention period and is aged out of the workspace.

It is possible to retain data in a Log Analytics workspace for up to 730 days (2 years), but the default data retention is set to 30 days. When you activate Azure Sentinel on a Log Analytics workspace, you receive up to 90 days of free data retention. Azure Sentinel is priced on ingestion and log retention, so if you choose to retain logs in your workspace for more than 90 days, fees will be assessed. It is recommended that you choose a retention period in your workspace that balances how far back you are likely to actively query your security logs against the cost of retention.

TIP **DATA RETENTION**

You must manually alter the data retention to 90 days after you activate Azure Sentinel on a Log Analytics workspace; it is not changed automatically. This is important because when data reaches its configured retention limit, it will be automatically purged by Log Analytics, and you wouldn't want to not take advantage of your free 90 days of retention!

Remember that you can set retention periods in Log Analytics on a per-table basis, so you can opt to retain certain tables for longer than others to reduce the cost of retaining an entire workspace for a longer period. A table that is often kept for longer than others is the `SecurityIncident` table, as this stores details of the security incidents that have been raised by Azure Sentinel and querying this table allows for SOC managers to see their SOC's performance metrics, number of incidents raised over time, and so on. Ultimately, a cost/benefit analysis will have to be performed to decide what works best for your implementation of Azure Sentinel; there are tools such as the Azure Sentinel pricing calculator that can help you with this.

MORE INFO **AZURE SENTINEL PRICING CALCULATOR**

You can learn more about Azure Sentinel pricing at *https://azure.microsoft.com/pricing/calculator/.*

To change the data retention settings in your workspace perform the following steps:

1. Navigate to the Azure portal by opening *https://portal.azure.com.*

2. In the **Search** bar, type **Log Analytics**, and under **Services**, click **Log Analytics Workspace**. The **Log Analytics Workspace** page appears.

3. Select your workspace, and the **Usage And Estimated Costs** page appears, as shown in Figure 3-10.

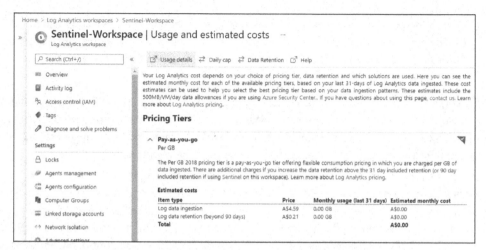

FIGURE 3-10 Navigating to the Data Retention settings in a Log Analytics workspace

4. Select the **Usage And Estimated Costs** blade.

5. Select **Data Retention** and move the slider on the **Data Retention** blade to your desired retention period for your workspace (shown in Figure 3-11) and select **OK**.

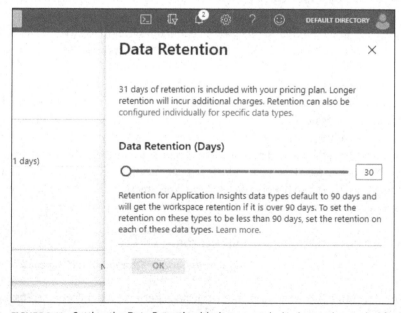

FIGURE 3-11 Setting the Data Retention blade to your desired retention period for your workspace

Long-term storage of Azure Sentinel data

Many organizations must adhere to strict data retention requirements for regulatory and compliance purposes that exceed the maximum 730 days that can be configured in Log Analytics. Additionally, keeping data in Log Analytics for the full 730 days that can be configured could be prohibitively expensive for a security operations team's budget.

There are two options to consider if long-term storage of Azure Sentinel logs is required for an implementation:

- Moving to blob storage
- Moving to Azure Data Explorer (ADX)

Sending data directly to blob storage is effectively archiving them and putting them in a cold store. This is the cheapest storage option, but the data will require "rehydrating" if they are needed to be actively queried again. ADX can be considered a warm store, which means data can be queried there. (It even uses the same query language—KQL.) However, the features are basic compared to Log Analytics and Azure Sentinel's rich feature set for security operations.

> **MORE INFO   LONG-TERM RETENTION OF AZURE SENTINEL DATA**
>
> You can learn more about long-term retention options for Azure Sentinel data at
> *https://techcommunity.microsoft.com/t5/azure-sentinel/using-azure-data-explorer-for-long-term-retention-of-azure/ba-p/1883947*.

Configure Azure Sentinel service security

Azure Sentinel relies on other services for some of its functionality. This means that to use these features, additional permissions other than the built-in Azure Sentinel roles need to be used:

- **Using Playbooks for automation**   In order to use Playbooks in Azure Sentinel, you will also need to assign the **Logic App Contributor** built-in role because Playbooks are part of Azure Logic Apps, which is considered to be a separate Azure resource and thus, has its own set of permissions.

- **Connecting data sources to Azure Sentinel**   A user must have write permissions on the Azure Sentinel workspace to be able to add a data source. They might also need additional permissions specific to each data source; these are listed on the connector's page.

- **Guest users assigning incidents**   To assign incidents in Azure Sentinel, guest users require the **Directory Reader** permissions to be assigned to them. Note that this role is not an Azure role but an Azure Active Directory role and that regular (non-guest) users have this role assigned by default.

- **Creating and deleting workbooks**   In order to create and delete workbooks in Azure Sentinel, a user will need to be assigned the Azure Monitor role of **Monitoring Contributor**. This is not required for using workbooks. It's only necessary for creating and deleting workbooks.

Skill 3-2: Plan and implement the use of data connectors for the ingestion of data sources into Azure Sentinel

This objective deals with the planning and implementation of connecting data sources to Azure Sentinel. No SIEM solution can function without data sources, so this is a critical aspect of creating an effective Azure Sentinel implementation that will successfully protect your IT environment.

Identify data sources to be ingested into Azure Sentinel

Identifying which data sources to ingest into Azure Sentinel is a critical activity that should ideally be decided upon before you begin your implementation. Azure Sentinel makes it easy to identify data sources that can be connected to the product via the built-in data connectors in the data connector gallery.

As a starting point, we recommend that you review the data connector gallery and identify which of these data sources you have in your environment and which ones you want to connect. Azure Sentinel has an extensive collection of built-in data connectors for both Microsoft and third-party products that can be utilized.

Follow these steps to review the data connector gallery:

1. Navigate to the Azure portal by opening *https://portal.azure.com.*

2. In the **Search** bar type **Sentinel**, and under **Services**, click **Azure Sentinel**. The **Azure Sentinel workspace** page appears, as shown in Figure 3-12.

FIGURE 3-12   Selecting the correct Azure Sentinel workspace

3. Select the workspace you want to use. The **Azure Sentinel | Overview** page appears, as shown in Figure 3-13.

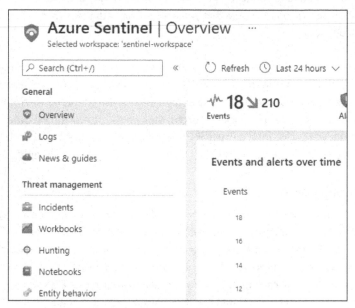

FIGURE 3-13 The Azure Sentinel | Overview page

4. Click **Data Connectors**, which opens the **Data Connectors** page, as shown in Figure 3-14.

FIGURE 3-14 Data Connectors gallery

5. Scroll through the gallery and note the data sources that are in your IT environment and that you want to ingest.

6. Add these data sources to your design document.

Although Azure Sentinel has many built-in data connectors, there might be data sources that you need to connect that are not in the gallery. We will cover how you can configure a custom connector to ingest these data sources into Sentinel later in the chapter. Meanwhile, we will continue to focus on identification of data sources. Many organizations have older, on-premises SIEMs that they are migrating away from, and you should review whether the data sources ingested by these SIEMs should be redirected to be ingested by Azure Sentinel.

> **NOTE MICROSOFT GRAPH SECURITY API**
>
> Organizations who have an incumbent SIEM solution are unlikely to want to migrate all their data sources to Azure Sentinel in a big bang approach. It is more likely that the organization runs both SIEMs side-by-side and gradually migrates more and more sources to Azure Sentinel, and in due course, the on-premises SIEM is decommissioned. Using the Microsoft Graph Security API, Azure Sentinel can integrate with popular on-premises SIEM solutions to support this approach while still maintaining a holistic view of security events. You can learn more about the Microsoft Graph Security API at *https://docs.microsoft.com/en-us/graph/security-concept-overview*.

After reviewing the data connector gallery and the current data sources that are being monitored by an organization's incumbent SIEM solution, the last stage of the process is to verify whether there are other data sources that need to be connected to Azure Sentinel from the IT environment. When setting up or migrating to a new SIEM, it is worthwhile to verify there aren't any blind spots in your monitoring setup and that there aren't any assets that have not been monitored previously. This can occur for various reasons, including:

- Difficulty in integrating the data source
- Volume or noisiness of data source
- Human error/oversight

If a data source was previously unable to be integrated into a SIEM, the data source should be reassessed to see whether it is more viable to connect it to the SIEM to reduce as many blind spots as possible in the environment when moving to a modern solution.

> **TIP** You might be familiar with the phrase "collection is not detection." Remember, ingestion charges increase as more data is sent to your workspace, so it is important to only ingest data that has use in a security monitoring context. As a rule of thumb, if you're not going to run a detection against it or use the data source for hunting, you need to reassess whether you should be ingesting it at all. Blindly ingesting as many data sources as possible will lead to a very large Azure bill!

Free data sources in Azure Sentinel

There are some data sources that can be ingested into Azure Sentinel free of charge. At the time of writing, the following sources could be ingested into a workspace completely free of charge when using the built-in Azure Sentinel connector:

- Azure Activity logs
- Office 365—Exchange, SharePoint, and Teams logs
- Security alerts (not raw logs) from Microsoft security products—MCAS, Azure Defender, Defender for Identity, Defender for Endpoint, and so on

> **NOTE   ONLY THE INGESTION IS FREE**
>
> These data sources would accumulate a retention charge if they were retained for more than 90 days in a workspace; only the ingestion is free.

> **TIP   CHECK THE FREE DATA SOURCES**
>
> From time to time, Microsoft might change the data sources that are free to ingest. Make sure that you check this prior to your exam and—arguably more importantly—prior to an implementation, so you or your customer don't get a nasty billing shock!

Identify the prerequisites for a data connector

Azure Sentinel makes it easy to understand what prerequisites you need before you can use a data connector: they are all listed on each data connector's page. Some data connectors require Syslog/CEF connectors or Windows Event collectors to be set up as a prerequisite for use, but we'll dive into that in more detail later in this chapter.

Follow these steps to view the prerequisites for using a data connector:

1. Navigate to the Azure portal by opening *https://portal.azure.com*.
2. In the **Search** bar, type **Sentinel**, and under **Services**, click **Azure Sentinel**. The **Azure Sentinel Workspace** page appears.
3. Select the workspace you want to use. The **Azure Sentinel | Overview** page appears.
4. Click **Data Connectors**, which opens the **Data Connectors** page.
5. Select the data connector for which you want to view the prerequisites and click the **Open Connector** page button.

6. The connector's overview page appears, as shown in Figure 3-15.

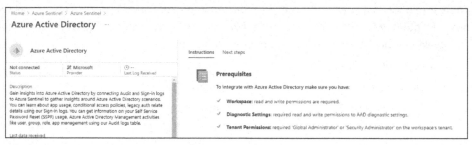

FIGURE 3-15 Data connector prerequisites

7. The prerequisites to be able to use the selected data connector can be found in the top-right part of the connector's page.

> **TIP NOTE ADDITIONAL PERMISSIONS NEEDED**
>
> Some data connector prerequisites will require you to have Azure AD permissions in other parts of Azure—not just Azure Sentinel—so take careful note of what additional permissions you need to be granted to be able to use a data connector.

Configure and use Azure Sentinel data connectors

Now that you've identified which data connectors you want to use and have all the prerequisites in hand, it's time to start configuring your Azure Sentinel data connectors. As always, Azure Sentinel tries to make this process as easy and painless as possible for you (you're probably noticing a theme here!).

Following are some examples of the Azure Sentinel data connectors you might connect in this manner:

- Microsoft Cloud App Security (MCAS)
- Azure Defender
- Azure Defender for IoT
- Microsoft Defender for Endpoint
- Microsoft Defender for Identity
- Microsoft Defender for Office 365
- Azure Active Directory Identity Protection

To configure a data connector:

1. Navigate to the Azure portal by opening *https://portal.azure.com*.

2. In the **Search** bar, type **Sentinel**, and under **Services**, click **Azure Sentinel**. The **Azure Sentinel Workspace** page appears.

3. Select the workspace you want to use. The **Azure Sentinel | Overview** page appears.

4. Click **Data Connectors**. The **Data Connectors** page appears.

5. Select the data connector that you want to configure and click the **Open Connector** page button.

6. The configuration steps to activate the selected data connector can be found on the bottom-right of the connector's page. Configuration steps vary from data connector to data connector, as shown in Figures 3-16 and 3-17.

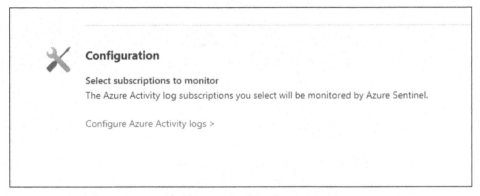

FIGURE 3-16 Configuration steps for the Azure Activity data connector

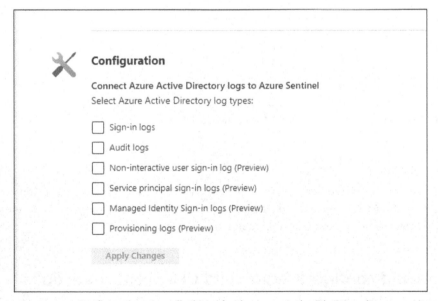

FIGURE 3-17 Configuration steps displayed for the Azure Active Directory data connector

7. Follow the configuration steps detailed to connect your data source to your workspace.

8. After you've connected the data source to your workspace, you can use the data connector's page to check the status of the connector, when the last log was received, and the like, as shown in Figure 3-18.

FIGURE 3-18 Checking the status of the Azure Activity data connector in Azure Sentinel

> **NOTE BE PATIENT**
>
> After you have connected a data source, don't be concerned if you don't see logs being received immediately. Depending on the data source, it might take up to a few hours before logs will start being ingested from that source into your workspace.

Design and configure Syslog and CEF event collections

Syslog and CEF formats are used by a huge range of systems for logging. You'll notice that if you review the prerequisites for the built-in Azure Sentinel data connectors that several of them use Syslog or CEF collection to ingest logs.

Before we dive in to how to design a collector for these types of logs, let's quickly step back and understand what Syslog and CEF are.

Syslog

Syslog has been around for a long time in computing terms—it first came into existence in the 1980s—and was documented in RFC 3164 in the early 2000s by the IETF. I deliberately use the word "documented" rather than "standardized," as you might be more used saying when referring to RFCs. This is because the only consistent part of a Syslog message is the beginning portion, where there is a timestamp and IP address or hostname. The contents of the remaining message can vary from source to source. Syslog logs are sent to the Syslog table.

Common Event Format (CEF)

CEF is also known as "Syslog CEF" because CEF is a normalized version of Syslog. It is already parsed and formatted, so it requires less work when the log is ingested into a SIEM solution. If a data source you want to connect to Azure Sentinel can output in Syslog or CEF, choose CEF! CEF logs are sent to the CommonSecurityLog table. CEF logs are formatted like this:

```
CEF:Version|Device Vendor|Device Product|Device Version|Signature
ID|Name|Severity|Extension
```

Syslog/CEF collector architecture options

The great news is that it doesn't matter whether you're collecting Syslog or CEF, the agent used and architectural considerations are exactly the same. A Syslog/CEF collector for Azure Sentinel uses the Linux version of the Log Analytics agent, also known as the OMS agent.

With regard to the architecture choices for your Syslog/CEF collector, you have two choices: Deploy on-premises or deploy in the cloud. Both architectures are supported, so ultimately, you will need to decide what works best for your environment. A cloud-based collector offers the elasticity and resiliency of cloud resources but might require more on-premises configuration. For example, if there is a firewall between the on-premises environment and the network connection to the Azure cloud (such as via Express Route, VPN, and so on), then ports would need to be opened for every Syslog/CEF source to be allowed through to reach the cloud. This might not be feasible or acceptable for security teams. In this case, an on-premises collector could better serve the implementation. As with so many things in IT implementations, there are pros and cons to each choice. These architecture options are shown below in Figures 3-19 and 3-20.

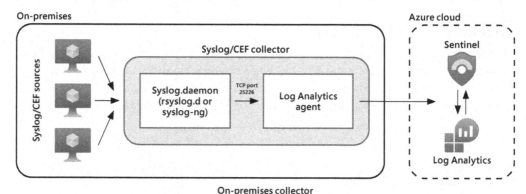

FIGURE 3-19 Architecture for an on-premises-based Syslog/CEF collector

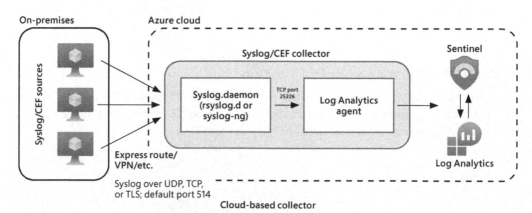

FIGURE 3-20 Architecture for a cloud-based Syslog/CEF collector

Design and configure Windows Events collections

Windows security events are events logged by devices using the Windows OS (servers and endpoints, physical and virtual) and can be sent to an Azure Sentinel workspace for analysis and for correlation with other events in your environment. Azure Sentinel provides a built-in connector where you can stream Windows security events to your workspace, as shown in Figure 3-21. Logs collected using this data source go into the SecurityEvents table.

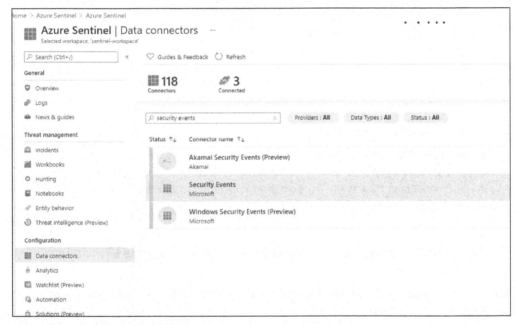

FIGURE 3-21 The built-in Security Events connector

As we did with collecting Syslog and CEF events, we will be using the Log Analytics agent to collect Windows security events, but we will be using the Windows version (unsurprisingly!). Unlike Syslog/CEF collection, we won't be creating a centralized collector. When using the Windows version of the Log Analytics agent, each agent streams directly to the Azure Sentinel workspace. There is no intermediary device. In Figure 3-22, you can see how Windows systems stream security events to a Sentinel workspace.

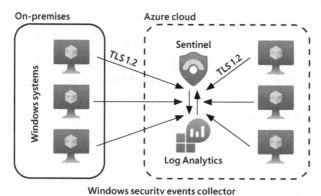

FIGURE 3-22   Streaming Windows security events to Azure Sentinel

> **NOTE   LOG ANALYTICS GATEWAY**
>
> If you have Windows systems that have no Internet access in your environment, you can use a Log Analytics gateway to act as a forward proxy for your Windows security events. You can learn more about the Log Analytics gateway at *https://docs.microsoft.com/en-us/azure/azure-monitor/agents/gateway*.

Configuring Windows security event collection for Azure Windows Virtual Machines

Folow these steps to configure the Security Events connector in Azure Sentinel for Azure Windows Virtual Machines:

1. Navigate to the Azure portal by opening *https://portal.azure.com*.
2. In the **Search** bar, type **Sentinel**, and under **Services**, click **Azure Sentinel**. The **Azure Sentinel Workspace** page appears.
3. Select the workspace you want to use. The **Azure Sentinel | Overview** page appears.
4. Click Data Connectors, which opens the **Data Connectors** page.
5. Select the **Security Events Data Connector** and click the **Open connector Page** button. The **Security Events Data Connector | Overview** page appears.

6. The shortcuts to install the Log Analytics agent on your Windows system can be found on the bottom-right part of the connector's page. Figure 3-23 shows the shortcuts to installation on the connector page.

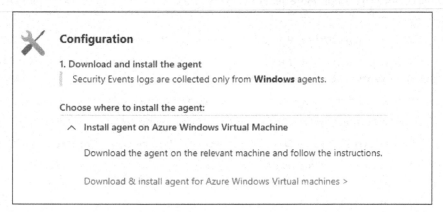

FIGURE 3-23 Log Analytics agent connector installation locations

7. Click **Download & Install Agent For Azure Windows Virtual Machines**.

8. On the **Virtual Machines** page, select the machine(s) that you want to connect.

9. On the **AzureWindowsServer** page, click **Connect**. You will see the connection to your Sentinel workspace taking place, as shown in Figure 3-24.

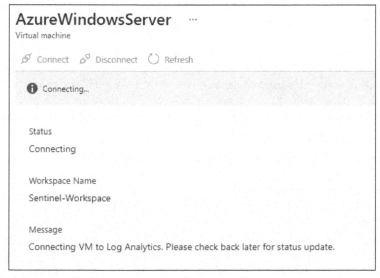

FIGURE 3-24 Connecting an Azure virtual machine to Azure Sentinel for Windows security event streaming

Configuring Windows security event collection for non-Azure Windows Machines

Follow these steps to configure the Security Events connector in Azure Sentinel for non-Azure Windows machines:

1. Navigate to the Azure portal by opening *https://portal.azure.com*.

2. In the **Search** bar, type **Sentinel**, and under **Services**, click **Azure Sentinel**. The **Azure Sentinel Workspace** page appears.

3. Select the workspace you want to use. The **Azure Sentinel | Overview** page appears.

4. Click **Data Connectors**. The **Data Connectors** page appears.

5. Select the **Security Events Data Connector** and click the **Open Connector** button.

6. The shortcuts to install the Log Analytics agent on your Windows system can be found on the bottom-right of the connector's page. Figure 3-25 shows the installation shortcuts on the connector page.

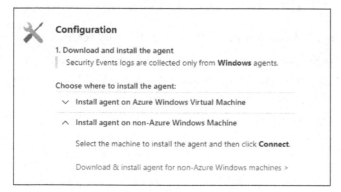

FIGURE 3-25 Downloading the Log Analytics agent for non-Azure Windows machines

7. Click **Download & Install Agent For Non-Azure Windows Machines**. The **Agents Management** page appears, as shown in Figure 3-26.

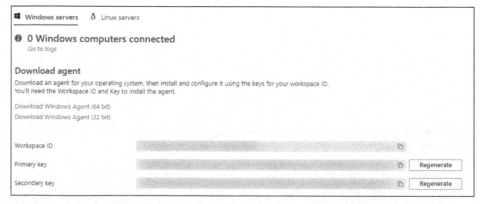

FIGURE 3-26 Retrieving Workspace ID and workspace keys

8. Make a note of your **Workspace ID** and workspace keys (**Primary Key** and **Secondary Key**) to input into the agent later.

9. Run the installer package on your target system, and it will launch the **Microsoft Monitoring Agent Setup Wizard**, as shown in Figure 3-27.

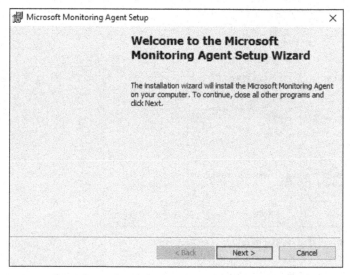

FIGURE 3-27 Microsoft Monitoring Agent Setup Wizard

10. Agree to the Microsoft software license terms and select a folder in which to install the agent.

11. In **Agent Setup Options**, select **Connect The Agent To Azure Log Analytics (OMS)**, as shown in Figure 3-28.

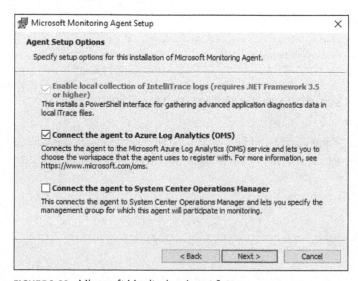

FIGURE 3-28 Microsoft Monitoring Agent Setup

12. After clicking **Next**, you will asked to provide your **Workspace ID** and **Workspace Key** for your Sentinel workspace, as shown in Figure 3-29.

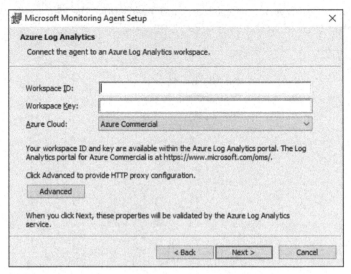

FIGURE 3-29 Adding the Workspace ID and Workspace Keys

13. Click **Next** and complete the installation of the agent.

14. Return to the Azure portal and check the **Agents Management** page where you should now see your non-Azure machine connected, as shown in Figure 3-30.

FIGURE 3-30 Agents Management page

Choosing Windows security events to stream to an Azure Sentinel workspace

There are thousands of Windows Events, and it can be hard to choose which ones you need to ingest, so Microsoft provides preset options in the connector itself (shown in Figure 3-31):

- All Events
- Common
- Minimal
- None

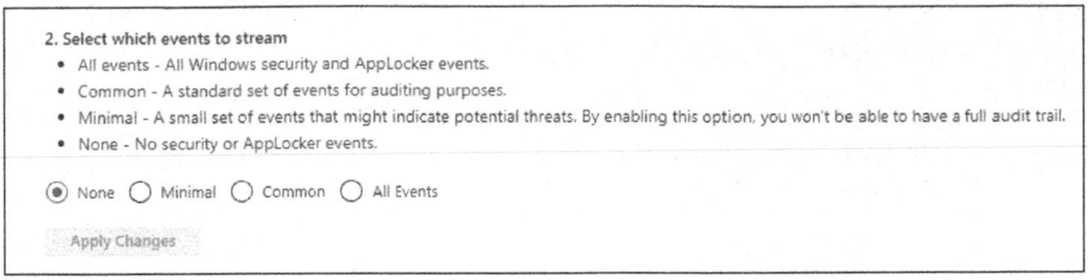

2. Select which events to stream

- All events - All Windows security and AppLocker events.
- Common - A standard set of events for auditing purposes.
- Minimal - A small set of events that might indicate potential threats. By enabling this option, you won't be able to have a full audit trail.
- None - No security or AppLocker events.

◉ None ○ Minimal ○ Common ○ All Events

Apply Changes

FIGURE 3-31 Preset streaming options available for the Security Events connector

> ***MORE INFO*** **WINDOWS SECURITY EVENTS INCLUDED IN EACH PRESET OPTION**
>
> You can learn more about the Event IDs included in each preset streaming option at *https://docs.microsoft.com/en-us/azure/sentinel/connect-windows-security-events*.

Configure custom threat intelligence connectors

Using threat intelligence (TI) feeds enriches the information a SIEM collects and thus enhances your security operations. TI feeds contain information about cyberthreats. Most typically, we see these expressed as indicators of compromise (IOCs). An IOC could be a known malicious IP, URL, hash value, and the like. If this IOC is matched to values in the data from your IT environment, it could indicate that an attacker is (or has been) in your environment. This is why IOCs from threat intelligence are often used for proactive hunting. From an incident perspective, if an incident is raised where some entities have matches to your threat intelligence, an SOC might choose to raise the severity of the incident because there is a higher likelihood that known attackers are part of the incident.

IOCs often have an expiration date attached to them. We know that attackers will change how they present their attacks frequently to avoid detection, which is why IOCs need frequent updating via a TI feed. TI feeds can be purchased from a vendor, but there are also open-source and free-to-use TI feeds available in the community.

In Azure Sentinel, when TI feeds are connected, the IOCs from the feed will be stored in the `ThreatIntelligenceIndicator` table, and you'll be able to review them in a more user-friendly format on the **Threat intelligence** page in the Sentinel UI. You can also add IOCs manually on the **New Indicator** blade, as shown in Figure 3-32.

FIGURE 3-32 Manually adding an IOC

If you are using a threat intelligence feed, it is likely to be sent from a STIX/TAXII setup:

- **STIX (Structured Threat Information eXpression)**   STIX is a standardized language that has been developed by MITRE in a collaborative way to represent structured information about cyber threats.

- **TAXII (Trusted Automated eXchange of Indicator Information)**   TAXII is a transport vehicle for STIX-structured threat information that allows STIX information to be exchanged between parties.

STIX and TAXII were created to allow easy and consistent sharing of threat information between individual people or organizations worldwide.

Azure Sentinel has a built-in threat Intelligence data connector that can be used to connect to TAXII servers and import IOCs into the `ThreatIntelligenceIndicator` table.

> **TIP**   **OLDER TAXII VERSIONS NOT SUPPORTED**
>
> Azure Sentinel only supports connections to the most recent versions of TAXII: 2.0 or 2.1. Older versions of TAXII are not supported.

Follow these steps to configure the Threat Intelligence Connector in Azure Sentinel:

1. Navigate to the Azure portal by opening *https://portal.azure.com*.

2. In the **Search** bar, type **Sentinel**, and under **Services**, click **Azure Sentinel**. The **Azure Sentinel Workspace** page appears.

3. Select the workspace you want to use. The **Azure Sentinel | Overview** page appears.

4. Click **Data Connectors**. The **Data Connectors** page appears.

5. Select the **Threat intelligence (TAXII) Data Connector** and click the **Open Connector** button. The **Threat Intelligence (TAXII) Data Connector** appears, as shown in Figure 3-33.

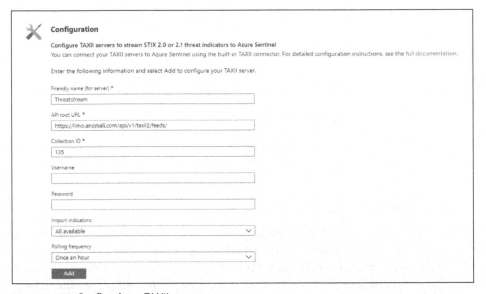

FIGURE 3-33   Configuring a TAXII server

6. Under **Configuration**, complete the details required to connect your TAXII server to Azure Sentinel. (This is standard information and should be provided by the threat intelligence feed provider.) Click **Add**.

7. You can check which TAXII servers you have connected to your Sentinel workspace by scrolling down to the bottom of the **Threat Intelligence Connector** page and checking the **List Of Configured TAXII Servers**, as shown in Figure 3-34.

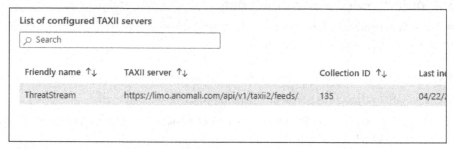

FIGURE 3-34 Checking configured TAXII servers on the Threat intelligence connector page

8. You can view IOCs on the **Threat intelligence** page in the Sentinel UI, as shown in Figure 3-35.

FIGURE 3-35 Viewing imported IOCs on the Threat Intelligence page

> **NOTE ACTIVE COLUMN**
>
> IOCs that have expired will still appear in the `ThreatIntelligenceIndicator` table because of the immutable nature of Log Analytics and will only age out when they reach the workspace's configured retention period. To combat this, the `ThreatIntelligenceIndicator` table has an **Active** column; when an IOC's expiry date is reached, a new entry will be added with **False** in the **Active** column, and it will no longer be used by Azure Sentinel for IOC matching.

Create custom logs in Azure Log Analytics to store custom data

Sometimes, it won't be possible to use any of the native methods described in the previous sections to connect your data source...so what then? The main method by which you can ingest custom logs into Azure Sentinel is to use the HTTP Data Collector API, but there are different ways to interact with it—direct via the API or via Azure Logic Apps. Depending on the use case, volume, and type of data you need to ingest, it will likely become obvious which method is better to use.

Custom log ingestion via the Azure Monitor HTTP Data Collector API

Azure Monitor provides the HTTP Data Collector API that can ingest data from a REST API client. Remember, Log Analytics is part of the wider Azure Monitor platform, so don't be put off by the name! Data must be sent to the HTTP Data Collector API in JSON format, and from there, it will be parsed into a custom table. When you submit the data, an individual record is created in the repository for each record in the request payload, as shown in Figure 3-36.

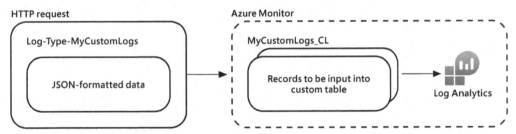

FIGURE 3-36 Sending data to the Azure Monitor HTTP Data Collector API

You have many options when choosing how to interact with this API; typically this would be via an existing REST API client or a serverless function written in Powershell, Python, C#, and so on. There really are no limits to how you interact and send data as long as you stick to the rules and formats required by the API.

Custom log ingestion via Azure Logic Apps

We'll be covering more about Azure Logic Apps and automation later in this chapter, but in this section we'll talk about how you can configure a Logic App to ingest custom data into your workspace. If you're unfamiliar with this product, Logic Apps provides a GUI-based interface to write automation scripts called Playbooks. If you've ever used Microsoft Flow, you'll have a good idea of what you'll be doing in Azure Logic Apps.

Let's walk through an example of pulling data from an external API to store in a custom table in Log Analytics. In my example, we're going to be pulling weather data, but in real life security operations this is more likely to be threat intel or something else that enriches the data in your workspace.

1. Navigate to the Azure portal by opening *https://portal.azure.com*.

2. In the **Search** bar, type **Sentinel**, and under **Services**, click **Azure Sentinel**. The **Azure Sentinel Workspace** page appears.

3. Select the workspace you want to use. The **Azure Sentinel | Overview** page appears.

4. Click **Automation**. The **Automation** page appears, as shown in Figure 3-37.

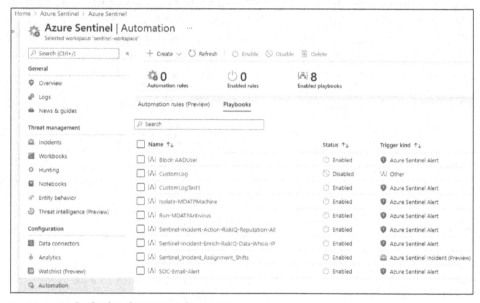

FIGURE 3-37   Reviewing the Automation page

5. Click **Create** > **Add New Playbook**. The **Create A Logic App** page appears, as shown in Figure 3-38.

6. Fill out the **Subscription**, **Resource Group**, **Region**, and **Name** of the Playbook and click **Review + Create** to validate your template.

7. When your template has validated, click **Create**.

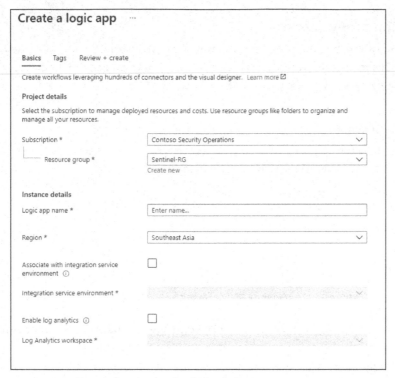

FIGURE 3-38 Completing the details of a Logic App

8. Open the blank Playbook you have created. You will be given the option to choose from various predefined templates. This time, select **Blank Logic App**. The **Logic Apps Designer** page appears.

9. We can now search for a trigger to kick-off the Playbook in the **Logic App Connector Gallery**. In Figure 3-39, you can see that we are searching for the **Schedule** trigger.

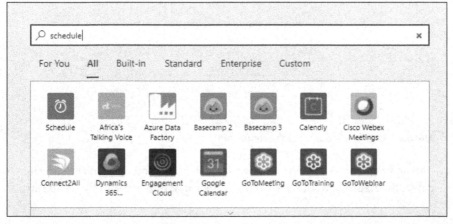

FIGURE 3-39 Searching for the Schedule trigger in the Logic App connector gallery

10. Select the **Schedule** connector and choose the **Recurrence** trigger.

11. Configure how frequently you want this Playbook to run. In my example, I'm going to configure it to run every 5 minutes, as you can see in Figure 3-40.

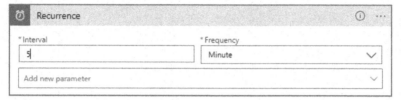

FIGURE 3-40 Configuring the frequency of the Playbook running in the Logic App Designer

12. For the next step in the Playbook, select **HTTP Logic App Connector** > **HTTP Action**. This is where we will configure the call to the external API for the custom data to be ingested.

13. Select **GET** for Method and add the URI for the API, plus any other necessary parts of the request such as authentication, headers, and so on. You can see the completed one for my weather API in Figure 3-41.

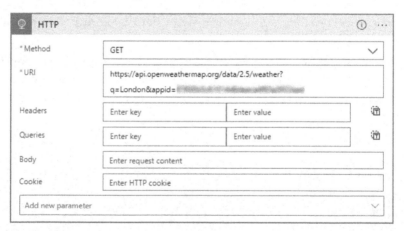

FIGURE 3-41 HTTP request to the external API

14. The final step in the Playbook will be to send this data into Log Analytics. Search for and select the **Azure Log Analytics Data Collector** and then select the **Send Data** action.

15. You will be asked to complete the details of the workspace to which you want to send the data (see Figure 3-42). Give the connection a memorable name and provide your workspace ID and key. (Earlier in this chapter, we explained how to obtain these.)

16. Click **Create**.

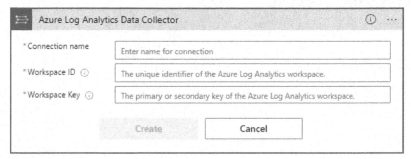

FIGURE 3-42 Completing the connection with the workspace

17. As shown in Figure 3-43, you will need to provide the **JSON Request Body** details that will be received by the Playbook. This allows the Playbook to parse the data correctly when it is received. You will also need to specify the name of the custom table that the data will be sent to in the **Custom Log Name** field.

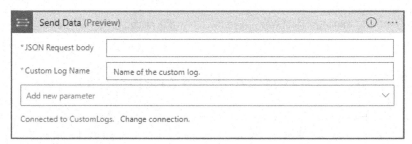

FIGURE 3-43 Completing the JSON Request Body format and custom table names in the Playbook

18. Click **Save** at the top left of the Logic App Designer page.

19. Navigate to the Playbook's **Overview** page and select **Run Trigger** > **Recurrence** to test your Playbook (see Figure 3-44). You will be able to see whether the Playbook ran successfully by looking at the bottom-right of the page.

FIGURE 3-44 Manually running a Playbook to test it

20. Now it's time to check to see whether our logs were received properly into our custom table: Navigate to the **Logs** page. As you can see in Figure 3-45, on the **Tables** tab, we now have an extra drop-down menu, **Custom Logs**. Whatever name you specified in **the Custom Log Name** will be appended with _CL. This prevents overlaps with the naming of built-in-in tables in Log Analytics.

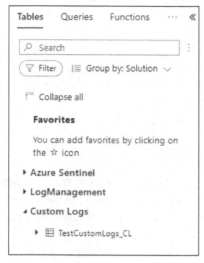

FIGURE 3-45 Custom logs listed alongside other tables on the Logs page

Skill 3-3: Manage Azure Sentinel analytics rules

Analytics rules are the Sentinel rules that correlate the logs that have been sent to the underlying Log Analytics workspace. Analytics rules run on a periodic basis with the intention of correlating specific patterns of events and activities in your environment logs. If a match to the rule is found, an alert and/or an incident is created, which your security operations team can act upon. (This is covered in more detail later in this section.)

Design and configure analytics rules

As with the rest of the product, you'll find that Azure Sentinel has many out-of-the-box analytics rules to start you off in your implementation. If you've worked with other SIEMs before, you might know them as "detection rules." These rules have been written by Microsoft security experts and, while they are fully customizable to your environment, they are a great way to get started with your base analytics rules in your Azure Sentinel implementation. It's worth reviewing the out-of-the-box templates regularly to check if there are new ones; Microsoft adds more on a regular basis. There are five types of analytics rules in Azure Sentinel:

- **Scheduled query**   These queries run on a fixed schedule (every 5 minutes, every hour, and the like), and you can see the query logic and can make changes to it. We will discuss how to do this later in this section.

- **Microsoft security**   These rules automatically create incidents based on alerts from other Microsoft security products. These rules are a great way to get your Azure Sentinel deployment up and running quickly.

- **Fusion**   Fusion uses scalable machine learning algorithms that can correlate many low-fidelity alerts and events across multiple products into high-fidelity and actionable incidents. Fusion is enabled by default. Because the logic is hidden and therefore not customizable, you can only create one rule with this template.

- **Machine learning (ML) behavioral analytics**   These templates are based on proprietary Microsoft machine learning algorithms, so you cannot see the internal logic of how they work and when they run. Because the logic is hidden and therefore not customizable, you can only create one rule with each template of this type.

- **Anomaly**   These rules use SOC-ML (machine learning) to detect specific types of anomalous behavior. Each rule has its own unique parameters and thresholds appropriate to the behavior being analyzed, and while its configuration can't be changed or fine-tuned, you can duplicate the rule and change and fine-tune the duplicate.

First, let's look at the **Analytics** page in the portal, which can be seen in Figures 3-46 and 3-47.

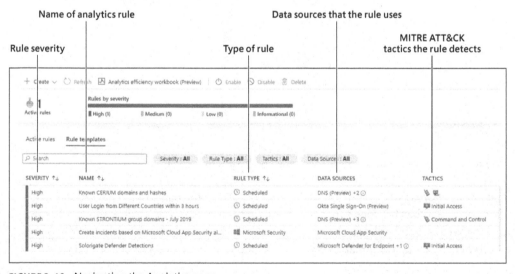

FIGURE 3-46   Navigating the Analytics page

We recommend that you enable all out-of-the-box templates that use data sources that you ingest into your workspace. It's very easy to do: You can use the filters to filter rule templates by a specific data source, or you can just look at the rule template summary (see Figure 3-47) and look at **Data Sources**.

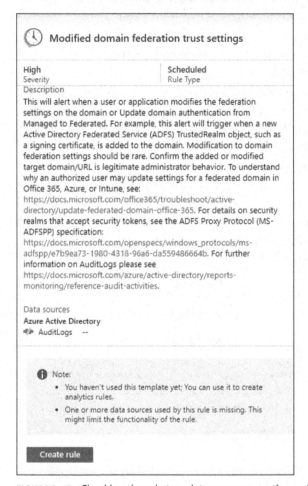

FIGURE 3-47   Checking the rule template summary on the analytics page

Pay attention to the color of the connector icon next to the name of the data source. If it's green, then Sentinel has found that type of logs in the workspace; if it's gray, then you need to add that log type for the rule to work properly. Figure 3-48 shows examples of both green (AzureActivity) and gray (Amazon Web Services) icons, with the green icon shown first.

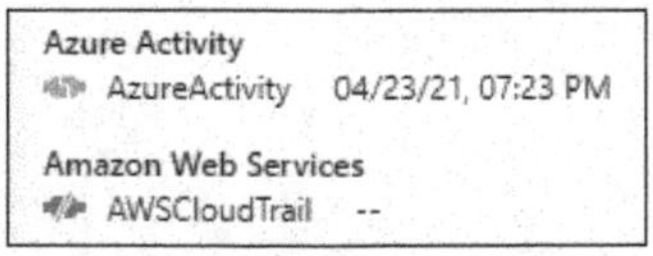

Azure Activity
AzureActivity   04/23/21, 07:23 PM

Amazon Web Services
AWSCloudTrail   --

FIGURE 3-48   Data source indicator on the rule template summary

To activate an analytics rule template:

1. Navigate to the Azure portal by opening *https://portal.azure.com.*

2. In the **Search** bar, type **Sentinel**, and under **Services**, click **Azure Sentinel**. The **Azure Sentinel Workspace** page appears.

3. Select the desired workspace. The **Azure Sentinel | Overview** page appears.

4. Click **Analytics**. The **Analytics** page appears, as shown in Figure 3-49.

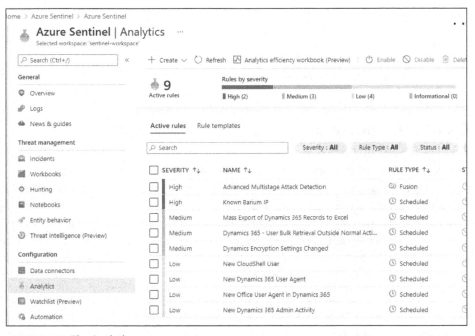

FIGURE 3-49 The Analytics page

5. Select the **Rule Templates** tab.

6. Select the rule template you want to activate and at the bottom of the rule template summary, click **Create Rule**.

7. You will be taken to the **Analytics Rule Wizard**. Work your way through the tabs of the wizard. (These tabs are all prefilled when using a rule template.) After the validation check, click **Create**.

8. You will return to the main **Analytics** page. Under the **Active Rules** tab, you should now see your newly created rule, as shown in Figure 3-50.

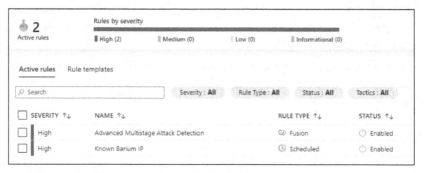

FIGURE 3-50 Checking active rules on the Analytics page

Create custom analytics rules to detect threats

Although the out-of-the-box analytics rules are a great way to start off your implementation, they aren't optimized for a specific environment and therefore, you might want to customize these rules to make them more specific to your thresholds, operational procedures, and so on. There are many reasons for customizing query logic, but the most common reason is to reduce false positives (such as when a rule triggers an incident but further investigation indicates there wasn't a security issue). SOCs are always trying to reduce false positives and noise because it wastes SOC analyst time. It is common for SOCs to not have enough analysts to look at alerts as it is, so they certainly don't want them looking at false positives!

In this section, we will look at how you can customize analytics rules to optimize them. Let's go back to the **Analytics** page and the analytics rule templates:

1. Navigate to the Azure portal by opening *https://portal.azure.com*.

2. In the **Search** bar, type **Sentinel**, and under **Services**, click **Azure Sentinel**. The **Azure Sentinel Workspace** page appears.

3. Select the workspace you want to use. The **Azure Sentinel | Overview** page appears.

4. Click **Analytics**. The **Analytics** page appears.

5. Select the **Rule Templates** tab.

6. Select the rule template you want to use and click **Create Rule** at the bottom of the rule template summary at the bottom-right of the page. For our example, I'm going to use the **Failed AWS Console Logons But Success Logon To AzureAD Rule** template. You will be taken to the **Analytics Rule Wizard**, as shown in Figure 3-51.

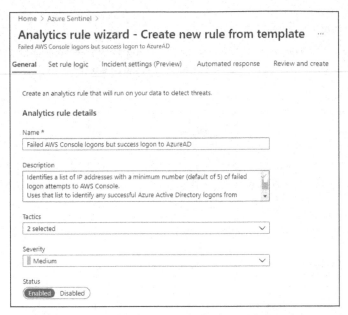

Analytics rule wizard - Create new rule from template ···
Failed AWS Console logons but success logon to AzureAD

General   Set rule logic   Incident settings (Preview)   Automated response   Review and create

Create an analytics rule that will run on your data to detect threats.

Analytics rule details

Name *

Failed AWS Console logons but success logon to AzureAD

Description

Identifies a list of IP addresses with a minimum number (default of 5) of failed
logon attempts to AWS Console.
Uses that list to identify any successful Azure Active Directory logons from

Tactics

2 selected

Severity

Medium

Status

Enabled   Disabled

FIGURE 3-51 Customizing the General tab of an analytics rule

7. On the **General** tab, you can customize the **Name**, **Description**, and the **MITRE Tactics** that this rule detects on, as well as the **Severity** of the rule. In this example, I'm planning to change the failed login attempts in the rule's logic, so I'm going to update the description of the number of failed logins from 5 to 10.

8. On the **Set Rule Logic** tab, you will see various aspects of the rule logic can be customized.

   - **Rule Query**   The Kusto Query Language (KQL) of the query. (See the "Define incident creation logic" section later in this chapter for further details on this.) This is fully editable, and in this example, I'm going to change the variable named `signin_ threshold`, which can be seen in Figure 3-52. This threshold is currently set to 5 failed logins, but I'm going to change it to 10. What this means is that until there have been 10 failed logins for a user in AWS followed by a successful Azure login by the same user, this rule will not trigger and create an alert.

   - **Alert Enrichment**   This is where you can define entities that can be classified for further analysis by Azure Sentinel.

   - **Query Scheduling**   In this section, you can configure how frequently your query runs and how far back in the logs the rule will look for matches (known as the *lookback window*). You can run queries in Azure Sentinel as frequently as every minute.

   - **Threshold**   This allows you to define how many rule "hits" need to occur before an alert is raised. Generally, this can almost always be left on the default setting, **Is Greater Than 0**.

   - **Event Grouping**   where you can configure how rule query results are grouped into alerts.

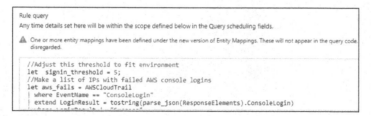

FIGURE 3-52 Customizing the KQL of an analytics rule

9. Let's move to the **Incident Settings** tab, as shown in Figure 3-53.

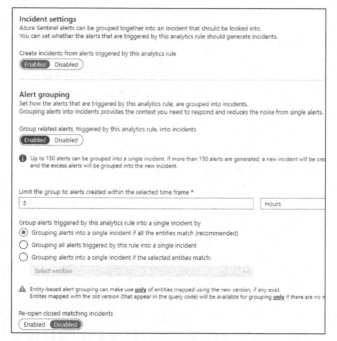

FIGURE 3-53 Customizing the incident settings of an analytics rule

10. The **Incident Settings** tab has many options that can be customized, and how these are configured is largely going to come down to the individual SOC and operational processes in an organization:

■ **Incident Settings** Here, you can enable/disable whether an incident in Azure Sentinel is triggered by an analytics rule. Often, people will say: "Of course I need an incident triggered from an analytics rule. That's the whole point of the rules!" However, sometimes an alert is sufficient enough for an SOC to take note, but there is no need for a full-scale incident. A Playbook can be run on an alert, and automation might be able to take care of the actions that need to take place without having any human intervention. (More on that later in this chapter.) The SOC might decide that an incident is triggered only when a collection or threshold of multiple alerts occur. Again, the aim here is to maximize the efficiency of the SOC and to ensure that SOC analysts spend their time on the right events that haven't been seen before and that require human intervention.

- **Alert Grouping** If you've worked in security operations (or any other kind of monitoring, for that matter), you'll likely have seen when a single event raises multiple incidents, overwhelming the analysts and your monitoring panel. Alert grouping can prevent this in an SOC by telling Azure Sentinel to group identical alerts into the same incident in a specified timeframe and thereby reducing noise.

- **Re-open closed matching incidents** As the name suggests, this setting will allow Azure Sentinel to re-open a closed incident if an alert matching the alert grouping configured on the rule matches.

11. The **Automated Response** tab is where either automation rules or Playbooks can be attached to a rule. We discuss this in more detail later in this chapter.

12. After the validation check, click **Create**. You will return to the main Analytics page. On the **Active Rules** tab, you should now see your newly created rule.

Activate Microsoft security analytics rules

Microsoft security services perform in-depth analysis of the logs they process and generate high-fidelity alerts. The services in this suite are:

- Microsoft Cloud App Security (MCAS)
- Azure Defender
- Azure Defender for IoT
- Microsoft Defender for Endpoint
- Microsoft Defender for Identity
- Microsoft Defender for Office 365
- Azure Active Directory Identity Protection

As we learned earlier in this section, these products' alerts can be connected to Azure Sentinel using built-in data connectors. Instead of performing further analysis on these alerts, as they have already had a significant amount of analysis done in the service, you might want to create an Azure Sentinel incident right away. This can be achieved quickly and simply by using Microsoft security analytics rules.

Let's learn how to activate these rules:

1. Navigate to the Azure portal by opening *https://portal.azure.com*.

2. In the **Search** bar, type **Sentinel**, and under **Services**, click **Azure Sentinel**. The **Azure Sentinel Workspace** page appears.

3. Select the workspace you want to use. The **Azure Sentinel Overview** page appears.

4. Click **Analytics**. The **Analytics** page appears.

5. Click **Create** and select **Microsoft Incident Creation Rule**, as displayed in Figure 3-54.

FIGURE 3-54 Creating a Microsoft security analytics rule

6. The **Microsoft Incident Creation Rule Wizard** appears, as shown in Figure 3-55.

FIGURE 3-55 Configuring a Microsoft security analytics rule in the Analytics Rule Wizard

7. The wizard has several fields that need completing, but you will notice that it has far fewer configurables than a scheduled query rule:

- **Name**   The name of the rule.

- **Description**   The description of the rule.

- **Status**   Set to **Enabled** or **Disabled**.

- **Microsoft Security Service**   This is where you select the type of Microsoft security service alerts that the rule will listen for. You must have one rule per Microsoft security service; they cannot be combined into one.

- **Filter By Severity**   You can choose to only create incidents for alerts of a certain severity. For example, you might only choose to create incidents for high- and medium-severity alerts using the rule.

- **Include/Exclude Specific Alerts**   This is where you can explicitly include or exclude certain alerts. This can be useful if a security service generates a noisy alert that does not require an incident to be raised.

TIP   **INCLUDE/EXCLUDE SPECIFIC ALERTS FEATURE**

Be careful when using the **Include/Exclude Specific Alerts** feature. While this is an effective way to reduce noise coming from your environment, it means that every instance of the alert specified will not raise an incident, so it is important to be sure that by using this feature, you won't inadvertently miss a real incident.

8. The **Automated Response** tab is where either automation rules or Playbooks can be attached to a rule. We will cover this in more detail later in this chapter.

9. After the validation check, click **Create**.

10. You will return to the main **Analytics** page. On the **Active Rules** tab, you should now see your newly created rule.

Configure connector-provided scheduled queries

We do often seem to start a section with a statement like this, but once again, I'll be referring to Azure Sentinel's out-of-the-box capabilities and how Microsoft makes it straightforward to configure relevant analytics rules. Earlier in the chapter, we already looked at the data source connector page and analytics rule templates, and in this section, we'll again be looking at these parts of Azure Sentinel.

If you open a **Data Connector** page, you can see the instructions that tell you how to connect that data source to the workspace. You might have noticed the **Next Steps** tab, which
contains links to workbook templates, query samples, and **Relevant Analytics Templates**
(see Figure 3-56).

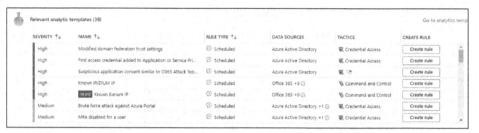

FIGURE 3-56   Relevant Analytic Templates

Here, you can click **Create Rule**, and you will be taken to the **Analytics Rule Wizard—
Create New Rule From Template** page. From there, you can create and customize this rule.
(We walked through using this wizard earlier in this chapter in "Create custom analytics rules
to detect threats.")

> **TIP   IN USE**
>
> When checking relevant analytic rule templates, rules that have already been deployed will
> be marked with **IN USE** (see Figure 3-56).

Although this isn't showcasing functionality that can't be found elsewhere in Azure Sentinel—especially on the Analytics page—it is strongly recommended that you activate all rule
templates that use the data sources you are choosing to connect to your workspace, so having
another method to verify this has been done correctly is never a bad thing!

Configure custom scheduled queries

Earlier in this skill, we discussed how to customize analytics rule templates. Now let's discuss
how to create a custom scheduled query from scratch. If you've been following along using
Azure Sentinel and testing out the steps earlier in this section, you've probably got a good idea
what's coming in this section. We'll be using the Analytics Rule Wizard on the **Analytics** page
to create our brand-new rule. This time—rather than deploying or amending an existing rule
template—we will be completing the entire rule ourselves.

So why do we need these rules? Aren't the rule templates enough to cover most likely
security events? Although the analytics rule templates are written by experts and cover a wide
range of scenarios, it is likely that a large, complex IT environment will need to have custom
analytics rules for detections that are very specific to that environment or that are for data
sources that don't have any rule templates.

Let's step through creating an analytics rule from scratch:

1. Navigate to the Azure portal by opening *https://portal.azure.com*.

2. In the **Search** bar, type **Sentinel**, and under **Services**, click **Azure Sentinel**. The **Azure Sentinel Workspace** page appears.

3. Select the workspace you want to use. The **Azure Sentinel Overview** page appears.

4. Click **Analytics**. The **Analytics** page appears.

5. Click **Create** > **Scheduled Query Rule**. The **Analytics Rule Wizard—Create** page **New Rule** page appears, as shown in Figure 3-57.

FIGURE 3-57 A blank analytics rule wizard to create a new analytics rule

6. The wizard is the same as the Analytics Rule Wizard used for templates, except this time, it is completely blank for you to fill in as you please.

7. We covered the different fields and how to complete them in the wizard in the "Create custom analytics rules to detect threats" section, earlier in this chapter.

8. After the validation check, click **Create**.

9. You will return to the main **Analytics** page. On the **Active Rules** tab, you should now see your newly created rule.

Define incident creation logic

For the final part of this section, we're going to address how to create incident creation logic, which is something we've skipped over to leave for the grand finale of this section. It's important to remember that although the exam outline (and hence, the title of this section) calls for learning how to define incident creation logic, what we're going to discuss in this section is the use of the KQL query language, which is used to define queries, events, alerts, and incidents.

Kusto Query Language (KQL)

Kusto Query Language (KQL) is a query language used in several Microsoft products, so if you're learning about Microsoft security services, then it's worthwhile investing some time to become familiar with the language. A not-so-well-known fact is that Kusto Query Language is named after Jacques Cousteau, the famous underwater explorer. KQL is a high-level language (meaning that it is closer to human language), but it has the flexibility and power to perform complex queries. Although not identical, if you've spent time using SQL, then learning KQL should be a straightforward task.

KQL is a complex language with many operators, so in this section, we will cover the basics of KQL and some of the operators commonly used to form incident creation logic.

EXAM TIP

For the SC-200 exam, make sure that you are comfortable reading KQL queries that typically might be found in an Azure Sentinel analytics rule. Aside from this study guide, study the rule templates in Azure Sentinel as examples of real-life incident/alert creation logic, and make sure you understand the KQL in them.

Let's start with the basics. In KQL, you must define the table that you are searching in. In this example, I'm searching the OfficeActivity table (shown in Table 3-1) for Exchange workloads. The where operator is used to filter the table to a subset of rows. In this case, that means any rows that have Exchange in the OfficeWorkload column.

```
OfficeActivity
| where OfficeWorkload == "Exchange"
```

> **NOTE KQL SPACING**
>
> We have spaced-out the KQL to make it easier to read, but you can put KQL on one line with correct spacing and syntax.

A very commonly used operator (and one of my personal favorites) is take. This operator returns the number of rows you specify:

```
OfficeActivity
| take 10
```

In this case, the query would return 10 rows from the OfficeActivity table. This operator is especially useful for testing queries when you're not sure how many results it might bring back. Also, it's helpful for looking at the structure and a few examples of rows from the specified table.

> **NOTE GUARANTEEING A SORT ORDER**
>
> When only the take operator is used by itself, the rows that are returned aren't guaranteed to be the same each time the query is run. You can only guarantee the sort by using the take operator in conjunction with a sort by operator, which is covered next.

Sort is a powerful operator that does exactly as the name suggests: It sorts rows of the table by one or more specified columns in ascending or descending order:

```
OfficeActivity
| sort by OfficeWorkload, UserId asc
```

In this example, we're sorting the OfficeActivity table (see Table 3-1) in ascending order by the OfficeWorkload and UserId columns. A close relative of this operator is top, which will return the top values after the sort (for example, the top 10 or top 100). This can be very useful for making queries more efficient if you don't require the entire contents of the table to be sorted, which is often the case in security queries. Often, searches will be looking for things such as the top number of failed logins in an environment and the users associated with them.

TABLE 3-1 OfficeActivity table

KQL Operator	Description	Syntax	Example query
Where	Filters on a specific predicate	T | where Predicate	OfficeActivity | where OfficeWorkload == "Exchange"
Take	Returns the specified number of records	T | take NumberOfRows	OfficeActivity | take 10
Sort	Sorts rows of the table by one or more specified columns in ascending or descending order	T | sort by expression1 [asc|desc], expression2 [asc|desc], ...	OfficeActivity | sort by OfficeWorkload, UserId asc
Top	Returns the first N rows of the dataset when the dataset is sorted using a column or expression	T | top numberOfRows by expression [asc|desc] [nulls first|last]	OfficeActivity | top 10 by OfficeWorkload asc
Count	Counts the number of records in the specified table	T | count	OfficeActivity | count
Summarize	Groups the rows according to the by group columns, and calculates aggregations over each group	T | summarize Aggregation [by Group Expression] Aggregation functions: count(), sum(), avg(), min(), max()	OfficeActivity | where OfficeWorkload == "Exchange" | summarize count(UserId)
Extend	Creates additional, calculated columns and adds them into the table	T | extend [ColumnName]	–
Project	Selects the columns to include in the query result in the order specified	T | extend [ColumnName]	OfficeActivity | where OfficeWorkload == "Exchange" | project Operation, UserType, UserId
Let	Creates a variable that can be referenced in queries	let Name = ScalarExpression | TabularExpression	let threshold = 10

> **NOTE QUERIES DON'T CHANGE UNDERLYING DATA**
>
> All extra columns and tables created when queries run are ephemeral and exist only for the duration of the query. They are not stored in the underlying workspace. Remember that Log Analytics is immutable and thus, queries cannot change the underlying data.

Let's break down one of the query templates to better understand how KQL works in practice. In Figure 3-58, the **Failed AWS Console Logons But Success Logon To AzureAD** rule is shown.

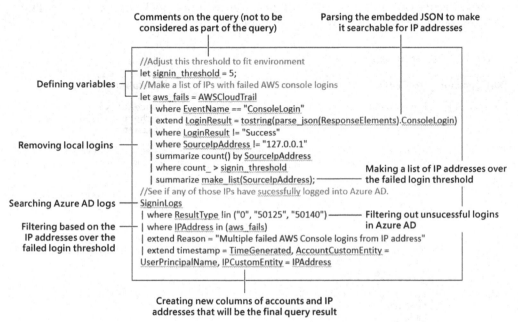

FIGURE 3-58 Breaking down the Failed AWS Console Logons But Success Logon To AzureAD analytics rule

The KQL in the rule is shown in Listing 3-1.

Listing 3-1 Failed AWS Console Logons But Success Login to AzureAD

```
//Adjust this threshold to fit environment
let signin_threshold = 5;
//Make a list of IPs with failed AWS console logins
let aws_fails = AWSCloudTrail
| where EventName == "ConsoleLogin"
| extend LoginResult = tostring(parse_json(ResponseElements).ConsoleLogin)
| where LoginResult != "Success"
| where SourceIpAddress != "127:0:0:1"
| summarize count() by SourceIpAddress
| where count_ > signin_threshold
| summarize make_list(SourceIpAddress);
```

```
//See if any of those IPs have sucessfully logged into Azure AD.
SigninLogs
| where ResultType !in ("0", "50125", "50140")
| where IPAddress in (aws_fails)
| extend Reason = "Multiple failed AWS Console logins from IP address"
| extend timestamp = TimeGenerated, AccountCustomEntity = UserPrincipalName,
IPCustomEntity = IPAddress
```

Let's break this rule down step-by-step:

1. The `signin` threshold variable is declared as 5 and is named `signin_threshold`.

2. A second variable is declared as `aws_fails`, but this variable is a list of IP addresses, so there are more lines of KQL to filter out these IP addresses.

3. Note that comments can be added to the query and prepended with //, and they will be ignored by the query parser.

4. To find a list of IP addresses from AWS Cloudtrail, the query first searches for `ConsoleLogin` events.

5. A new column is created using the `extend` operator called `LoginResult`. As part of the creation of this column, the query is using the `parse_json` operator is used to parse the embedded JSON in the `ResponseElements` column, so the query can search for records that do not contain `Success`.

6. Local logins are removed (127.0.0.1).

7. The number of unsuccessful logins are summarized by the `SourceIpAddress` column.

8. A list is created of any IP addresses that have been counted by the query as having more than the threshold (5) unsuccessful login attempts.

9. This list of IP addresses is now our `aws_fails` variable.

10. Moving to the second part of the query, it searches Azure AD logs to see if there have been any successful logins to Azure from the list of IP addresses we made in the first part of the query.

11. Finally, any matching results will be presented in a user-friendly manner and mapped to entities using the `extend` operator and custom entities.

> **TIP UNCODER.IO**
>
> If you're trying to translate rules from another SIEM to KQL, uncoder.io is a great free tool to use (see *https://uncoder.io/*). It provides rule "translations" from other SIEM languages and is a great way to pick up KQL if you have previously worked on other SIEMs.

Skill 3-4: Configure Security Orchestration, Automation, and Response (SOAR) in Azure Sentinel

Security orchestration, automation, and response (SOAR) is a powerful tool that can help streamline security operations and is sometimes overlooked in the content of Azure Sentinel. People forget that Azure Sentinel is both a SIEM and a SOAR product. In the past, SIEM and SOAR products were separate, had to be purchased separately, and might have not come from the same vendor. In this section, we'll learn about how to work with the SOAR capabilities in Azure Sentinel.

Create Azure Sentinel Playbooks

If you've used other Azure products, you might already be familiar with Azure Logic Apps, which is the main "engine" that drives automation in Azure Sentinel. Azure Logic Apps is a GUI-based tool that can create complicated automation Playbooks with little-to-no programming and coding knowledge required. This is great for SOC analysts and SOC engineers who might have little previous knowledge of how to make automation scripts. If you've used Microsoft Flow before, you'll also have a good idea of what to expect when it comes to creating automation in Azure Sentinel.

Before we go any further, let's have a terminology check to clarify our understanding:

- **Azure Logic Apps**   This is the name of the Azure service that provides automation throughout the Azure cloud, including for Azure Sentinel. Because Azure Logic Apps is a separate service to Azure Sentinel, it requires separate permissions for a user to create and run Playbooks (which are discussed earlier in the chapter).
- **Playbook**   A Playbook is a collection of automated actions in a workflow.
- **Logic App connector**   This is not the same as an Azure Sentinel data connector. Instead, a Logic App Connector is a predefined trigger or action that can be added into a Playbook. At the time this book was written, there were more than 300 Logic App connectors.

> *MORE INFO*   **LOGIC APP CONNECTOR LIST**
>
> You can look at the full current list of Logic App connectors here: *https://docs.microsoft.com/en-us/connectors/connector-reference/connector-reference-logicapps-connectors*.

There are three main scenarios for which automation is used in Azure Sentinel:

- **Alerting**   This is the most used type of automation and the most straightforward to configure. When an incident or alert is triggered, Playbooks can be configured to send emails, Teams messages, and the like to alert the on-call team that an incident has been raised.
- **Remediation**   This is where automation takes remedial action in the IT environment to contain or even stop a security incident. Examples here could be isolating a virtual ma-

chine that has an Azure Defender alert raised against it, blocking the account of a user in Azure AD when their activity indicates the account has been compromised, or taking a malicious IP address from an incident in Azure Sentinel and writing a block rule back to the firewall to stop traffic from that IP address.

TIP **ALERTING AND REMEDIATION**

Although they can be configured independently of each other, alerting and remediation can—and usually should be—contained in one Playbook.

- **Enrichment** This is where supplementary data is used to "enrich" raw logs and results. This can be done as an alert, when an incident is triggered, or during an investigation. For example, after an incident has been raised, a SOC analyst could run an enrichment Playbook to check if the IP address entities in the incident match third-party threat intel feeds (for example, VirusTotal).

Let's look at how to create a simple email alert Playbook in Azure Sentinel:

1. Navigate to the Azure portal by opening *https://portal.azure.com*.

2. In the **Search** bar, type **Sentinel**, and under **Services**, click **Azure Sentinel**. The **Azure Sentinel Workspace** page appears.

3. Select the workspace you want to use. The **Azure Sentinel | Overview** page appears.

4. Click **Automation**. The **Automation** page appears, as shown in Figure 3-59.

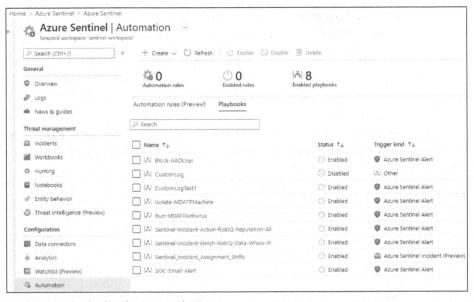

FIGURE 3-59 Reviewing the Automation page

---

5. Click **Create** > **Add New Playbook**. The **Create A Logic App** page appears, as shown in Figure 3-60.

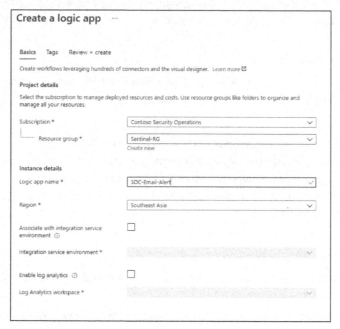

FIGURE 3-60 Completing the details of a Logic App

6. Fill out the **Subscription**, **Resource Group**, **Region**, and **Name** of the Playbook and click **Review + Create**, as shown previously in Figure 3-60.

7. When your template has validated, click **Create**.

8. Open the blank Playbook you have created; you will be given the option to choose from various predefined templates. This time, we will select **Blank Logic App**. The Logic Apps Designer page appears.

9. We can now search for a trigger to kick-off the Playbook in the **Logic App Connector** gallery. In Figure 3-61, you can see that we are searching for an Azure Sentinel trigger.

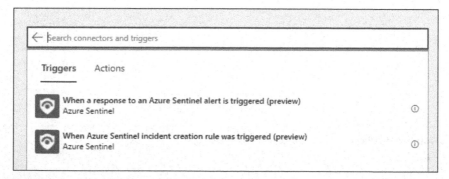

FIGURE 3-61 Searching for an Azure Sentinel trigger in the Logic App Connector gallery

10. Select the **When A Response To An Azure Sentinel Alert Is Triggered** trigger.

11. Sign in to create a connection to your Azure Sentinel workspace from the Playbook, as shown in Figure 3-62. You can also use a service principal or managed identity if you would prefer.

FIGURE 3-62   Signing in to Azure Sentinel from the Logic App designer

12. For the next step in the Playbook, I'm going to select the **Outlook.com** connector and under **Actions**, I will choose **Send An Email (V2)**. This is where we will configure the email to be sent when an alert is raised in Azure Sentinel (see Figure 3-63).

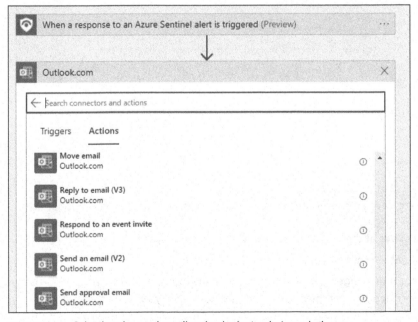

FIGURE 3-63   Selecting the send email action in the Logic Apps designer

Sign in to the Outlook account; the connector will allow you to configure the email that will be sent when the Playbook is triggered. Add the address(es) to which you want the email to be sent, the title of the email, and the body of the email. There are other optional parameters that you can choose to configure at this point. It is possible to add dynamic content from the alert, such as the name of the alert, the severity, a description, and so on that will be populated dynamically from the alert when the Playbook is triggered. This helps give SOC analysts a better idea of what is happening in the initial notification, as shown in Figure 3-64.

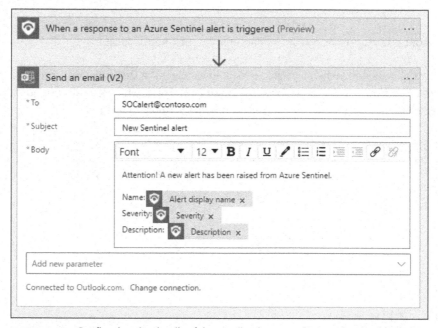

FIGURE 3-64 Configuring the details of the email to be sent when an alert is triggered

13. Click **Save** at the top-left of the Logic App Designer page.

14. Navigate to the **Overview** page of the Playbook.

15. Select **Run Trigger** > **Run** to test-run your Playbook, as shown in Figure 3-65. Look to the bottom-right of the page to see whether the Playbook ran successfully.

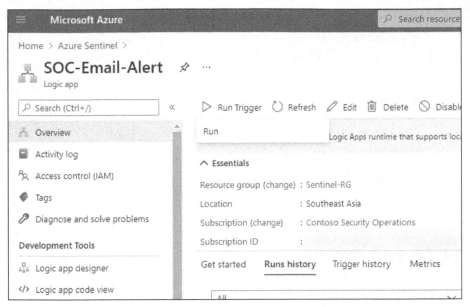

FIGURE 3-65 Manually running a Playbook to test it

Arguably, the most attractive aspect of a SOAR capability is the automation aspect. Rather than relying on a human resource to take actions, automation can do things quicker and more reliably. We already touched on this during the analytics rule section of this chapter, but let's dive into how to configure analytics rules and incidents to trigger Playbooks.

Why do we want to attach Playbooks to an analytics rule? Quite simply, this is the quickest and easiest way to alert and/or respond to a threat that Azure Sentinel detects. By attaching a Playbook to an analytics rule, when that rule is triggered, the Playbook will automatically run and take the specified actions. Even before an SOC analyst goes to look at the incident or alert, the Playbook could have taken remedial action. Some SOCs who have a mature automation capability can use automation to entirely resolve incidents without human intervention. Microsoft's own SOC tries to do this where possible. Of course, there will be incidents or attacks that have never been seen before and cannot be automated away, but this means that SOC analysts can be more efficient in the time they spend on investigations rather than repetitive tasks.

In this section, we will look at how you can customize analytics rules to optimize them. Let's go back to the **Analytics** page and the analytics rule templates:

1. Navigate to the Azure portal by opening *https://portal.azure.com*.

2. In the **Search** bar, type **Sentinel**, and under **Services**, click **Azure Sentinel**. The **Azure Sentinel Workspace** page appears.

3. Select the workspace you want to use. The **Azure Sentinel | Overview** page appears.

4. Click **Analytics**. The **Analytics** page appears.

5. Select the rule you want to attach a Playbook to and click **Edit** at the bottom of the rule template summary .

6. You will be taken to the **Analytics Rule Wizard**. Select the **Automated Response** tab.

7. Under **Alert Automation**, you can select Playbooks that are configured to run when the rule is triggered (see Figure 3-66).

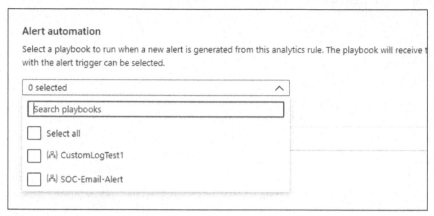

FIGURE 3-66 Attaching a Playbook to an analytics rule

8. On the **Review And Create** tab, click **Save** after the validation check.

> **NOTE   ONLY ENABLED PLAYBOOKS APPEAR**
>
> Only Playbooks that are enabled will show in the drop-down menu to be attached to an analytics rule.

Use Playbooks to remediate threats

As we discussed earlier in this section, one of the most powerful aspects of a SOAR capability is the ability to remediate threats automatically. Even with the best and smartest SOC analysts in the world, they will never be able to respond as quickly or efficiently to an incident as automation can, which means automation can reduce the potential impact of an incident. Using Playbooks to remediate threats also frees up SOC analysts' time to concentrate on incidents that haven't been seen before, cannot be remediated automatically, and therefore need human intervention.

Although this is not an exhaustive list, here are some examples of the kind of security incident remediation that are possible using Azure Logic Apps:

- Blocking a user account in Azure AD to prevent an account that might have been compromised from being able to access resources in the IT environment
- Writing a rule to a firewall to block an IP address from which malicious traffic is being sent
- Isolating a virtual machine in Azure that might have been compromised to prevent further lateral movement

- Taking a snapshot of an Azure virtual machine for evidence gathering purposes when the machine exhibits suspicious activity

- Blocking a malicious IP address on an on-premises Exchange server to prevent further access to the server from that specific address if suspicious traffic and/or activity has been seen originating from there

It can be challenging to decide what remediation action might be appropriate—especially if automated remediation is something that hasn't been part of your security operations previously—so it's important to take a step back and work out your use cases. Consider your most-raised security incidents and any repetitive tasks that SOC analysts undertake to resolve those incidents. Could these be automated? Are there some actions that you'd always like to take no matter what the incident is? What automation an organization chooses to take can vary widely. For example, a highly risk averse organization might choose to immediately block any Azure AD user accounts that exhibit suspicious activity, but this will put an additional burden on the service desk, which will have to re-enable accounts, posibly reducing productivity. There is also the risk of an account being blocked as a false positive because no SIEM can get things right 100 percent of the time.

EXAM TIP

If you're stuck for remediation Playbook ideas, check out the Azure Sentinel GitHub repo for Playbooks. It has many free examples of Playbooks that have been made by the community and are templatized so you can easily deploy them in several clicks. Before your SC-200 exam, make sure you have deployed a few of these Playbook templates to your own demo environment and that are familiar with how they can be constructed. See *https://github.com/Azure/Azure-Sentinel/tree/master/playbooks*.

Use Playbooks to manage incidents

In this chapter, it's already been mentioned several times that even the best and most efficient SOC analysts don't always have enough time to fully investigate every alert and incident that comes into an SOC. SOC analysts commonly undertake repetitive, time-consuming tasks to close incidents, change statuses, assign out incidents to on-shift analysts, and so on.

Aside from remediation, Azure Sentinel's SOAR capabilities can help to reduce the administrative overhead of dealing with incidents. In this section, we'll detail some examples—not an exhaustive list—of how overhead on incident management can be reduced using automation:

- **Automatically assigning incidents to on-shift analysts**   Using the shifts feature in Teams, a Playbook can be used to decide which analyst is on-shift and available and automatically assign that ticket to that analyst. The Playbook can also send a notification to that analyst to let them know an incident has been assigned to them using a messaging system, email, and the like.

- **Automatically assigning incidents to an entity owner** Similar to the previous example, a Playbook can be used to look up the owner of an entity (for example, a host) that is involved in an incident and assign the incident for them to investigate. As in the previous example, the Playbook can also send a notification to the asset owner to let them know an incident has been assigned to them using a messaging system, email, and so on.

- **Creating a ticket in a third-party ticketing system** Many organizations utilize SaaS ticketing systems to manage their IT operations and can draw statistics and reporting from that system about the number of incidents, time to resolve, and so on. Although the incident system in Azure Sentinel is robust, it might make more sense for incidents to be managed in a third-party system (such as ServiceNow) to align with the wider organization's IT operations and reporting. A Playbook can be used to create a ticket in a third-party system when an incident is triggered and populate all the details of the incident in that third-party system. This saves SOC analysts' time and effort copying and pasting the details across from one system to another.

- **Syncing third-party incident system updates with Azure Sentinel incidents** Related to the previous example, if a third-party system is being used to track and manage incidents, a Playbook can be used to sync the information between Azure Sentinel and the third-party ticketing system, so there is no time-consuming copying and pasting between two systems (Copying and pasting between systems is not a good use of SOC analyst time!)

- **Enrich incident details from third-party systems** When an incident is raised, a Playbook can be used to enrich the details of the entities involved in an incident and post a comment to give the analyst additional context. This saves the SOC analyst time and effort to log in to another portal or system to look up these details manually. Typical examples of enrichment include looking up the asset owner of a host or checking if an IP address matches any threat intelligence feeds (such as VirusTotal).

- **Add a user/host/IP address to a Watchlist** A Playbook can take entities from an incident and add them into a watchlist so that they can be flagged in other analytics rules that refer to the watchlist. This saves an SOC analyst from having to do this manually.

Use Playbooks across Microsoft Defender solutions

If you're using other Microsoft Defender solutions, using Playbooks is an ideal way to create a conjoined response to security events and incidents across your Microsoft product suite. As one would expect, Azure Logic Apps provides many ways to do this with Logic App connectors. As a reminder, when we're discussing Microsoft Defender solutions, we're talking about:

- Azure Defender
- Azure Defender for IoT
- Microsoft Defender for Endpoint
- Microsoft Defender for Identity
- Microsoft Defender for Office 365

As you can see in Figure 3-67, when you search for **defender** in the Logic Apps designer, there are already many built-in triggers and actions that you can select from.

FIGURE 3-67 Searching for Microsoft Defender triggers and actions

Let's look through an example to demonstrate how simple this can be. Rather than starting from scratch, as we have done earlier in this section, I'm going to use a template from the Azure Sentinel GitHub repo:

1. Navigate to the **Azure Sentinel GitHub repo** page by opening *https://github.com/ Azure/Azure-Sentinel.*

2. Click **playbooks** to be taken to the Playbooks section of the repo.

3. Select the Playbook that you want to deploy. For this example, I'll be selecting **Isolate- MDATPMachine**, as seen in Figure 3-68.

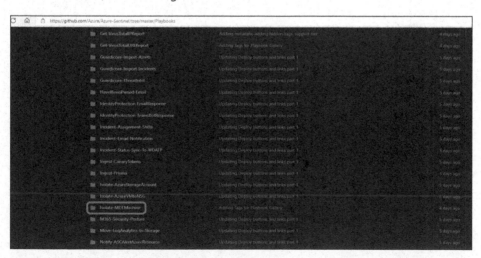

FIGURE 3-68 Selecting a Playbook template to deploy in the Azure Sentinel GitHub repo

4. Click **Deploy To Azure**, and you will be taken to the Azure portal and the **Custom Deployment Template**.

> **NOTE** **ARM TEMPLATES**
>
> Playbook templates from the Azure Sentinel GitHub repo are all Azure Resource Manager (ARM) templates. You can read more about ARM templates at *https://docs. microsoft.com/en-us/azure/azure-resource-manager/templates/*.

5. As shown in Figure 3-69, you need to complete the parameters of the Playbook template so that it can be deployed. The exact parameters each template will ask for will depend on the Playbook contents, but you will always be asked for **Subscription**, **Resource Group**, **Region**, and **Playbook Name**.

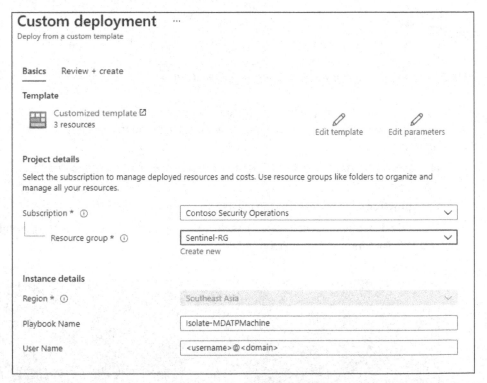

FIGURE 3-69 Entering parameters into a Playbook template for deployment

6. Let the validation check complete and then click **Create**.

7. Wait for your template to deploy successfully. Once complete, you will see the message shown in Figure 3-70.

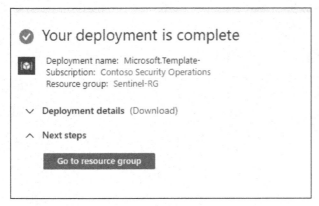

FIGURE 3-70 A completed template deployment

8. Navigate to Azure Sentinel in the Azure portal and open the **Automation** page. You should find that your newly deployed Playbook should now be listed under **playbooks**.

> **NOTE AUTHORIZING THE CONNECTION**
>
> Playbook templates will deploy connections, but sometimes you will need to authorize the connection after deployment before the connection is made. This is expected behavior and does not mean the Playbook template is broken.

9. Open the Playbook and open the Logic App Designer.

10. Expand the steps of the Playbook, and you will see the triggers and actions have already been prepopulated and configured by the ARM template that we deployed, as shown in Figure 3-71.

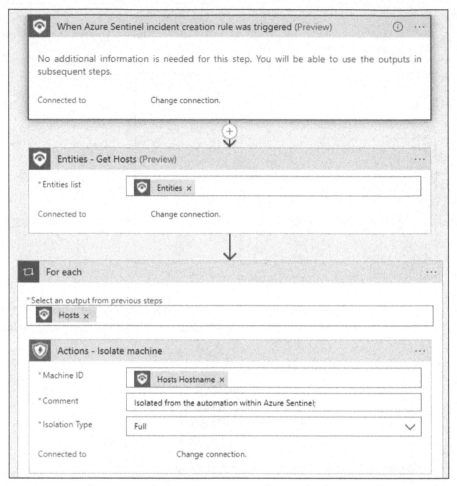

FIGURE 3-71 Checking a template deployment in Logic Apps designer

11. This Playbook is ready to go and can now be attached to an analytics rule, as we discussed earlier in this section.

Let's walk through what this Playbook is doing:

1. When an incident creation rule is triggered, the Playbook will run.

2. Details about the host entities from the Azure Sentinel incident that has been raised are sent to Microsoft Defender for Endpoint.

3. Subsequently, those machines are isolated.

Far quicker than any human, Azure Sentinel and Microsoft Defender for Endpoint have worked together to isolate the hosts that are part of a security incident to reduce the "blast radius" or impact of an incident and—if these machines have been breached by an attacker— are stopping the attackers from being able to cause any more damage or from moving laterally in your IT environment.

Skill 3-5: Manage Azure Sentinel incidents

If you've only seen one part of Azure Sentinel before you started studying for the SC-200 exam, the incident part is likely to have been it. Incidents are the first thing that comes to mind for most people when they think of what a SIEM does, and this is entirely understandable because incidents are where the action takes place. This is where an SOC analyst will investigate what is happening or what has happened in the IT environment to trigger an incident, verify whether the incident is a false-positive, understand the blast radius of the incident, and so on. The core function of an SOC (and the SOC analysts who work in that department) is to deal with security incidents.

This section of the chapter covers the skills necessary to investigate single- and multi-workspace incidents, triage and respond to Azure Sentinel incidents, and use User and Entity Behavior Analytics (UEBA) to detect threats according to the SC-200 exam outline.

Investigate incidents in Azure Sentinel

Investigating incidents is critical for an SOC analyst to understand the severity and scope of a potential security issue. The investigation graph in Azure Sentinel allows an SOC analyst to quickly and efficiently investigate and query alerts and entities in an incident, and Azure Sentinel assists by suggesting additional context-aware queries to be run.

First, let's look at the **Incidents** page in Azure Sentinel that is shown in Figure 3-72.

FIGURE 3-72 Navigating the Incidents page in Azure Sentinel

The Incidents page that lists all the open incidents in Azure Sentinel is self-explanatory and contains details of each open incident such as the title, severity, created time, and the owner of the incident. An incident is a collection of alerts.

> **NOTE SECURITYINCIDENTS TABLE**
>
> The SecurityIncidents table contains details of all incidents that have occurred in your Azure Sentinel workspace—open or closed—and is commonly used for reporting SOC performance statistics, such as trends in the number of incidents raised over time, time to triage, and so on. Azure Sentinel only stores the details of incidents for as long as your workspace retention is set to, so remember to align your SecurityIncidents table retention period with your SOC reporting needs.

So we've selected our incident that we want to investigate; let's dig into how we do this:

1. Navigate to the Azure portal by opening *https://portal.azure.com*.

2. In the **Search** bar, type **Sentinel**, and under **Services**, click **Azure Sentinel**. The **Azure Sentinel Workspace** page appears.

3. Select the workspace you want to use. **The Azure Sentinel | Overview** page appears.

4. Click **Incidents**. The **Incidents** overview page appears.

5. Select the incident you want to investigate and click **View Full Details**. The **Incident** page appears.

6. Click **Investigate**. You will be taken to the investigation graph. What you see on this page depends on the incident itself, but the structure of the interface is shown in Figure 3-73.

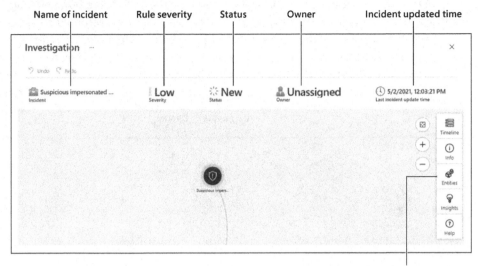

FIGURE 3-73 The incident investigation graph in Azure Sentinel

7. Figure 3-74 shows that alerts contained in the incident are denoted by a large circle containing an exclamation point. If you click the circle, a summary of the alert is shown on the left side of the investigation graph.

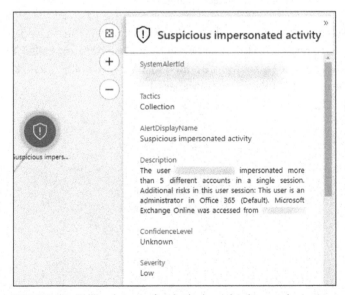

FIGURE 3-74 Drilling into an alert in the investigation graph

8. Figure 3-75 shows the entities that are related to the alert in question. They are linked in the investigation graph with lines. If you hover over an entity, Azure Sentinel will suggest further context-aware further queries that an SOC analyst might want to run to understand and investigate the incident further. In Figure 3-75, Azure Sentinel is suggesting that a number of different queries could be run against the account in question; let's look at the **Hosts The Account Failed To Log In To The Most** query. If a user account has been compromised, understanding which hosts it has tried and failed to log in to can help an SOC analyst understand what other devices might be compromised and what kind of resources an attacker is looking to access in an organization's environment.

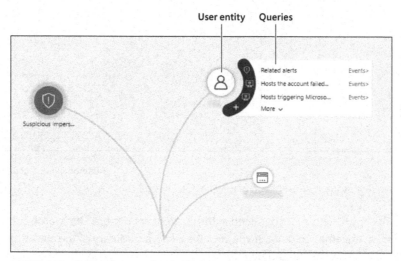

FIGURE 3-75   Drilling into an alert in the investigation graph

9. Clicking the suggested query will display the results of that query in the investigation graph, too. Figure 3-76 shows that after running the **Hosts The Account Failed To Log In To The Most** query, additional entities are added to the investigation graph, and their relationship to the rest of the incident is displayed.

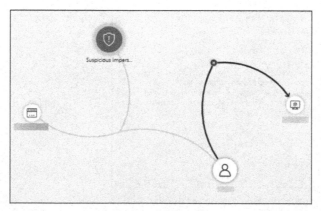

FIGURE 3-76   Additional host entities added to the investigation graph

10. These additional entities can also be queried further to dig even deeper into what is happening in an incident. This can help an SOC analyst get a full picture of what is happening. Theoretically, this querying of entities could go on ad infinitum, but an SOC analyst usually will need to dig only a few "layers" deep to perform an effective investigation.

11. Let's review the additional investigation panels that can also be used for investigation:

- **Timeline** The Timeline panel will order all alerts in date and time order so that an SOC analyst can understand the order in which events in the incident happened (see Figure 3-77).

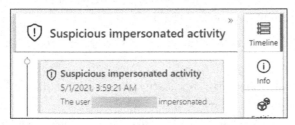

FIGURE 3-77 The timeline panel in the investigation graph

- **Info** The Info panel provides more in-depth information about the selected alert or entity.

- **Entities** The Entities panel provides a summary of the entities being displayed in the investigation.

- **Insights** The Insights panel (see Figure 3-78) shows other insights about an entity that Azure Sentinel's built-in UEBA engine thinks is relevant and useful for an SOC analyst to know.

FIGURE 3-78 The insights panel in the investigation graph

Triage incidents in Azure Sentinel

Most of us are familiar with the concept of triage from a medical perspective, but how does that work in security operations? This is the dictionary definition of triage:

"The process of examining problems in order to decide which ones are the most serious and must be dealt with first."

Therefore, it's easy to see why triaging incidents is a critical activity for an SOC to decide how to prioritize which incidents to work on first.

How can we triage incidents in Azure Sentinel? There are several ways that this can be done, and a real-life SOC analyst would use a combination of these methods to maximize their triage effectiveness. It's important to remember that triage won't look the same for every organization: What one organization considers to be a high-severity incident might be another's medium- or low-severity incident. SOC managers and analysts must work closely with their business stakeholders and technology risk professionals to align severity ratings with their security posture and risk tolerance.

When an incident is raised in Azure Sentinel, it can be triaged in several areas. Following is a chronological look at the lifecycle of an incident:

- **In an analytics rule**   As discussed earlier in this chapter, when you configure an analytics rule, you must set the initial severity. This initial severity rating will help an SOC analyst decide how to triage the incident.

- **In a watchlist**   If entities in the incident match a watchlist (for example, VIP users), an analytics rule can be configured to make the incident higher or lower severity.

- **How many alerts are part of the incident**   As shown earlier in this chapter, it's possible to configure an analytics rule to collect alerts in a set time period to be collected into one incident. An incident that involves many alerts is likely to be set at a higher priority than one with fewer alerts.

- **Using TI matching**   Threat intelligence can be used to check if there are IOC (indicators of compromise) matches with any TI feeds that Azure Sentinel is ingesting. For example, if an IP address is raised in an incident, an analyst could run a Playbook to determine if this was a known-malicious IP and reference a third-party service such as Virus Total. If the IP was found to be a known-malicious IP, then the severity could be increased, and it could be prioritized.

- **Using enrichment from third-party sources** Similar to the previous point, enrichment doesn't just have to be about TI. Enrichment could be an inventory management system that stores the criticality of an asset. This means an incident raised against a single user desktop might only be classified as being a low-priority incident. However, an incident raised against an e-commerce company's web servers could be critical to investigate and resolve, and thus, it might be considered to be a high-priority incident. Once again, this could be automated in either a Playbook that is run as the incident is triggered, or it could be a manually run Playbook during the course of an investigation.

Respond to incidents in Azure Sentinel

Now we've investigated and triaged an incident, we need to respond to resolve it. Azure Sentinel makes this easy with automation. In this section, we will look at how you can run Playbooks to resolve incidents, so we're not talking about how we can trigger automation to happen when an incident is raised; instead, we're talking about the next step.

Let's work through an example incident:

1. Navigate to the Azure portal by opening *https://portal.azure.com*.

2. In the **Search** bar, type **Sentinel**, and under **Services**, click **Azure Sentinel**. The **Azure Sentinel Workspace** page appears.

3. Select the workspace you want to use. The **Azure Sentinel | Overview** page appears.

4. Click **Incidents**, which opens the **Incidents** overview page.

5. Select the incident you want to respond to and click **View Full Details**.

6. A list of all alerts that are part of an incident are shown on the **Timeline** tab (see Figure 3-79).

FIGURE 3-79 Viewing alerts on the Timeline tab

7. Click **View Playbooks**, and you will be taken to the **Alert Playbooks** page where all Playbooks that have been configured in the workspace will be listed. By clicking **Run**, you can trigger one or more Playbooks to run in the context of the selected alert (see Figure 3-80).

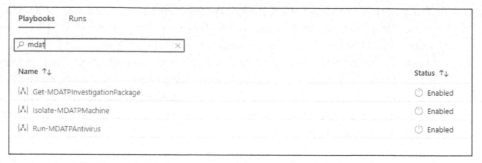

FIGURE 3-80   Selecting a Playbook to run against an alert in an incident

8. The SOC analyst who has been assigned the incident can then update the case notes as appropriate on the **Comments** tab of the incident's page (see Figure 3-81).

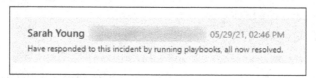

Sarah Young   05/29/21, 02:46 PM
Have responded to this incident by running playbooks, all now resolved.

FIGURE 3-81   Posting comments on the incident tab

EXAM TIP

Remember, for your SC-200 exam, everything rolls up to Azure Sentinel, so this is where you should always be driving incident investigations toward triage and response from Azure Sentinel. If necessary, you might need to drill down into individual Microsoft security service portals.

Investigate multi-workspace incidents

When preparing for the SC-200 exam, it's important to remember that there are two types of multi-workspace scenarios that you might be asked about in relation to Azure Sentinel:

- **Cross-tenant scenario**   Where multiple Azure tenancies each have Azure Sentinel workspaces that need to be centrally managed
- **Cross-workspace scenario**   Where there are multiple workspaces in one Azure tenancy that need to be centrally managed

At the beginning of this chapter, we discussed the considerations when designing Azure Sentinel workspaces and why some organizations might require more than one workspace in their deployment. Some customers might also choose to outsource the running of their SOC to a Managed Security Service Provider (MSSP) that will handle security operations on their behalf.

Aside from Azure Lighthouse, there are several Log Analytics and Azure Sentinel features that allow you to investigate incidents across workspaces in the same Azure tenant.

- **Cross-workspace analytics rules** Analytics rules can be configured to search other workspaces when they are correlating logs. To enable this capability, we have to use the workspace and union KQL operators. Using the queries we used in the "Define incident creation logic"section earlier in this chapter, let's see how we would need to update them to make them cross-workspace. This is the original query:

```
OfficeActivity
| where OfficeWorkload == "Exchange"
```

To make convert this to a cross-workspace query, it would become:

```
union
workspace('<workspaceA>'.OfficeActivity
| union workspace('<workspaceB>').OfficeActivity
| where OfficeWorkload == "Exchange"
```

- **Cross-workspace hunting queries** Like cross-workspace analytics rules, the workspace and union KQL operators can be used in hunting queries to proactively detect threats and anomalies across multiple workspaces in an environment.
- **Cross-workspace workbooks** The **workspace and union KQL operators** can also be used to display consolidated statistics and visualisations from different workspaces. This is particularly useful for centralized reporting for an SOC that uses more than one workspace.

NOTE **CROSS-WORKSPACE ANALYTICS RULES**

There are a few things to be mindful of when using cross-workspace analytics rules. All the workspaces involved in the query must have Azure Sentinel installed. (You can't do it with just a Log Analytics workspace.) You can search a maximum of 20 workspaces in one rule. The incidents and alerts raised by the cross-workspace analytics rule will only appear in the originating workspace from which the rule is being run.

Identify advanced threats with user and entity behavior analytics (UEBA)

Traditionally, user and entity behavior analytics (UEBA) was not incorporated into a SIEM solution. Instead, you would have to buy a third-party product or add-on to be able to get these insights. Having the power of UEBA built into Azure Sentinel—and have it as part of the same interface—allows SOC analysts to focus on a particular entity as part of their investigation. Also, Azure Sentinel's UEBA can provide insights about an entity's anomalous activities and behaviors. These insights are based on that entity's previous behavior, and those behaviors are with the behavior of its peers (if a user) or similar endpoints (if a host). Figure 3-82 takes a look at the architecture of the UEBA feature.

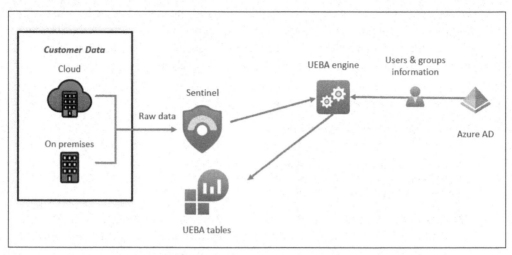

FIGURE 3-82   UEBA architecture overview

As you can see in Figure 3-82, Azure Sentinel's UEBA engine takes in raw data sources—from both the cloud and on-premises—that has already been ingested into the workspace, and it then takes users and groups information from Azure AD, enriches it all, and then populates the dedicated UEBA tables in Log Analytics. You will find these UEBA tables in your workspace (listed under **Azure Sentinel UEBA**) after you have enabled this feature.

By default, UEBA is not enabled in Azure Sentinel, so let's first look at how to enable it:

1.   Navigate to the Azure portal by opening *https://portal.azure.com*.

2.   In the **Search** bar, type **Sentinel**, and under **Services**, click **Azure Sentinel**. The **Azure Sentinel Workspace** page appears.

3.   Select the workspace you want to use. The **Azure Sentinel | Overview** page appears.

4.   Click **Entity Behavior**. The **Entity Behavior** page appears, as shown in Figure 3-83.

5.   Click **Configure UEBA**.

FIGURE 3-83 The Entity Behavior page in Azure Sentinel

6. You will be taken to the **Entity Behavior Analytics Settings** page. Click **Configure UEBA** one more time, which will open the **Entity Behavior Configuration** page, as shown in Figure 3-84.

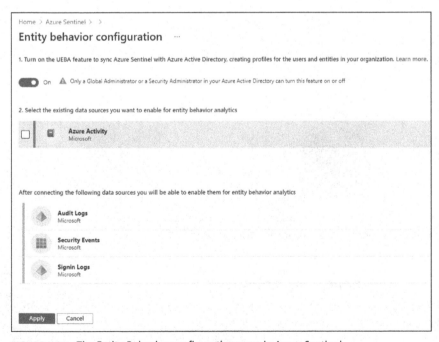

FIGURE 3-84 The Entity Behavior configuration page in Azure Sentinel

7. Select the data sources that you want to enable for UEBA. You can only enable data sources for UEBA that are already being ingested into your Azure Sentinel workspace.

8. Click **Apply**. You have now enabled UEBA for the data sources you selected in your Azure Sentinel workspace.

> **NOTE ADDITIONAL INGESTION CHARGES**
>
> Be mindful that turning on UEBA will generate additional ingestion charges for your Azure Sentinel workspace because new UEBA tables are created, and data is stored in them for the feature to work.

9. Now let's explore the entity pages that use the UEBA feature: Return to the **Entity Behavior** page, as shown in Figure 3-85.

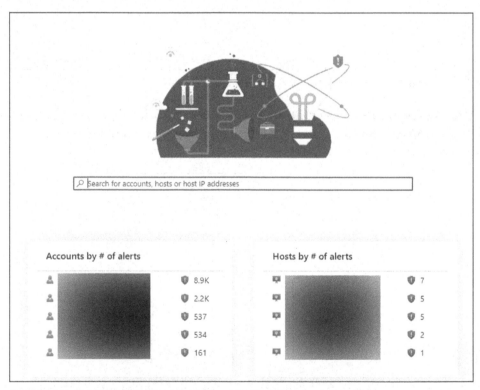

FIGURE 3-85 The Entity Behavior page in Azure Sentinel

> **TIP ENTITY BEHAVIOR PAGE POPULATION**
>
> In real life, after you have turned on UEBA, it can take an up to an hour for the Entity Behavior page to start being populated.

10. The top accounts and hosts by number of alerts will be shown. You can click them to be taken to that entity's page, as shown in Figure 3-86.

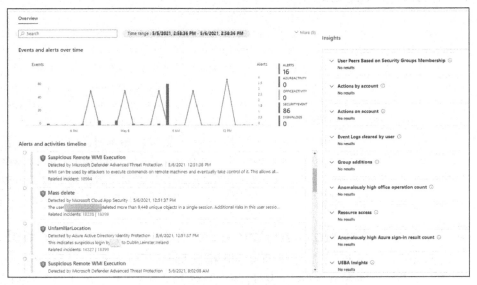

FIGURE 3-86 User entity page in Azure Sentinel UEBA

Both entity and host pages are similar, follow a theme that is familiar to other pages in Azure Sentinel, and have a focus on timeline and insights: The page will show all the alerts related to that entity in a timeline fashion. Insights about that entity are found on the left side of the page. Insights are based on the following data sources:

- Syslog (Linux)
- SecurityEvent (Windows)
- AuditLogs (Azure AD)
- SigninLogs (Azure AD)
- OfficeActivity (Office 365)
- BehaviorAnalytics (Azure Sentinel UEBA)
- Heartbeat (Azure Monitor Agent)
- CommonSecurityLog (Azure Sentinel)

Entity pages and UEBA functionality are designed to fit into a larger incident investigation and management piece when an SOC is using Azure Sentinel, and they highlight anomalous behaviors and help with triaging.

EXAM TIP

For the SC-200 exam, make sure you understand what UEBA is and how it can be used to assist in investigations.

Skill 3-6: Use Azure Sentinel workbooks to analyze and interpret data

If you used Azure Sentinel during its initial public preview phase back in 2019, you might remember that the workbooks page in the user interface was simply called "dashboards." While workbooks in Azure Sentinel do provide the basis for displaying data and information from the product in various formats that could be used as a dashboard, the reality is that workbooks are much, much more than that. They can be used for guided querying and assisting SOC analysts to focus their attention on the most critical incidents and events in their environments.

This section of the chapter covers the skills necessary to activate and customize Azure Sentinel workbook templates, create custom workbooks from scratch, configure advanced visualizations, analyze data using workbooks, and track incident and SOC metrics using the security operations efficiency workbook according to the SC-200 exam outline.

Activate and customize Azure Sentinel workbook templates

As s you spend more time getting familiar with Azure Sentinel, Microsoft has provided out-of-the-box templates for workbooks that you can add to your workspace and customize them with minimal time spent on overhead. Workbook templates typically exist for any built-in data source for which you can find a connector in the data connectors gallery. Remember, there are workbook templates that aren't directly related to a single specific data source, so make sure that you look through the workbook template gallery carefully and activate any workbooks that are relevant to your environment.

> **NOTE   MANAGING AZURE SENTINEL WORKBOOKS**
>
> Azure Sentinel workbooks use Azure Monitor workbooks as their base, so if you've used those workbooks before, you will know how to manage Azure Sentinel workbooks.

Let's look at how to activate a workbook template in your Azure Sentinel workspace:

1. Navigate to the Azure portal by opening *https://portal.azure.com*.
2. In the **Search** bar, type **Sentinel**, and under **Services**, click **Azure Sentinel**. The **Azure Sentinel Workspace** page appears.

3. Select the workspace you want to use. The **Azure Sentinel | Overview** page appears.

4. Click **Workbooks**. The **Workbooks** gallery appears, as shown in Figure 3-87.

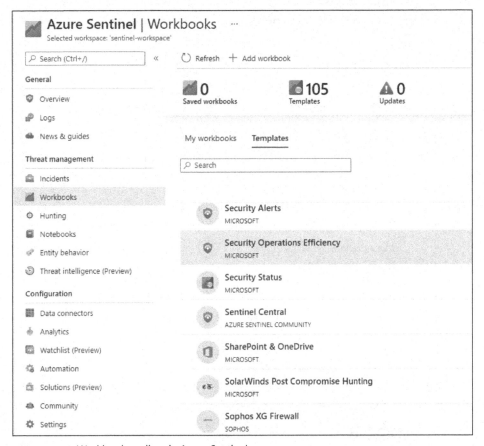

FIGURE 3-87 Workbooks gallery in Azure Sentinel

5. Select the workbook you want to activate in your Azure Sentinel workspace, and the preview bar appears on the left side of the screen, as shown in Figure 3-88.

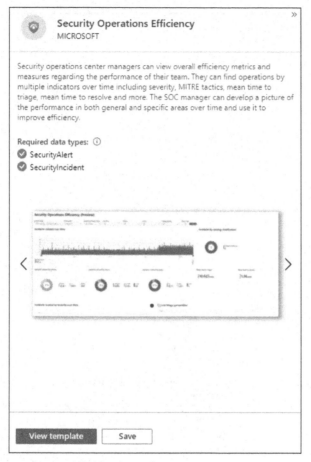

FIGURE 3-88 Workbook template summary

6. Click **View Template**. This will show you a preview of the workbook using the data in your workspace.

> *NOTE* **REQUIRED DATA TYPES**
>
> A workbook template displays **Required Data Types** and will indicate if the logs required for the workbook to function properly are available in your workspace. Be prepared for a few errors if you activate the template and don't have all the logs that the workbook uses!

7. Return to the workbooks gallery, and this time, select the workbook you want to activate and click **Save**.

8. You will be prompted select what location you want to save the workbook to, as shown in Figure 3-89.

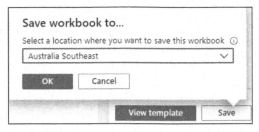

FIGURE 3-89 Saving a workbook in the workbooks gallery

9. Choose your desired location and click **OK**.

10. You will notice that the button options for that workbook have changed, and you now have the **View Saved Workbook** option, as shown in Figure 3-90.

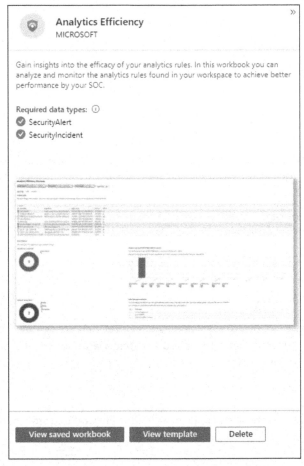

FIGURE 3-90 A saved workbook in the workbooks gallery

11. Click **View Saved Workbook**.

12. You will be taken to your saved workbook template, which is populated with the data from your workspace, as shown in Figure 3-91.

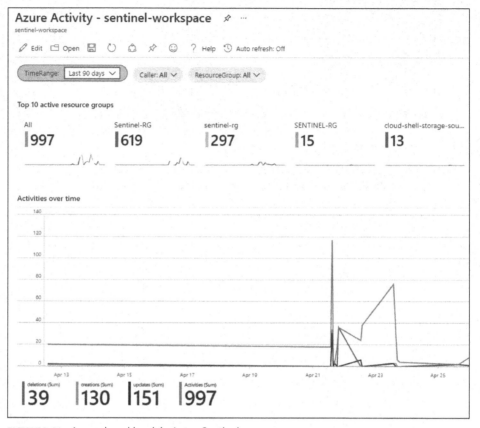

FIGURE 3-91   A saved workbook in Azure Sentinel

13. If required, you can now use the **Edit** button and customize this template.

Create custom workbooks

Although workbook templates cover many use cases and eventualities in Azure Sentinel, in a large, complex organization, it is likely that you might need to create a workbook for reporting specific items for your organization from scratch.

EXAM TIP

It's important that you know how to effectively create a useful, custom workbook for your SC-200 exam.

Let's look at how to create a useful, custom workbook:

1. Navigate to the Azure portal by opening *https://portal.azure.com.*

2. In the **Search** bar, type **Sentinel**, and under **Services**, click **Azure Sentinel**. The **Azure Sentinel Workspace** page appears.

3. Select the workspace you want to use. The **Azure Sentinel | Overview** page appears.

4. Click **Workbooks**. The **Workbooks Gallery** appears.

5. Click **Add Workbook**. The **New Workbook** page appears, as shown in Figure 3-92.

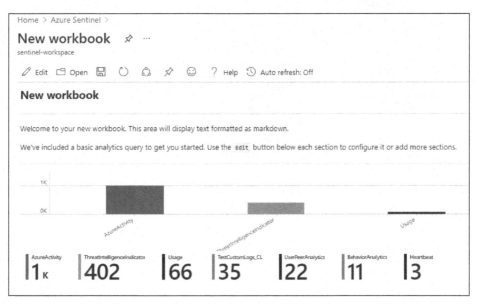

FIGURE 3-92 Opening a new custom workbook

6. Click **Edit**, and you will now be able to add items to your custom workbook, as shown in Figure 3-93.

FIGURE 3-93 Adding new items to a custom workbook

7. Let's briefly explain the items in the **Add** column:

- **Add Text** As this self-explanatory option implies, text can be added to your workbook to explain the purpose of the workbook or any additional explanation of the visualizations being shown. Text in workbooks is formatted as markdown.

- **Add Parameters** This is where parameters that can be iterated throughout the workbook are defined as shown in Figure 3-94.

FIGURE 3-94 Adding parameters to a custom workbook

- **Add Links/Tabs** This self-explanatory option allows you to add relevant links and tabs to your workbook.

- **Add Query** Arguably, the most important aspect of customizing workbooks, this is where you can add KQL queries that will bring back data to the workbook to be displayed. If you've learned KQL for searching logs and writing analytics rules, you'll have a good idea what is required here from a query language perspective. There are several different visualizations that you can choose to use, which can be set in the user interface or in the query itself using the render KQL operator shown in Figure 3-95.

EXAM TIP

Study some of the workbook templates and how they structure their KQL queries to help you understand how to construct KQL queries for visualizations in workbooks.

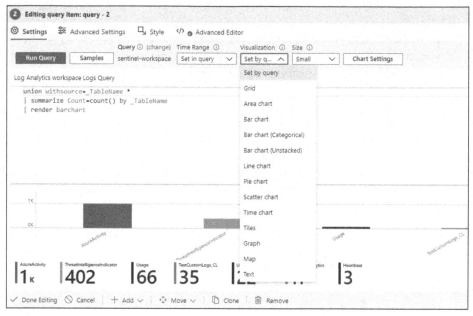

FIGURE 3-95 Choosing a visualization in a workbook query

- **Add Group** This is where workbook items can be grouped logically to make management of the workbook easier.

8. When you've finished creating your custom workbook, click **Save**.

9. Choose where you want to save your custom workbook to, as shown in Figure 3-96.

FIGURE 3-96 Saving a custom workbook

Configure advanced visualizations

There are many visualization options to choose from in Azure Sentinel when creating workbooks. Choosing the "correct" visualization for the data being displayed will be—to a large extent—a personal preference for those individuals creating the workbook and the organization's preferences for how the data is to be displayed.

Having said this, certain query results don't display well (or at all) in certain types of visualizations. In preparation for your SC-200 exam, make sure you are familiar with what does and doesn't work in terms of the different visualization options and query results in Azure Sentinel. For example, queries that use the `bin` operator to summarize query results usually display best with a line or bar chart.

EXAM TIP

The Visualizations Demo workbook template found in Azure Sentinel (see Figure 3-97) is a template specifically designed to showcase different types of workbook visualizations. Make sure that you use it to help your SC-200 studies!

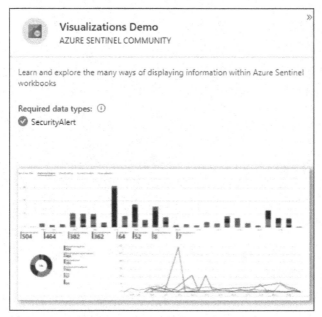

FIGURE 3-97 The Visualizations Demo workbook template

Let's look at some of the visualization options available for you to use in workbooks:

- **Charts** Available chart types include line, bar, pie, and time. You can customize the chart's height, width, color palette, legend, titles, and so on. Also, you can customize axis types and series colors using the chart settings. Figure 3-98 shows an example pie chart in a workbook:

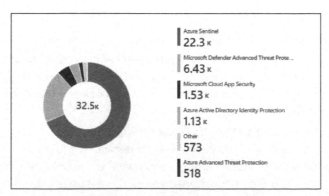

FIGURE 3-98 Pie chart in an Azure Sentinel workbook

- **Grids** Grids display the results of a query not unlike the results seen in the Log Analytics query interface, so using KQL you can choose the columns that appear in the grid. Figure 3-99 shows an example grid in a workbook.

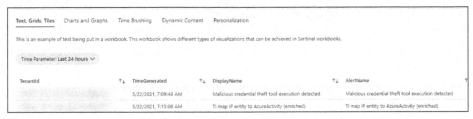

FIGURE 3-99 Example grid in an Azure Sentinel workbook

- **Tiles** Tiles are a method of presenting summarized data in workbooks. Figure 3-100 shows an example of tiles in a workbook:

FIGURE 3-100 Example tile in an Azure Sentinel workbook

- **Graphs** Graphs can show the relationships between entities in the logs they are analyzing. See Figure 3-101 for an example of a graph visualization:

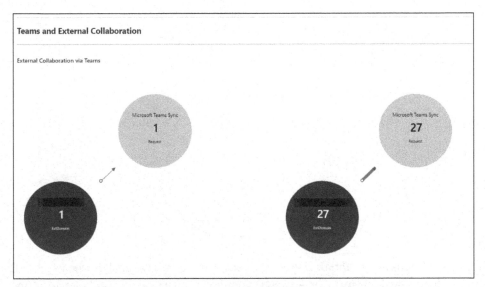

FIGURE 3-101 Example graph in an Azure Sentinel workbook

View and analyze Azure Sentinel data using workbooks

So far in this part of the chapter, we have discussed how you can configure and create workbooks, but next we'll focus on how to use workbooks in the context of an SOC analyst responding to or investigating incidents. How an SOC uses workbooks is, of course, highly contextual and will depend on the organization's wider IT operations processes, so this section will look at how workbooks can be used by an SOC in a more general context and explore some of the main analytical concepts.

For this example, we're going to be using one of the built-in workbook templates, the Azure AD Sign-In Logs workbook:

1. Navigate to the Azure portal by opening *https://portal.azure.com*.

2. In the **Search** bar, type **Sentinel**, and under **Services**, click **Azure Sentinel**. The **Azure Sentinel Workspace** page appears.

3. Select the workspace you want to use. The **Azure Sentinel | Overview** page appears.

4. Click **Workbooks**. The **Workbooks** gallery appears.

5. Click the **Azure AD Sign-In Logs Workbook**.

6. Click **View Saved Workbook**. The **Sign-in Analysis Workbook** appears, as shown in Figure 3-102.

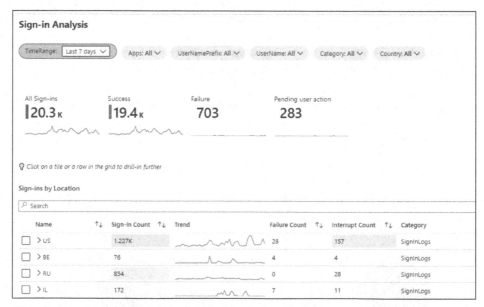

FIGURE 3-102 Azure AD Sign-in Analysis workbook

7. Let's look at this workbook from the perspective of an SOC analyst who wants to look for unusual activity in the Azure AD sign-in logs. As we can see in Figure 3-102, the number of sign-ins for each country is shown, as well as the trend for sign-ins from each country for the time range specified. The **TimeRange** is set to **Last 7 Days**.

8. Clicking in the **Sign-Ins By Location** box allows you to drill-in to more specific locations in the U.S., as shown in Figure 3-103.

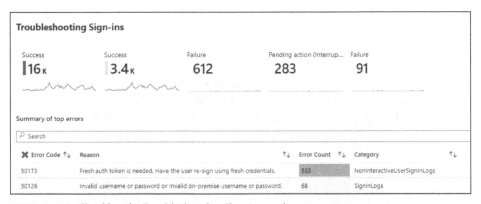

Sign-ins by Location

Name	Sign-in Count	Trend	Failure Count	Interrupt Count	Category
∨ US	1.227K		28	157	SigninLogs
Pflugerville	43		4	18	SigninLogs
Pflugerville	43		4	18	SigninLogs
Redmond	52		1	14	SigninLogs
Redmond	52		1	14	SigninLogs

FIGURE 3-103 Drilling into sign-in locations detail by country

9. We can see that both Redmond and Pflugerville are the most recorded locations for sign-ins in this workspace in the past 7 days and that there have been a couple of small spikes in sign-ins from these locations in the past week. (We can observe this by looking at the **Trend** column.)

10. Moving further down the workbook, the SOC analyst can analyze the number of successful versus unsuccessful sign-ins, as shown in Figure 3-104.

Troubleshooting Sign-ins

Success	Success	Failure	Pending action (Interrup...	Failure
16 k	3.4 k	612	283	91

Summary of top errors

✗ Error Code	Reason	Error Count	Category
50173	Fresh auth token is needed. Have the user re-sign using fresh credentials.	535	NonInteractiveUserSigninLogs
50126	Invalid username or password or Invalid on-premise username or password.	68	SigninLogs

FIGURE 3-104 Checking the Troubleshooting Sign-Ins section

11. The workbook also shows the **Summary Of Top Errors** for the selected time period. Figure 3-104 shows that in this instance, the top sign-in error was **Fresh Auth Token Is Needed. Have The User Re-Sign Using Fresh Credentials**, followed by **Invalid Username Or Password Or Invalid On-Premises Username Or Password**. This information can assist an SOC analyst in understanding the baseline of the environment they manage, as well as help them look for anomalies.

12. The SOC analyst can choose to focus in on a specific user or change the time period that the workbook displays; this can be done via the parameters tabs—**TimeRange**, **Apps**, **UserNamePrefix**, and **UserName**—at the top of the workbook, as shown in Figure 3-105.

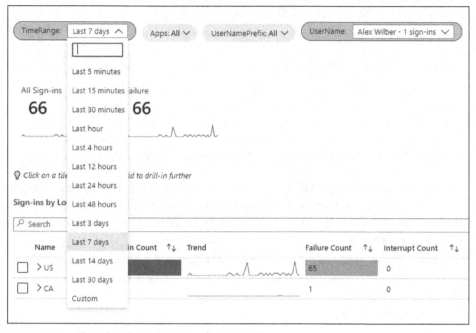

FIGURE 3-105 Changing the parameters of a workbook

13. Finally, it might be necessary to print a hard or soft copy of the workbook to give to management for reporting purposes. This can be done by clicking the ellipsis (three dots) to the right of the workbook's title, as shown in Figure 3-106.

FIGURE 3-106 Printing a workbook in Azure Sentinel

Track incident metrics using the security operations efficiency workbook

Although all the Azure Sentinel workbook templates are very useful—they've all been written by experts in their field—they are often tied to a particular data source and will not be useful if you are not ingesting that data source into your Azure Sentinel workspace. However, the

Security Operations Efficiency workbook is a workbook that uses the SecurityIncidents table to allow you to track key SOC metrics, such as the number of incidents raised, their severity, mean time to triage, and so on. Regardless of your organization's security operations processes and the data sources you ingest, you will want to track key performance indicators (KPIs) of your SOC. (And even if you don't, your management probably will!)

EXAM TIP

For the SC-200 exam, it's important that you're familiar with the Security Operations Efficiency workbook and the metrics that it can provide for reporting on an SOC's performance.

Let's walk through this workbook to learn more about reporting:

1. Navigate to the Azure portal by opening *https://portal.azure.com*.

2. In the **Search** bar, type **Sentinel**, and under **Services**, click **Azure Sentinel**. The **Azure Sentinel Workspace** page appears.

3. Select the workspace you want to use. The **Azure Sentinel | Overview** page appears.

4. Click **Workbooks**. The **Workbooks** gallery appears.

5. Click the **Security Operations Efficiency** workbook. The **Security Operations Efficiency** workbook appears, as shown in Figure 3-107. Here, you can see various SOC operational metrics for reporting purposes. In Figure 3-107, we can see that there was a large spike in new incidents on about May 2 and that most incidents are being raised as high-severity incidents.

FIGURE 3-107 Security Operations Efficiency workbook

6. Scrolling further into the workbook, we can see two key SOC operational metrics. **Mean Time To Triage** and **Mean Time To Closure** are—along with the number of incidents and severity—very commonly used SOC reporting metrics. (The example in Figure 3-108 shows a very slow SOC team. **Mean Time To Triage** should be much less than one day in real life. Fortunately, this is not a real SOC!)

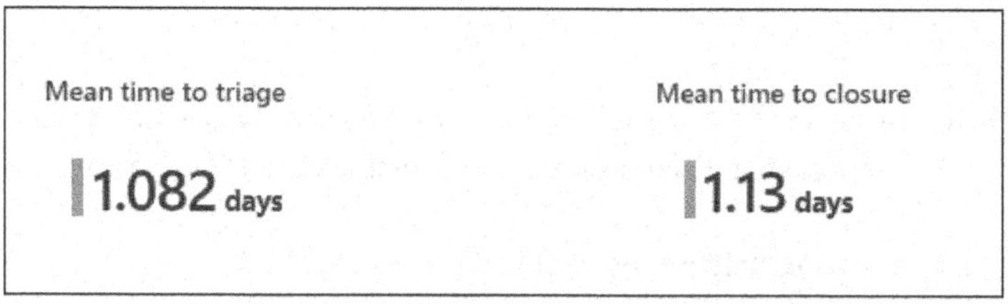

Mean time to triage

1.082 days

Mean time to closure

1.13 days

FIGURE 3-108   Mean Time To Triage and Mean Time To Closure

EXAM TIP

Make sure that you are familiar with the typical metrics that SOC managers use for KPIs and how to display these in a workbook in Azure Sentinel. Most of this should be covered in the security operations efficiency workbook, but you should study the queries behind the workbook so that you understand how to query the `SecurityIncidents` table to obtain these metrics.

Skill 3-7: Hunt for threats using the Azure Sentinel portal

Hunting is the proactive side of threat detection in security operations. While much focus is put on the reactive side of detection (creating alerts and incidents in response to patterns of behavior being correlated across log sources), as an SOC increases in maturity, it should be moving toward proactive threat hunting and looking for potentially suspicious activity before it triggers a detection rule.

This section of the chapter covers the skills necessary to create custom hunting queries; manually run hunting queries; monitor using Livestream; perform hunting using notebooks; track query results with bookmarks; use those bookmarks in investigations; and convert a hunting query into an analytics rule.

Create custom hunting queries

If you're reading this chapter from start to finish, you probably already know what this topic is going to start with: Microsoft includes many Sentinel hunting queries that you can use right out of the box that have been written by security experts. Before you take the time and effort to write a custom query, do look through the built-in hunting queries to see if they will meet your requirements. Hunting queries don't have templates. The out-of-the-box queries exist in your hunting queries list, and you can't edit them like you are able to with analytics rules and workbooks. If you want to edit an out of the box hunting rule, you will need to re-create the whole rule with your edited KQL query.

> **TIP HUNTING QUERIES VERSUS ANALYTICS RULES**
>
> If you're unsure about the differences between a hunting query and an analytics rule, use the out-of-the-box hunting query templates to give you an idea. Typically, hunting queries are looking for a single or limited series of events that might be an indicator of a security issue, but in isolation, they would not necessarily be sufficient to raise an incident immediately.

Let's look at how to create a custom hunting rule in Azure Sentinel:

1. Navigate to the Azure portal by opening *https://portal.azure.com.*

2. In the **Search** bar, type **Sentinel**, and under **Services**, click **Azure Sentinel**. The **Azure Sentinel Workspace** page appears.

3. Select the workspace you want to use. The **Azure Sentinel | Overview** page appears.

4. Click **Hunting**. The **Hunting** page appears, as shown in Figure 3-109.

FIGURE 3-109   The Hunting page in Azure Sentinel

5. Click **New Query**. The **Create Custom Query** page appears, as shown in Figure 3-110.

Home > Azure Sentinel >

Create custom query ...

🗑 Delete Query

ℹ Do not use fixed time ranges, either directly or in a function, in your query. Otherwise, we cannot show changes in query results over time.

Name *

Powershell use

Description

Checking for Powershell use in logs

Custom query

```
SecurityEvent
| where ParentProcessName contains "powershell.exe"
```

View query results >

Entity mapping

Map the entities recognized by Azure Sentinel to the appropriate columns available in your query results.
This enables Azure Sentinel to recognize the entities that are part of the alerts for further analysis.
Entity type must be a string.

Entity Type	Column
Account	AccountName
Host	Choose column
IP	Choose column
URL	Choose column
Timestamp	Choose column

Tactics

2 selected

FIGURE 3-110 Create Custom Query

Following is the KQL of the query shown in Figure 3-110:

```
SecurityEvent
| where ParentProcessName contains "powershell.exe"
```

6. On the Create Custom Query page, you can define the **Name**, **Description**, **Custom Query**, **Entity Mapping**, and **MITRE Tactics** for your hunting query.

> **NOTE AVOID REFERENCES TO TIME RANGES**
>
> Unlike an analytics rule, hunting query logic should not include any reference to time ranges because this prevents Azure Sentinel from showing you the change in query results over time to create a baseline for monitoring.

7. Click **Create**.

8. You will be returned to the **Hunting** page, and if you search for your custom hunting query by name, it should now appear in your hunting **Queries** list, as shown in Figure 3-111.

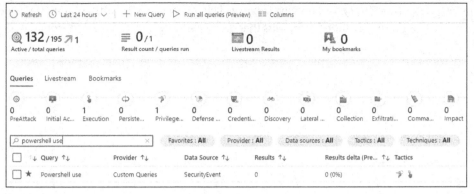

FIGURE 3-111 Searching for a custom hunting query

Run hunting queries manually

Hunting queries will almost always be run manually in Azure Sentinel, which we will explore in this topic:

1. Navigate to the Azure portal by opening *https://portal.azure.com*.

2. In the **Search** bar, type **Sentinel**, and under **Services**, click **Azure Sentinel**. The **Azure Sentinel Workspace** page appears.

3. Select the workspace you want to use. The **Azure Sentinel | Overview** page appears.

4. Click **Hunting**, which opens the **Hunting** page.

5. Select the query that you want to run manually. The **Hunting Query Preview** pane appears, as shown in Figure 3-112.

FIGURE 3-112 The Hunting Query Preview pane

6. Click **Run Query**. The hunting query will be run, and the **Results** column will be populated with the number of results that query has returned, as shown in Figure 3-113.

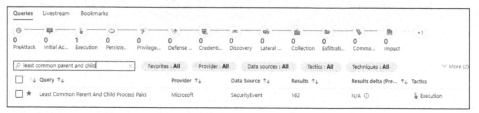

FIGURE 3-113 Checking the number of results a hunting query has returned

7. To see the hunting query results in more detail, click **View Results** in the **Hunting Query Preview** pane, and you will be taken to the Log Analytics page to see the raw results of the query.

8. To run multiple hunting queries at the same time, select the queries to be run on the **Hunting** page using the check boxes next to each query, as shown in Figure 3-114.

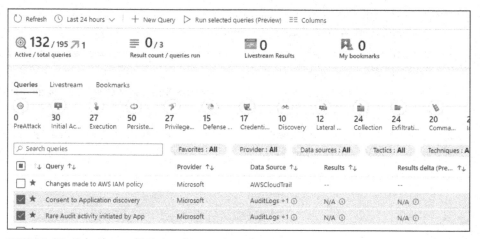

FIGURE 3-114 Selecting multiple hunting queries to be run

9. Click **Run Selected Queries**.

10. The selected queries will run, and the results will be displayed in the **Results** column in the same way they are shown when you run a single query.

Monitor hunting queries by using Livestream

Livestream is a way of running hunting queries continuously—every 30 seconds—and it will let you know if there are any new results matching the query. This is a great way to monitor for any baseline changes in your environment that can be indicative of a security issue but without raising any unnecessary false-positive incidents. Livestreams can also be useful for testing new queries, and it is also possible to "promote" a Livestream query to an analytics rule or just straight into an investigation.

Let's look at how to use a Livestream in Azure Sentinel:

1. Navigate to the Azure portal by opening *https://portal.azure.com*.

2. In the **Search** bar, type **Sentinel**, and under **Services**, click **Azure Sentinel**. The **Azure Sentinel Workspace** page appears.

3. Select the workspace you want to use. The **Azure Sentinel | Overview** page appears.

4. Click **Hunting**, which opens the **Hunting** page.

5. Click the **Livestream** tab, which opens the **Livestream** tab on the **Hunting** page, as shown in Figure 3-115.

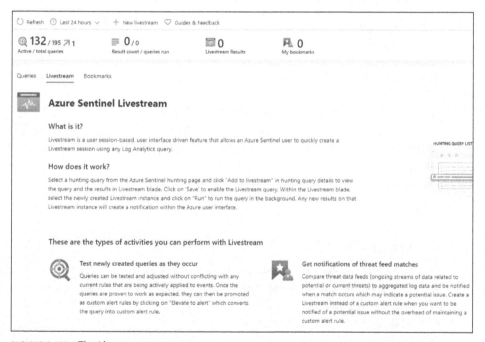

FIGURE 3-115   The Livestream page

6. The Livestream tab is not prepopulated with queries, so if this is your first time using the feature, it will be empty. To add a Livestream query, click **New Livestream**.

7. The **Livestream** page appears, as shown in Figure 3-116, using this the KQL:

```
SecurityEvent
| where EventID == 4625
```

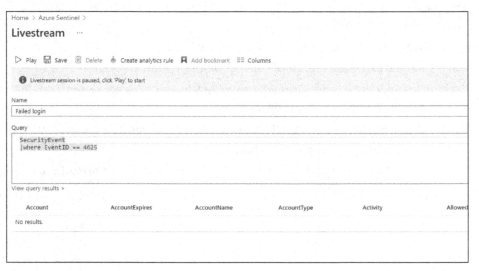

FIGURE 3-116 The Livestream page

8. Give your Livestream a **Name** and enter the **KQL** for the Livestream in the **Query** field. Remember, as for other hunting queries, you should not specify time periods in Livestream query logic because this prevents Azure Sentinel from detecting changes over time.

9. Click **Save**.

10. Click **Play** to start the Livestream.

> **TIP BE PATIENT!**
> If you are expecting immediate results with your livestream query, be patient! It can take up to 30 seconds for the Livestream to start and for results to be visible.

11. The Livestream will start running. Any results from the query will be displayed below on the Livestream page, as shown in Figure 3-117.

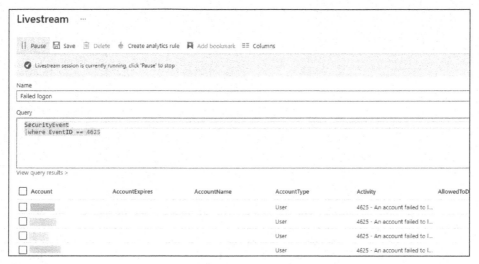

FIGURE 3-117 The Livestream page with query results

12. The Livestream results will be refreshed every 30 seconds.

13. You can pause the Livestream using the **Pause** button at the top of the **Livestream** page.

14. Return to the **Livestream** tab on the **Hunting** page, as shown in Figure 3-118.

FIGURE 3-118 The Livestream tab with saved Livestreams

15. The saved Livestream is now visible on the tab, and you can also see whether the Livestream is currently running by looking at the **Status** column.

16. You can pause and play livestreams from this page using the Livestream preview pane on the right side of the page, as shown in Figure 3-119.

FIGURE 3-119 The Livestream preview pane with the Play button visible

17. Click **Pause** or **Play** in this pane. (This button toggles between **Play** and **Pause**.)

Track query results with bookmarks

An SOC analyst might look through hundreds of thousands of logs during a shift, and the human brain can only process and remember a limited number of details. This is where bookmarks come in handy. They are a tool in Azure Sentinel that allows you to save specific records from a query result that an SOC analyst can revisit if they need to. Bookmarks can be attached to incidents to assist with investigation, and as with most things in Azure Sentinel, they also are stored in their own table—the HuntingBookmark table—and they can be searched through using KQL.

Let's look at how to create a bookmark in Azure Sentinel:

1. Navigate to the Azure portal by opening *https://portal.azure.com*.

2. In the **Search** bar, type **Sentinel**, and under **Services**, click **Azure Sentinel**. The **Azure Sentinel Workspace** page appears.

3. Select the workspace you want to use. The **Azure Sentinel | Overview** page appears.

4. Click **Hunting**, which opens the **Hunting** page.

5. Select a hunting query to run. The **Hunting Query Preview** pane appears on the right side of the screen, as shown in Figure 3-120.

FIGURE 3-120 The Hunting Query Preview pane in Azure Sentinel

6. Click **View Query Results** or **View Results**. (Both take you to the **Logs** page.)

7. You will be taken to the **Logs** page, where you can view the results of the hunting query, as shown in Figure 3-121. The KQL of the query is as follows:

```
AzureActivity
| where Category == "Administrative"
```

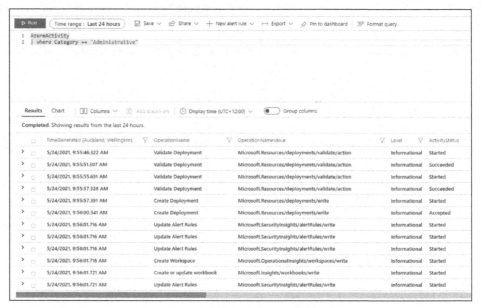

FIGURE 3-121 Viewing hunting query results on the Logs page

8. Select the record you want to bookmark by selecting that record and clicking **Add Bookmark**. The **Add Bookmark** pane appears, as shown in Figure 3-122.

9. You can enter details about the record you are saving as a bookmark, including the **Name**, **Entity Mapping**, **Tags**, and **Notes** to remind yourself or other SOC personnel what is important or noteworthy about this bookmark. When you've finished, click **Create**.

> **NOTE BOOKMARKS IN INVESTIGATION GRAPH**
>
> To view a bookmark in the investigation graph, you need to map at least one entity in the bookmark.

FIGURE 3-122 The Add Bookmark pane

10. To view your saved bookmarks, navigate to the **Hunting** page and click the **Bookmarks** tab, as shown in Figure 3-123.

FIGURE 3-123 The Bookmarks tab

11. You can also view saved bookmarks by navigating to the **Bookmark Logs** page and searching the `HuntingBookmark` table, as shown in Figure 3-124. The query being run is as follows:

```
HuntingBookmark
| take 10
```

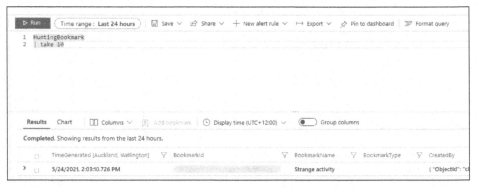

FIGURE 3-124 Searching saved bookmarks in the `HuntingBookmark` table

Use hunting bookmarks for data investigations

Bookmarking certain records can be useful in isolation, but to get the full value of the bookmarks feature in Azure Sentinel, you need to use them to assist in investigations. There are several ways that you can use bookmarks to enhance your threat hunting when using Azure Sentinel.

Adding bookmarks to a new or existing incident

1. Navigate to the Azure portal by opening *https://portal.azure.com*.
2. In the **Search** bar, type **Sentinel**, and under **Services**, click **Azure Sentinel**. The **Azure Sentinel Workspace** page appears.
3. Select the workspace you want to use. The **Azure Sentinel | Overview** page appears.
4. Click **Hunting**. The **Hunting** page appears.
5. Click the **Bookmarks** tab, as shown previously in Figure 3-123.
6. Select the bookmark and click **Incident Actions**, as shown in Figure 3-125.

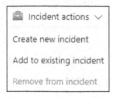

FIGURE 3-125 The Incident Actions button

7. You can select either:

- **Create New Incident** When this option is selected, the **Promoting Bookmark To An Incident** pane appears, as shown in Figure 3-126. From here, you can add a **Description** to the incident, select the **Severity** of the incident, add tags, and assign to an analyst. Once this information is added, clicking **Create** creates the incident.

FIGURE 3-126 The Promoting Bookmark To An Incident pane

- **Add To Existing Incident** When this option is chosen, the **Promoting Bookmark To An Existing Incident** pane appears, as shown in Figure 3-127, where you can select the incident to which you want to attach the bookmark. Click **Add** when you are ready.

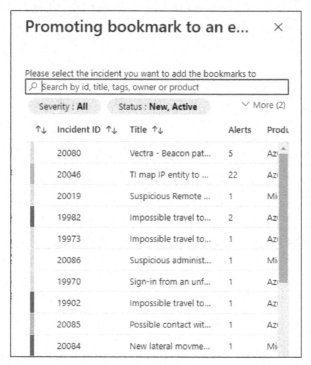

FIGURE 3-127 The Promoting Bookmark To An Existing Incident pane

8. To check an incident's attached bookmarks, navigate to the **Incidents** page in Azure Sentinel.

9. Select the incident you want to check bookmarks for and click **View Full Details**. The **Incident Overview** page appears.

10. Click the **Bookmarks** tab, as shown in Figure 3-128, to check the bookmarks attached to the incident.

FIGURE 3-128 Checking an incident's attached bookmarks

Exploring bookmarks in the investigation graph

The investigation graph can be used to explore a bookmark and the entities contained within it.

1. Navigate to the Azure portal by opening *https://portal.azure.com*.

2. In the **Search** bar, type **Sentinel**, and under **Services**, click **Azure Sentinel**. The **Azure Sentinel Workspace** page appears.

3. Select the workspace you want to use. The **Azure Sentinel | Overview** page appears.

4. Click **Hunting**, and the **Hunting** page appears.

5. Click the **Bookmarks** tab, as shown in Figure 3-129.

FIGURE 3-129 The Bookmarks tab

6. Select the bookmark you want to explore and click **Investigate** in the **Bookmark** preview pane. The **Investigation** graph appears, as shown in Figure 3-130.

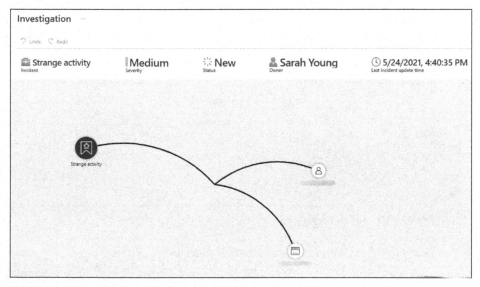

FIGURE 3-130 Investigating a bookmark

7. You can now use the investigation graph to explore the entities in the bookmark, just as you can use the investigation graph to explore an incident. If you need more information on how to use the investigation graph, refer to Skill 3-5, "Manage Azure Sentinel incidents."

Convert a hunting query to an analytics rule

We've spoken earlier in this section about how hunting is a proactive activity in security operations. But what if—during that proactive hunting activity—an SOC analyst finds an issue that needs to be escalated into an incident? This can be done quickly and easily on the Azure Sentinel hunting page either through a Livestream or direct from a hunting query.

Convert a Livestream to an analytics rule

1. Navigate to the Azure portal by opening *https://portal.azure.com*.
2. In the **Search** bar, type **Sentinel**, and under **Services**, click **Azure Sentinel**. The **Azure Sentinel Workspace** page appears.
3. Select the workspace you want to use. The **Azure Sentinel | Overview** page appears.
4. Click **Hunting**, and the **Hunting** page appears.
5. Click the **Livestream** tab, and the **Livestream** tab on the **Hunting** page appears, as shown in Figure 3-131.

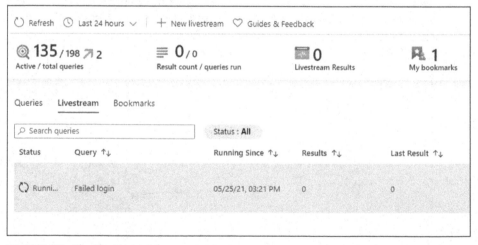

FIGURE 3-131 The Livestream tab

6. Select the Livestream you want to convert to an analytics rule.

7. Click **Open Livestream** at the bottom-right side of the page. The Livestream page appears, as shown in Figure 3-132. The KQL of this query is as follows:

```
SecurityEvent
| where EventID == 4625
```

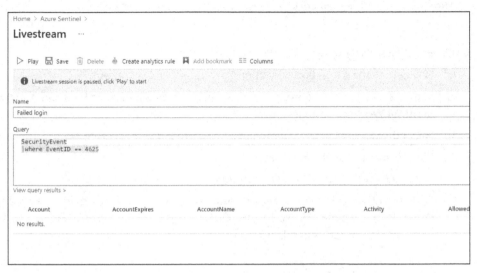

FIGURE 3-132   The Livestream page

8. Click **Create Analytics Rule**. The **Analytics Rule Wizard** appears, as shown in Figure 3-133.

FIGURE 3-133   The Analytics Rule Wizard

9. You can now fill in the details of the analytics rule as you would for any other rule that you would create in Azure Sentinel.

> **NOTE TITLE AND QUERY LOGIC**
>
> The Livestream title and query logic will be prepopulated in the wizard.

Convert a hunting query to an analytics rule

1. Navigate to the Azure portal by opening *https://portal.azure.com*.

2. In the **Search** bar, type **Sentinel**, and under **Services**, click **Azure Sentinel**. The **Azure Sentinel Workspace** page appears.

3. Select the workspace you want to use. The **Azure Sentinel | Overview** page appears.

4. Click **Hunting**. The **Hunting** page appears.

5. Select the hunting query you want to convert to an analytics rule.

6. Click **View Query Results** or **View Results** (both do the same thing) in the **Hunting Query Preview** pane. You will be taken to the **Logs** page, as shown in Figure 3-134. The KQL of the query is as follows:

```
AzureActivity
| where Category == "Administrative"
```

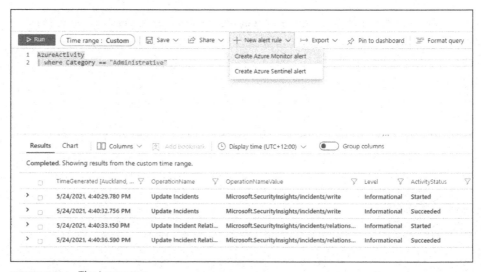

FIGURE 3-134 The Logs page

7. Click **New Alert Rule** > **Create Azure Sentinel Alert**.

8. The **Analytics Rule Wizard** appears, as shown in Figure 3-135. The KQL in the query is:

```
AzureActivity
| where Category == "Administrative"
```

FIGURE 3-135 The Analytics Rule Wizard

9. You can now fill in the details of the analytics rule as you would for any other rule that you would create in Azure Sentinel.

> **NOTE HUNTING QUERY LOGIC**
>
> The hunting query logic will be prepopulated in the wizard.

Perform advanced hunting with notebooks

The Jupyter Project is an open-source project that was developed to assist data science computing across many programming languages. A Jupyter notebook is an open-source web application that allows you to create and share documents that contain live code, equations, visualizations, and more. Because security operations can essentially be thought of as a security-focused data science—in other words, looking for patterns and anomalies in data—Jupyter notebooks are very well suited to assisting SOC analysts to interpret data.

In Azure Sentinel, Jupyter notebooks run on the Azure Notebooks platform, which is directly connected to the Azure Sentinel user interface. Notebooks allow an SOC analyst to conduct investigations and hunting using a huge collection of programming libraries for machine learning, visualization, and data analysis. Microsoft has developed a library called **KqlMagic** that allows you to take queries from Azure Sentinel and run them inside of a notebook. As the library name suggests, queries are still run using the KQL language.

As with the rest of Azure Sentinel, Microsoft have created notebook templates that can be used in production as they are, but they also give you some inspiration to make your own. Let's go through how to start using notebooks:

1. Navigate to the Azure portal by opening *https://portal.azure.com*.

2. In the **Search** bar, type **Sentinel**, and under **Services**, click **Azure Sentinel**. The **Azure Sentinel Workspace** page appears.

3. Select the workspace you want to use. The **Azure Sentinel | Overview** page appears.

4. Click **Notebooks**, and the **Notebooks** page appears, as shown in Figure 3-136.

FIGURE 3-136 The Notebooks page

5. If you haven't created an Azure Machine Learning **Workspace** yet, you'll need to do this by clicking **Create New AML Workspace**. You will be taken to the **Machine Learning** page, as shown in Figure 3-137.

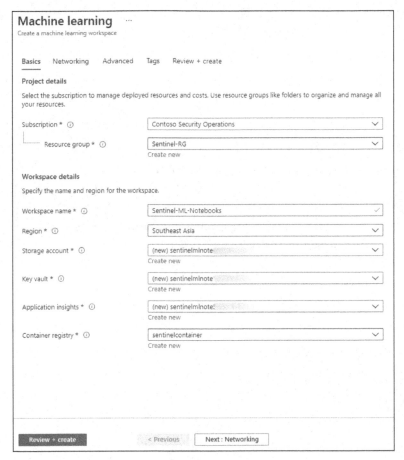

FIGURE 3-137 The Machine Learning page

6. Complete the details of the deployment, which include **Subscription**, **Resource Group**, **Workspace Name**, **Region**, and so on. When you've finished, click **Create**.

7. Return to the **Notebooks** page in Azure Sentinel, select the notebook that you want to launch, and select **Save Notebook**.

8. You will be asked which Azure Machine Learning (AML) workspace you want to save the notebook to, as shown in Figure 3-138.

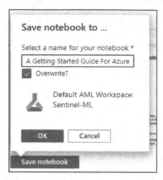

FIGURE 3-138 Saving a notebook template to an AML workspace

9. Click **OK**, and the notebook template will be saved to your AML workspace.

10. After the notebook has been saved, the **Launch Notebook** button will appear on the notebook preview pane, as shown in Figure 3-139.

FIGURE 3-139 Launch notebook button appears on the notebook preview pane after the notebook has been saved.

11. Click **Launch Notebook**. Your notebook will open in the AML interface, as shown in Figure 3-140.

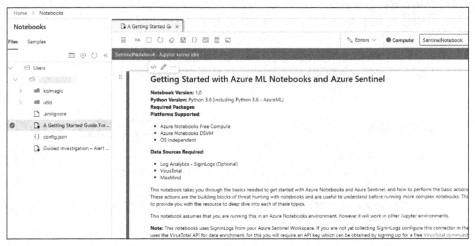

FIGURE 3-140 A notebook opened in the AML interface

12. If this is the first time you've used your AML interface, you'll also need to configure some compute to power your notebook before you can start running it.

13. At the top-right of the screen, you will see a + sign that displays **New Compute** when you hover your mouse over it. Click the + and you will be taken to the **Create Compute Instance** page shown in Figure 3-141.

FIGURE 3-141 Creating compute to run a notebook with

14. Select the VM you want to use for notebook compute, complete the **Compute Name** details, and click **Create**.

15. You can now launch a compute instance to run your notebook by selecting the compute instance and clicking the **Start Compute** triangle-shaped button, as shown in Figure 3-142.

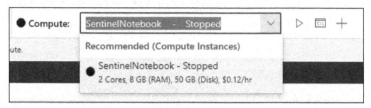

FIGURE 3-142 Choosing a compute instance to run a notebook with

16. You can now work through the notebook and execute the code in each cell by clicking the **Run Cell** button, as shown in Figure 3-143.

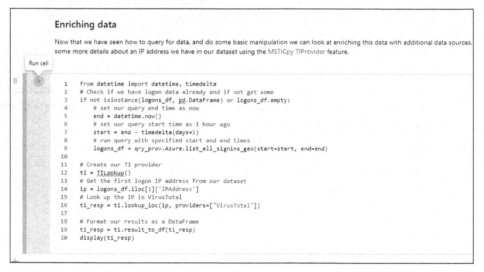

FIGURE 3-143 Executing code in a notebook cell

Thought experiment

In this thought experiment, demonstrate your skills and knowledge of the topics covered in this chapter. You can find answers to this thought experiment in the next section.

Security operations at Contoso Ltd.

You are the SOC manager for Contoso Ltd., a large global organization with offices and operations in several jurisdictions. The organization runs a hybrid environment with both on-premises and cloud IT infrastructure that needs to be monitored for any security breaches. Contoso Ltd. uses Azure Sentinel as its SIEM solution.

As a part of your duties for Contoso Ltd., you run a large follow-the-sun SOC across several countries with hundreds of staff: Tier 1 analysts run the initial triage and basic incident resolution; Tier 2 analysts handle incidents escalated to them from Tier 1; and Tier 3 analysts are the most experienced analysts who take on the most complex cases that Tiers 1 and 2 haven't been able to resolve. Sometimes, this involves the need for Tier 2 analysts to change the configuration of Azure Sentinel.

Looking at your SOC metrics, you can see that both the mean time to triage and mean time to closure of the Contoso SOC is longer than you expected and that SOC analysts aren't able to respond and close incidents as fast as your upper-management expects them to. Upon speaking to the SOC analysts, they tell you that they don't get notified when a new incident is raised, and they have to manually check the incidents page to see if new incidents have occurred since they last checked. You want to configure more automation into your SOC processes to notify the SOC analysts when a new incident has been triggered.

With this information in mind, answer the following questions:

1. How can you ensure that Tier 1 and Tier 2 SOC analysts cannot change the data sources that are connected to Azure Sentinel and that only Tier 3 analysts have access to do this?

2. How can you monitor the mean time to triage and mean time in Azure Sentinel?

3. How can you ensure that an alert notification is sent to the SOC team when an incident is triggered?

Thought experiment answers

This section contains the solution to the thought experiment. Each answer explains why the answer choice is correct.

1. You should assign the correct built-in Azure AD roles for Azure Sentinel. In this example, the Tier 1 and Tier 2 SOC analysts who do not need access to change Sentinel settings should be assigned the Azure Sentinel Responder role, where they can manage incidents and review data. Tier 3 analysts should be assigned the Azure Sentinel Contributor role, which allows them to edit settings in Azure Sentinel.

2. Mean time to triage and mean time to closure are calculated in the Security Operations Efficiency workbook in Azure Sentinel. This workbook uses the data found in the `SecurityIncidents` table to make its calculations.

3. You should configure a Playbook that sends an alert to the SOC team to inform them that a new incident has been raised in Azure Sentinel. This notification could be via email, Teams, and so on. Configure it so that it aligns with the team's operational processes.

Chapter Summary

- Azure Sentinel is both a SIEM and SOAR product.

- Azure Sentinel has out-of-the-box templates for almost every configurable part of the product. Make sure that you utilize these first before you create something new from scratch.

- Azure Sentinel can support a single workspace, multiple workspaces in one Azure tenancy, and multiple workspaces cross tenancy implementation models.

- Data sources are critical for a successful security operations procedure in an organization. Too much data is costly, but too little data can leave blind spots.

- Data sources have three main methods of ingestion in Azure Sentinel: built-in connector, CEF/syslog collection, and custom connectors.

- Azure Sentinel can support both the ingestion and matching of TI for enrichment of incidents, hunting, and analytics rules.

- Analytics rules can be configured as a schedule queries or Microsoft security analytics rules.

- KQL is the query language used for all logic definitions in Azure Sentinel.

- Azure Logic Apps provides automation capabilities for Azure Sentinel.

- Automation has three main uses in Azure Sentinel: alerting, remediation, and enrichment.

- Workbooks are the method by which data can be visualized in Azure Sentinel.

- Hunting is the proactive side of threat hunting and can be performed with queries, with livestreams, or in notebooks.

Index

A

T

U

Plug into learning at

MicrosoftPressStore.com

The Microsoft Press Store by Pearson offers:

- Free U.S. shipping

- Buy an eBook, get three formats – Includes PDF, EPUB, and MOBI to use with your computer, tablet, and mobile devices

- Print & eBook Best Value Packs

- eBook Deal of the Week – Save up to 50% on featured title

- Newsletter – Be the first to hear about new releases, announcements, special offers, and more

- Register your book – Find companion files, errata, and product updates, plus receive a special coupon* to save on your next purchase

Discounts are applied to the list price of a product. Some products are not eligible to receive additional discounts, so your discount code may not be applied to all items in your cart. Discount codes cannot be applied to products that are already discounted, such as eBook Deal of the Week, eBooks that are part of a book + eBook pack, and products with special discounts applied as part of a promotional offering. Only one coupon can be used per order.

 Pearson

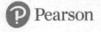